ROUTE 66 ACROSS ARIZONA

A Comprehensive Two-Way Guide for Touring Route 66

by

RICHARD & SHERRY MANGUM

Hexagon Press Publications

Sedona Hikes
135 Day Hikes
256 pages
Color photo section
Price $15.95

Flagstaff Historic Walk
Downtown District
64 pages
Historic photos
Price $6.95

Flagstaff Hikes
146 Day Hikes
288 pages
Color photo section
Price $16.95

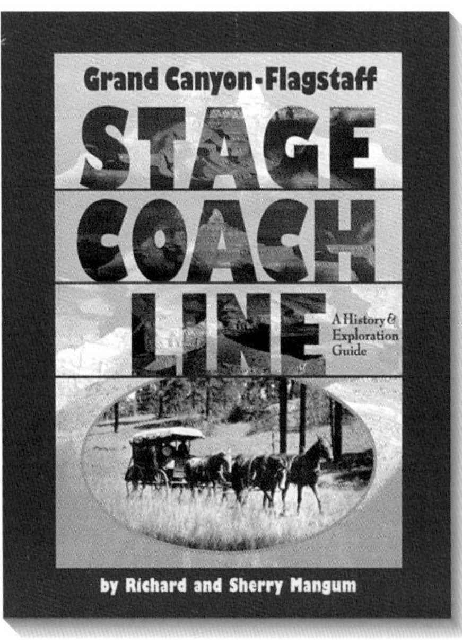

Grand Canyon-Flagstaff Stagecoach Line
A History & Exploration Guide
100 pages
Price $14.95

Buy direct from Hexagon Press, Inc. 300 E. Bennett, Flagstaff AZ 86001
Phone/Fax: 928-774-8800; e-mail: rsmangum@msn.com

Cover photos: *Twin Arrows and Route 66 Neon* (computer composite) by Sherry G. Mangum
Cover design: Joan Carstensen, Sullivan Santamaria Design, Inc., Flagstaff, AZ
Production: Northland Graphics, Flagstaff, AZ

First Edition 2001
ISBN 1-891517-66-X
Library of Congress #2001091278

Table of Contents

Foreword—Welcome to Arizona!

We hope you will have fun driving and exploring Route 66 in our state.

Native Knowledge
Many authors who have written about Route 66 in Arizona were here for a few hours or a few days on assignment. Dick and Sherry live in Flagstaff and know Arizona intimately.

Road-Tested
We have driven every inch of the Mother Road in Arizona, back and forth, many times, keeping careful logs. Our directions are reliable. Although we believe we found every scrap of Route 66 in Arizona, we have included only those that we believe make suitable detours.

Eastbound & Westbound Directions
Many Route 66 guidebooks are written from one direction of travel, most of them westbound. This causes problems for travelers going in the other direction. There is only one way to take care of this problem, and that is to write up each trip both ways, which we have done.

Maps, Maps, Maps
When you are on the road, written directions are not good enough. You need maps. That is why we have gone out of our way to prepare maps, and you will see that this book is stuffed with them, most of them in color.

What Arizona Has to Offer
The longest remaining stretch of Mother Road in the nation—159 miles, The Grand Canyon, The Petrified Forest, the Painted Desert, Meteor Crater, and many other roadside attractions. You'll find the best nostalgia here as well.

Thank You
We had plenty of help preparing this book, as we found lots of friendly people on the road. While there are many we could thank, we want to give recognition to Janice Griffith of the Old Trails Museum in Winslow, Paul and Sandi Taylor of *Route 66 Magazine* in Williams, Jaynell Chambers of the Mohave Museum in Kingman, Garnette Franklin at the Navajo County Museum in Holbrook, and Angel Delgadillo of Seligman.

Photo Credits—all by Sherry Mangum except as shown on a photo as follows: KFS—Kaibab Forest Service, MMHA—Mohave Museum of History and Arts, OTM—Old Trails Museum, OP—Old Postcard, NA—National Archives.

Meet the Authors

Dick was born in Flagstaff in 1936 and has lived there all his life. He well remembers the glory days of Route 66 in Arizona and believes that he has old motor oil in his blood. After graduating from Flagstaff High School in 1954, he became a lawyer, practicing in Flagstaff from 1961 until 1976, at which point he became a Superior Court Judge. He changed careers in 1993 to become a writer. "It's what I always wanted to do," he says.

Sherry moved to Flagstaff when she was seven years old and her parents built a house on the original alignment of Route 66 east of Flagstaff, running from Camp Townsend to Winona. She became a photographer, whose works have been featured in national and international publications. All photos in this book are hers unless otherwise indicated.

This outstanding team was given the Copper Quill Award by the Flagstaff Public Library in 2000.

Together the Mangums research, make the road trips and prepare their books. See you on the Route!

Arizona and Its Major Roads Today

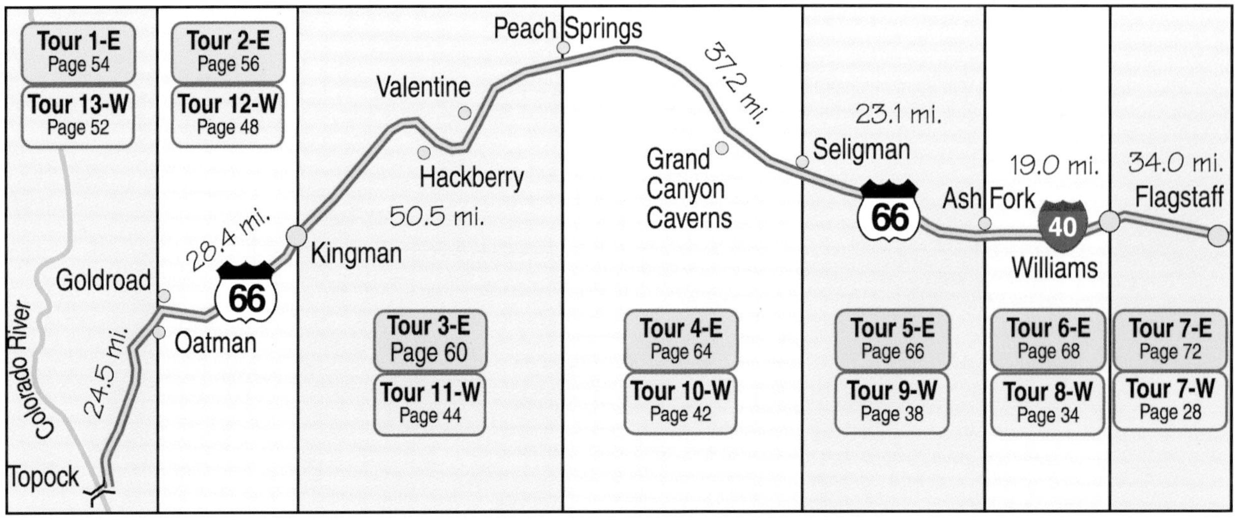

THE TOURS—AN OVERVIEW

TOUR I-E & 13-W TOPOCK-OATMAN

Distance: 24.5 miles. **Driving Time**: 45 minutes.
The Landscape: Low-lying desert at the Colorado River (500 feet), mountain heights of 2700 feet at Oatman.
Comments: This trip is located in the extreme western portion of Arizona and covers a varied landscape, from the low, sun-blasted desert of the Colorado River to the rugged mountains containing the wonderful old gold mining town of Oatman. There are memorable views from the mountains.
Highlights: The old bridge across the Colorado River, the Black Mountains, Oatman.
Suggestions: Few travelers will want to make any stops between Oatman and Topock.
Places to Eat in Oatman: Oatman Hotel.
Places to Sleep in Oatman: None recommended.

TOUR 2-E & 12-W OATMAN-KINGMAN

Distance: 28.4 miles. **Driving Time**: 1.5 hours.
The Landscape: Oatman is just below the crest of Sitgreaves Pass high in the Black Mountains, while Kingman is located in a vast plain surrounded by mountain ranges. The road is narrow and twisting going up and down the mountain, flat and fast on the plain. The road on both sides of Sitgreaves Pass is frightening to some people, but is a wonderful driving experience—the farthest thing imaginable from today's freeways.
Comments: Most travelers will want to stop in Oatman for an hour to browse the shops, feed the burros, and take some photos. There are a couple of cafes in Oatman, but it is not a good place to spend the night. Kingman, however, has many good motels and restaurants, so if you are in Kingman near the end of the day, plan to sleep there. Travelers can spend an interesting half day in Kingman, going to the Mohave County Museum, the Route 66 Association Museum, etc. See page 47.
Highlights: Visiting Oatman, Views from Sitgreaves Pass, Goldroad Mine Tour, Visiting Kingman.
Suggestions: We take our time on this stretch of road, because there are many interesting things to see and the views are wonderful. It is not a road for people in a hurry
Places to Eat in Kingman: See page 47.
Places to Sleep in Kingman: See page 47.

TOUR 3-E & 11-W KINGMAN-PEACH SPRINGS

Distance: 50.5 miles **Driving Time**: 1 hour
The Landscape: On both ends of these tours there are broad flat plains, but in the center the road passes through the interesting and scenic Crozier and Truxton Canyons.
Comments: There are interesting detours on this trip and one could spend half a day on the journey, particularly if you find yourself in love with the old Route 66 Visitor Center and General Store at Hackberry. At the end of the tour there is a good motel and restaurant at Peach Springs, but Peach Springs is a remote place.
Highlights: Hackberry and the General Store, Valentine.
Suggestions: Stop at Hackberry for at least one-half hour.
Places to Eat in Peach Springs: Hualapai Lodge.
Places to Sleep in Peach Springs: Hualapai Lodge.

TOUR 4-E & 10-W PEACH SPRINGS-SELIGMAN

Distance: 37.2 miles. **Driving Time**: 45 minutes.
The Landscape: Flat rangelands.
Comments: If you take the sidetrip to Grand Canyon Caverns, you will spend at least an hour and a half there. There isn't much to do on the way. In Seligman you will definitely want to visit Delgadillo's Snow Cap and Delgadillo's Route 66 Visitor Center. There are good places to eat and sleep in Seligman.
Highlights: Grand Canyon Caverns, Hualapai Indian Reservation.
Suggestions: Grand Canyon Caverns is not a must-see.
Places to Eat in Seligman: Copper Cart, Westside Lilo's.
Places to Sleep in Seligman: Route 66 Motel.

TOUR 5-E & 9-W SELIGMAN-ASH FORK

Distance: 23.1 miles. **Driving Time**: 30 minutes.
The Landscape: Flat rangeland.
Comments: There isn't much to slow you down between Seligman and Ash Fork.
Highlights: Crookton Overpass.
Suggestions: Pass through Ash Fork, where there is little of interest and spend your time in Seligman, where there is plenty.

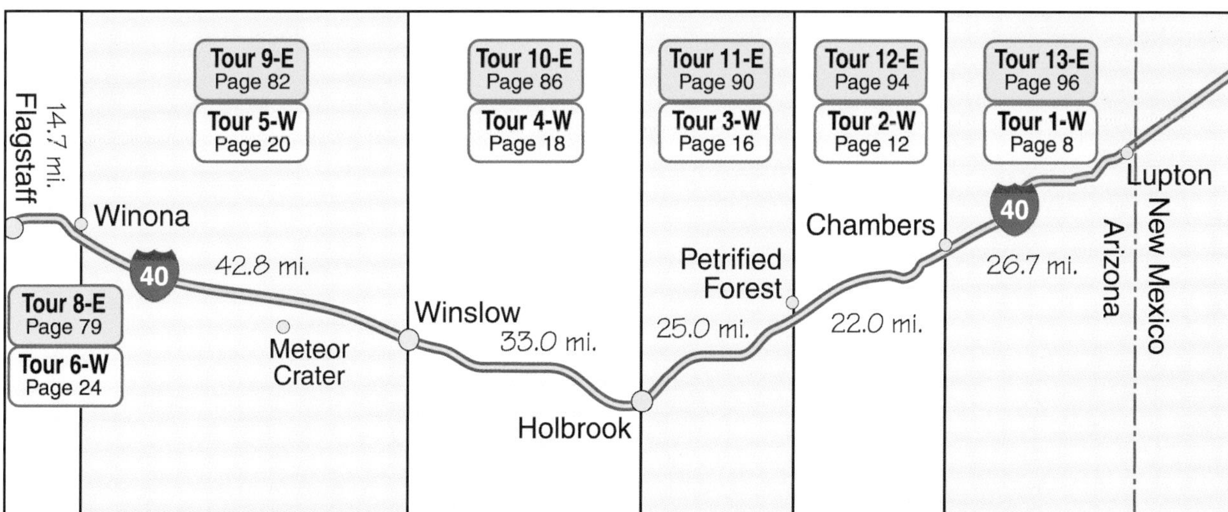

Places to Eat in Ash Fork: None recommended.
Places to Sleep in Ash Fork: None recommended.

TOUR 6-E & 8-W ASH FORK-WILLIAMS

Distance: 19.0 miles. **Driving Time**: 30 minutes.
The Landscape: The edge of the Mogollon Rim is located between these two towns. Williams perches on top of the Rim and Ash Fork on the bottom. Williams is pine-covered, while Ash Fork is in a scrub juniper belt.
Comments: There are great views off the Rim.
Highlights: Ash Fork Hill, several detours.
Suggestions: Allow some time to explore Williams.
Places to Eat in Williams: See page 70.
Places to Sleep in Williams: See page 70.

TOUR 7-E & 7-W WILLIAMS-FLAGSTAFF

Distance: 34.0 miles. **Driving Time**: 1 hour.
The Landscape: High plateau lands covered with heavy pine forests, dominated by the San Francisco Peaks.
Comments. There are several interesting detours and things to do on this tour.
Highlights: Good long bits of Route 66 to drive, the Arboretum, the Deer Farm.
Suggestions: Allow plenty of time for sidetrips.
Places to Eat in Flagstaff: See page 26.
Places to Sleep in Flagstaff: See page 26.

TOUR 8-E & 6-W FLAGSTAFF-WINONA

Distance: 14.7 miles. **Driving Time**: 30 minutes.
The Landscape: Flagstaff is in the heart of the pine forest, while Winona is at the edge.
Comments: This is a short tour but an interesting one.
Highlights: Long bits of old Route 66, Walnut Canyon, Detours.
Suggestions: See Walnut Canyon if you have time, and stop in at the Winona Trading Post.
Places to Eat in Winona: Snacks at trading post.
Places to Sleep in Winona: None.

TOUR 9-E & 5-W WINONA-WINSLOW

Distance: 42.8 miles. **Driving Time**: 1 hour.
The Landscape: Flat rangeland.
Comments: You will drive Interstate-40.
Highlights: Meteor Crater, highly recommended.
Suggestions: Stop at Twin Arrows for a photo, and visit Meteor Crater.

Places to Eat in Winslow: See page 19.
Places to Sleep in Winslow: See page 19.

TOUR 10-E & 4-W WINSLOW-HOLBROOK

Distance: 33.0 miles. **Driving Time**: 45 minutes.
The Landscape: Flat rangelands.
Comments: A straight drive on Interstate-40 with some interesting detours.
Highlights: Jack Rabbit Trading Post.
Suggestions: Take the Joseph City and Jackrabbit detours.
Places to Eat in Holbrook: See page 88.
Places to Sleep in Holbrook: See page 88.

TOUR 11-E & 3-W HOLBROOK-PETRIFIED FOREST

Distance: 25.0 miles. **Driving Time**: 40 minutes.
The Landscape: Flat rangeland.
Comments: This is an easy drive over Interstate-40.
Highlights: The Petrified Forest.
Suggestions: Allow two hours at least to see the Petrified Forest.
Places to Eat in Petrified Forest: Fred Harvey cafes at the north and south Visitor Centers.
Places to Sleep in Petrified Forest: None.

TOUR 12-E & 2-W PETRIFIED FOREST-CHAMBERS

Distance: 22.0 miles. **Driving Time**: 45 minutes.
The Landscape: Flat rangelands through Navajo country.
Comments: There are some good pieces of Route 66.
Highlights: Indian country.
Suggestions: Eat at the 66 Diner in Sanders.
Places to Eat in Chambers: Chieftan Inn
Places to Sleep in Chambers: Chieftan Inn

TOUR 13-E & 1-W CHAMBERS-LUPTON

Distance: 26.7 miles **Driving Time**: 1 hour
The Landscape: Flat rangelands through Navajo country. Interesting, beautiful red cliffs at the New Mexico line.
Comments: We have one 18.0 mile-long 66 tour here.
Highlights: Scenery, Trading Posts.
Suggestions: Photograph the kitschy displays at Lupton.
Places to Eat in Lupton: None recommended.
Places to Sleep in Lupton: None.

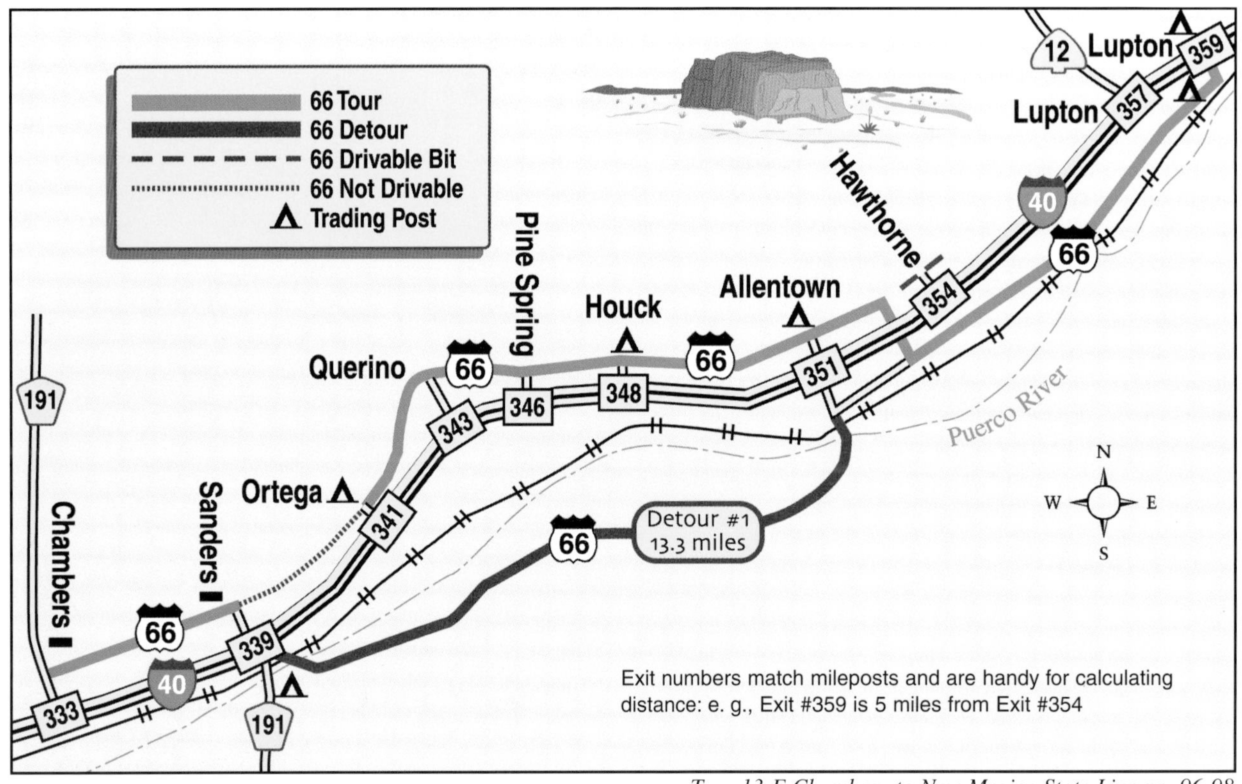

Tour 13-E Chambers to New Mexico State Line pp. 96-98

Tour 1-W New Mexico State Line to Chambers

Distance: 26.7 miles *42.7 km*

Highlights: Scenery, Navajo Indian Reservation, Trading Posts

Driving Time: 1 hour

Lupton

Tours 1-W and **2-W** take you through Navajo country. You will enjoy some beautiful scenery here and will see many Navajos, as you pass near some of their homesteads. Today, the Navajos are modernizing rapidly and many of their traditional ways are disappearing, so you should expect to see cars instead of horses, tract homes instead of hogans, and conventional dress rather than the old-style clothing. TV and other outside influences are changing the culture.

In addition to seeing Navajoland, many Indian country travelers relish the idea of being able to buy Native American arts and crafts from the artisans. Native artists are busier than they have ever been, and there is no shortage of Indian goods, and I-40 has a trading post at almost every exit on this tour. These posts are designed to cater to tourists and stock goods that the operators have found to appeal to tourists. You will want to stop and check out at least one of them in order to see what these trading posts are all about. They are part of the experience of road travel across northern Arizona.

Our image of Navajo life was created by photos like this from the 1950s. You shouldn't expect to see such a scene today—OP

If you have the time and are comfortable driving back roads, try our blue-line tour (the blue line on the map). If you are in a hurry drive straight through on I-40 so that you will have more time at the Petrified Forest, at which you will want at least half a day. If you start in the morning, we recommend spending half a day at the Petrified Forest with an overnight stay at Holbrook or Winslow. This will make a full and satisfying day.

START

EXIT #359—Lupton
Food, Gas, Trading Posts

At the border there are a number of trading posts. You will pass them as you enter Arizona and can't miss their kitschy signs and advertising gimmicks. Our favorite gimmick is the life-size plastic animals perched on the cliffs. If you want to inspect the posts take Exit #359-Lupton and turn right. Speedy's Truck Stop, with gas and food, is located among these businesses. These trading posts sell tourist goods. As of June 2000 the restaurant at the Tepee Trading Post has been closed and the only food you will find at Lupton is truck-stop fare at Speedy's.

When you are ready to begin driving our blue-line Route 66 tour, take Exit #359-Lupton, drive under I-40, set your **Zero** point midway through the underpass, and you will come to a stop sign. Turn right here. There is one more trading post, Ortega's Indian Market, a dome with a Mohawk haircut, located at this turn. It too stocks typical tourist goods. You will now drive Route 66 in a place where it is used as a frontage road.

The area of beautiful red cliffs at the border lasts for only a mile, and then you enter into an open landscape of low-growing juniper trees, and sparse grasslands. This is high desert country, with an average elevation of 6,000 feet *(1,800 meters)*. As you drive this section of Route 66 you will pass the connecting roads for Exit #357-Lupton and Exit #354-Hawthorne.

At the 5.6 mile *9.0 km* point turn right and go through one of the side-by-side tunnels under I-40. Route 66 actually swung to the north here, and the tunnels are intended to give drivers access to it. On the other side turn left, where you will find old cracked paving running west. This is the 1931 version of Route 66, and we think it is fun to drive. You will be amazed at how it winds around, rising and dipping, in contrast to the nearby I-40, where roadbuilders flattened everything. You will also appreciate how narrow the old road was and how many dangerous curves and blind spots it had. You will arrive at Allentown at the 8.0 mile *12.8 km* point. An interesting detour from Allentown to Sanders over the old road that was used by the National Old Trails and was 66 from 1923-1930 starts here. See Detour #1 on the next column.

Lupton today

Arizona-New Mexico border—fake animals on cliffs

EXIT #351—Allentown
Food, Trading Post

Allentown is not a town, just a trading post site. You will find two posts there, the largest one on I-40 in Arizona, called Indian City, and a small one called Chee's. Indian City is two-stories high and very modern. Indoors is a Taco Bell Express and a fountain with an eating area. The ground floor contains typical tourist goods, and there is an upstairs gallery, with additional merchandise. Chee's little place has three parts, a curio store with typical tourist goods, a rock shop and a book store. From Allentown continue to drive the northside frontage road to the west, to

DETOUR #1
EXIT #351-Allentown S&W
Oldest 66 to Sanders
13.3 mi. *21.3 km* one-way
Time 25 minutes

At Exit #351-Allentown, *Zero* at Indian City, cross I-40, and then drive south on County Highway 9402 for 0.5 miles *0.8 km*. You will cross the railroad and come to two bridges, side-by-side. The old bridge was built in 1923 as part of the Old Trails Highway, then used by 66 from 1926-1930, and is falling to pieces, very scenic for photos. Drive over the new bridge and turn right (W) on County Highway 7240. It runs west parallel to the railroad to Sanders, where you will cross another 1923 bridge, a good one, to return to I-40.

The Querino Canyon Bridge

the freeway is the large Indian Center Trading Post, which also bills itself as Indian Ruins. The advertising signs for this business remind us of one of the unsavory old-time practice of using misleading billboards advertising non-existent attractions. When we asked about Indian Ruins at the trading post, we were told that there are none. The merchandise sold here is typical. There is a gas station.

From Exit #341-Ortega Road, drive west on I-40. The next exit you will reach is Exit #339-Sanders.

Houck. Look carefully for it, as it is a little hard to see. You will continue to drive the frontage road parallel to I-40 and at the 11.1 mile *17.8 km* point will arrive at Houck.

EXIT #348—Houck

Food, Trading Post

Houck (pronounced "Howk" not "Hoke") is an historic spot, with James Houck establishing a trading post here in 1877, making it perhaps the oldest on Route 66. Today it is the site of Fort Courage, a big modern trading post, the main feature of which is a replica of the fort seen in the old TV series *F-Troop*. The series was not filmed here. We rate the goods in the trading post as typical tourist. There is also a convenience market and a post office. In a separate building is a restaurant and a gas station. Guests used to be able to climb the tower, but it is now closed.

From Houck stay on the north frontage road, old 66, heading west until at 12.9 miles *20.6 km* you reach Exit #346-Pine Spring. We continue the blue-line tour on old 66 here, but it requires driving about 5.0 miles *8.0 km* on a good dirt road from here. Some drivers will want to turn left and get onto I-40 westbound at Exit #346.

To continue the tour, drive the unpaved road uphill. At the 14.8 mile *23.7 km* point you will see the Querino Trading Post to your right where a sideroad meets old 66. This is an interesting place to visit, catering to local Navajos rather than to tourists. Shortly beyond this point, at 15.3 miles *24.5 km* you will reach the 1930 Querino Canyon Bridge, a great old steel span. Haul out the camera. The fire-destroyed ruins of the old Querino Trading Post are on the east side of the bridge. From the bridge continue west, coming downhill. You will reach paving again on a frontage road, turn right and follow it to the 18.0 miles *28.8 km* point, where there is a stop sign. From the sign you get onto I-40 West at Exit #341-Ortega.

If you return to I-40 from Exit #346-Pine Spring, drive I-40 west. At Exit #341-Ortega Road, on the north side of

EXIT #339—Sanders

Food (Classic Diner), Gas, Outstanding Trading Post

Take this exit and turn left, driving over I-40. Then drive the bridges over the railroad and the Puerco River. When you come to the end of the last bridge, take the first paved street to the left and drive east one block, turning right on the paved street past the post office. The **66 Diner** is on your left in the next block.

We route you to one of the main restaurant attractions for Arizona roadies, the 66 Diner, one of the famous old Valentine units, which was situated in Holbrook for many years and moved to Sanders recently. On the inside wall by the entrance you will see what appear to be a mail slot and a mail box. These were part of the Valentine system, and were actually strongboxes into which the day's receipts were deposited. As to the food, the portions served here are generous and the prices are low. We enjoyed our supper at the diner. It seems that the locals are extremely fond of Mexican food and Navajo tacos. You can also get huge hamburgers. There are Route 66 and Fifties memorabilia on the walls.

Sanders is more of a town than the places you have seen up to now, with a post office. Hwy. 191, leading to St. Johns, joins I-40 from the south here, so there are several businesses fronting Hwy. 191. Sanders is an education center for Navajo children with several big schools. Navajo families displaced by the Navajo-Hopi relocation controversy have found new homes around Sanders.

Travelers wanting a different trading post experience, one offering more traditional and less tourist-oriented goods will find a gem in Sanders along Highway 191, just one block west of the diner, at **R. B. Burnham & Co.** The Burnham family is now in its fourth generation of traders. When you enter the store it seems that it is nothing but a convenience market for the local Navajos. You will find some interesting goods in stock, including skeins of yarn for rug weaving, but the real treasure is in the back room.

Sanders 66 Diner after dark

You must have permission to enter it. Inside you will find real Navajo arts and crafts, authentic beautiful goods. This is the place to buy something that is really good, with confidence that you are getting quality. Across the highway and closer to I-40 there is a modern gas station, with the best prices we found in the area. Inside the gas station there is a convenience store for snacks and a Taco Bell Express, for fast food.

To continue the journey westward from Sanders, we are able to take a nice stretch of Route 66 used as a frontage road. From Exit #339-Sanders, **Zero** at the stop sign, turn right and then take an immediate left turn (W) onto the paved frontage road, marked Apache County Road 7060. As soon as you start driving it you will recognize it as Mother Road. There are quite a few homes along this passage from Sanders to Chambers. Drive 6.2 miles *9.9 km* to a stop sign at the junction with Highway 191. To the right is the Chambers Trading Post on Highway 191, with convenience market and tourist goods. In a separate building is the Kiyaaáánii Gallery. Turn left and go 0.5 miles *0.8 km* to Exit #333-Chambers.

EXIT #333—Chambers

Food, Lodging, Trading Post

Chambers is rather like Sanders without the schools. It does have a post office and an important road comes in from the north, Highway 191, which goes to Ganado and Chinle, deep in the Navajo nation.

The Chieftan Inn, located on the south side of I-40 at Chambers is a modern Best Western motel with a decent restaurant, the only motel between the New Mexico border and Holbrook. We tried it and can recommend it.

This tour ends at Chambers.

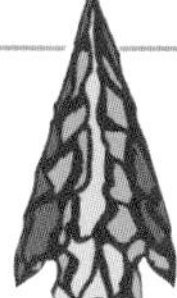

Tip: taking a side-trip to see Hubbell Trading Post National Historic Site, Canyon de Chelly or Monument Valley—all of which are accessible via Highway 191 north of Chambers—requires advance planning and many miles of driving, not a realistic detour for the Route 66 roadie. Don't attempt to do these as a day trip, especially Monument Valley. Foreign visitors who are unused to the Southwest are often told that Monument Valley is "near" Route 66. That is true only in the broadest sense. One can't really see and enjoy Canyon de Chelly or Monument Valley without taking the arranged tours available at each place. They require an overnight stay and accommodations are scarce in the high season. If you want to see these wonderful places be sure to make arrangements well in advance and plan to take a full day for Canyon de Chelly and two days for Monument Valley.

Canyon de Chelly

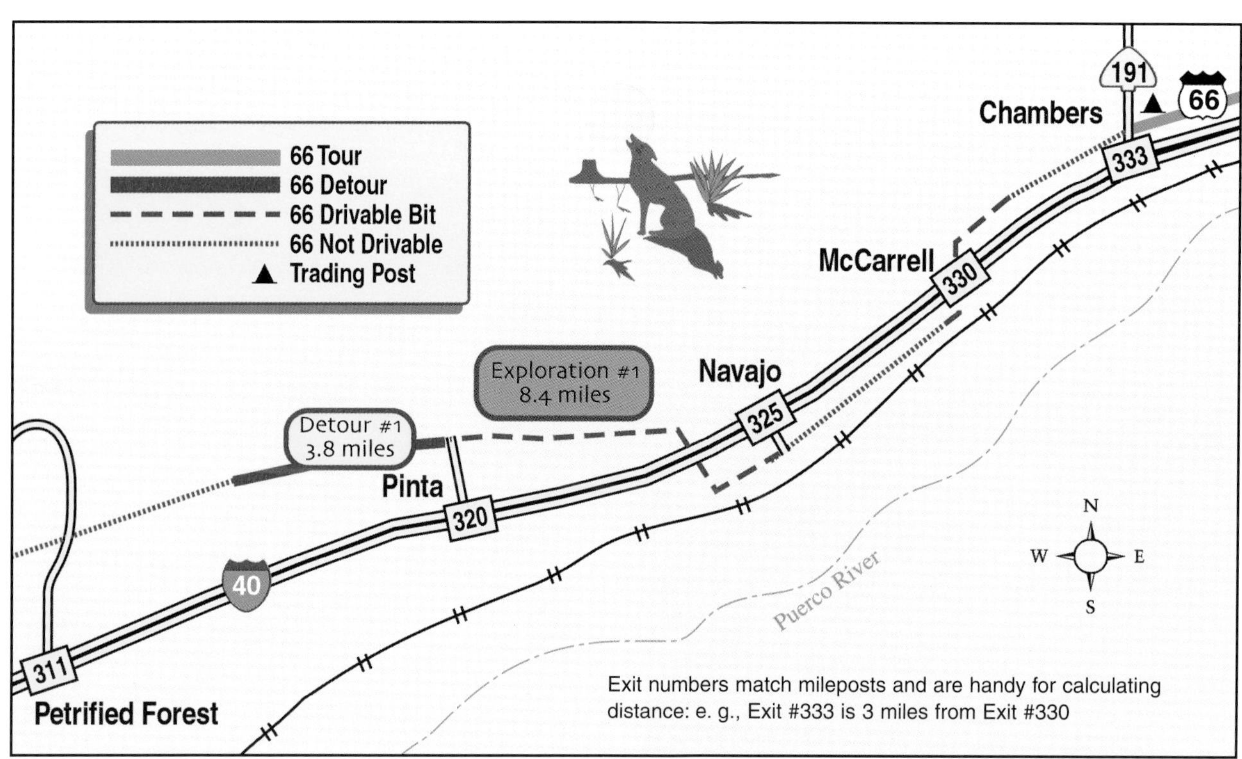

Tour 12-E Petrified Forest to Chambers pp. 94-95

Tour 2-W Chambers to The Petrified Forest

Distance: 22.0 miles *35.2 km*

Highlights: Scenery, Petrified Forest

Driving Time: 45 minutes

Navajo mother with infant—OP

Tour 2-W continues through Navajo Country, although the Navajo influence begins to diminish as you travel west of Chambers. You will stop for sightseeing at the Petrified Forest, one of the great natural wonders of the world, which no traveler should miss.

EXIT #333—Chambers

Food, Gas, Trading Posts

From Chambers we will not be able to drive any long portions of Route 66 on the regular tour, and will have to settle for I-40. Two drivable bits of Route 66 are available, but one of these, Exploration #1 west of Exit #325-Navajo, is not for the ordinary driver, or the ordinary car.

As you drive west of Chambers on I-40, you can see bits of Route 66 to your right (N). There are hills in this area and the old road does some pretty wild twisting to negotiate them, quite a change from the "flatten it all" approach of the 1960s freeway builders.

There are two drivable bits of Route 66 from Exit #330-McCarrell, but these are so short that they will be of interest only to the "see-very-inch" enthusiast. Both of these are paved and any car can handle them, but they are not very interesting and we suggest that most drivers will want to buzz on by them, so that they have more time to spend at the Petrified Forest.

EXIT #325—Navajo

Gas, Food

There is an Exploration available from this exit, but we recommend it only for the driver who has experience driving backcountry byways and who is driving a high-clearance vehicle. Also, the trip should not be undertaken if the ground is wet or if there is any danger of a sudden hard rain. Finally, we advise against driving this road after dark. Part of this old road is rough and where it crosses Crazy Creek there are a couple of washouts that could worsen. They are tricky to drive in the daytime and would be murder at night.

Today the traveler sees little at Navajo. In 1946, Rittenhouse described it as having a population of 52 and said that it, "Consists of Marty's Trading Post, with gas and groceries; a small neat cafe in a house back of the trading post, and five tourist cabins." Navajo is an historic

<*Westbound*

site, for at nearby Navajo Springs an important event took place. In 1863 during the depths of the Civil War, Arizona and New Mexico were joined in one giant territory named New Mexico. President Lincoln thought it wise to divide the territory and create the separate territory of Arizona, with its capital north of Tucson, because Tucson was a hotbed of southern sympathizers. Arizona was created and Lincoln appointed officials to govern the new territory sending the party to Arizona to take charge. The officials, accompanied by a group of scouts, left Santa Fe late in 1863, traveling west. They wanted to be certain they were on Arizona soil before undertaking any official acts. The scouts told them they were definitely in Arizona when they camped at Navajo Springs on December 29, 1863, and there Governor J. B. Goodwin declared that Arizona was officially established. Maps show that there is a marker at the springs, some 3.5 miles *5.6 km* SE of Exit #325. In May 2000 we tried to drive to the site and found that at the halfway point there was a seriously locked (six padlocks) gate barring the way. There is a bronze plaque south and east of Exit #325-Navajo.

EXPLORATION #1
EXIT #325-Navajo S&W
Route 66 to Petrified Forest
8.4 mi. *13.4 km* one-way
Time 25 minutes

Take Exit #325-Navajo, **Zero** and turn left at the stop sign and go south over I-40. Turn left and go to the bottom of the ramp, just before the gas station, where you turn right (S) on the paved road, immediately going over a cattle guard. You drive past a row of houses. At 0.5 miles *0.8 km* you drive over another cattle guard and come to a road junction. Turn right (W) on Apache County Road 7385, old 66. You'll see a Dead End sign, but ignore it. At 2.6 miles *4.2 km* turn right (N) and go through a tunnel under I-40. On the other side turn left on the sandy road. At the fork, go left. At 3.1 miles *5.0 km* you'll be at the top of a rise. From now on, this trip gets interesting. You will soon feel that you are way out in the desert. At 3.5 miles *5.6 km* you will find a narrow place where floods have washed out part of the road. The washout has been partly filled in so that you can drive the repaired place, but the road has steep crumbly banks. You will find another such washout at 3.8 miles *6.1 km*. Once you are past these two trouble spots, you will be on much better surfaces and can proceed confidently. Old paving now appears but it is rough. At 4.4 miles *7.0 km* you will pass through a gate in a wire fence into a wild life sanctuary, which you leave through another gate at 5.9 miles *9.4 km*. Beyond here you will enjoy good paving to the 7.2 mile *11.5 km* point. This is the place where the unpaved connecting road to Exit #320-Pinta comes in to your left (S). You can return to I-40 at 8.4 miles *13.4 km* or continue westward 2.6 miles *4.2 km* on Detour #1.

EXIT #320—Pinta

No Gas, No Food, No Lodging

The very interesting Detour #1 is available from this Exit, being the west half of Exploration #1, which we described from Exit #325-Navajo.

DETOUR #1
EXIT #320-Pinta N&W
Old Route 66
3.8 mi. *6.1 km* one-way
Time 20 minutes

At Exit #320-Pinta stop sign, **Zero**, turn right and take the offramp downhill. Don't worry about the Dead End sign. Follow the curving road west. The paving ends. Don't take the straight dirt road to the left, but stay on the main dirt road. At 1.2 miles *1.9 km* you will intersect old 66. Turn left and drive on the old paving. At about 3.8 miles *6.1 km* you will find the remains of the Painted Desert Trading Post (R) overlooking the valley of the Dead River—very scenic for photos. Just west of this is an old but still drivable bridge, a good place to stop. You can drive another 2.4 miles *3.8 km* west of the bridge, but the road is bad and is blocked at the boundary fence for the Petrified Forest. Return the way you came in and get on to I-40 westbound.

Once you are back on I-40 from Pinta get into the westbound lanes and head for Exit #311-Petrified Forest. When you get there, take Exit #311 to go into the park. You will find that all traffic is controlled so that it must go to the Visitor Center.

EXIT #311—Petrified Forest

Food, Gas, Trading Post

See the following pages for a tour guide to the Petrified Forest and Painted Desert. Be aware that most travelers will want to finish their visit and get to Holbrook by driving south out of the park to go west on Highway 180 rather than returning to I-40. To return to I-40 means backtracking through the park for 26.3 miles *42.1 km*. See the map on the following page for an understanding of the road situation.

Ruins of the Painted Desert Trading Post, Detour #1

The Petrified Forest National Park—North to South

Distance: 28.0 miles *44.8 km* plus detours **Time**: Depends on stops, but at least half a day

For the tour from South to North, see pp. 92-93

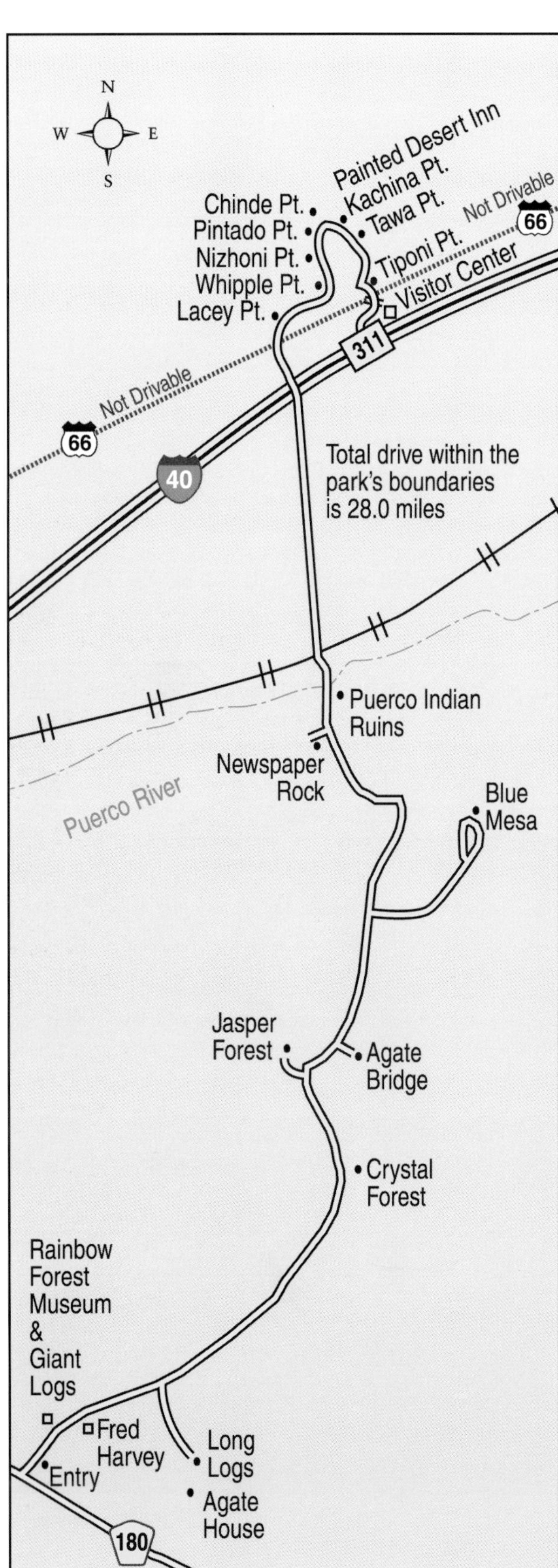

The Petrified Forest is an unforgettable sight, not to be missed, but be sure to allow enough time to see and enjoy it. How much time do you need? We think half a day is a minimum. We like to get out of our car and hike at places in the park, but some travelers will be content to settle for what they can see from the windows of their vehicles. Hours vary from 7-7 summer and 8-5 winter MST.

The National Park Service has designed the road system so that drivers are automatically directed to the Visitor Center, which consists of two parts, one operated by the Park Service, with an information desk, gift shop, bookstore, museum and toilets; and the other operated by Fred Harvey, with its own curio shop, cafeteria, convenience market, and gas station. The food here is much better than that found at the south end of the park and the setting is nice, so this is the place to eat. From I-40 to our Zero point is 0.5 miles *0.8 km.*

Once you leave the Visitor Center, you pass the Entrance Station, where you must pay an entrance fee. Set your odometer to 0.0 here and then use the following road log.

0.0 mi. *0.0 km* **Entrance Station—Zero Point**

0.4 mi. *0.6 km* **Old Route 66**. You will see an unpaved road to your right, which is barred to traffic. This is Route 66, which followed this alignment until about 1961.

0.5 mi. *0.8 km* **Tiponi Point** (R). This is the first of eight Painted Desert lookout points. Some, but not Tiponi, require walking. The views are gorgeous. We are big fans of the Painted Desert and can't get enough of it. It is questionable whether you will want to visit every viewpoint. If you have the time, you may want to do so, but if you are in a hurry, we suggest stopping at Tiponi, the Painted Desert Inn, Pintado and Lacey.

The Painted Desert from Kachina Point

1.4 mi. *2.2 km* **Tawa Point** (R). There's a short walk to a viewpoint. On the way, you will find a 0.5 mile-long *0.8 km* foot trail along the rim to the Painted Desert Inn. We have hiked this trail and find it to be easy and enjoyable.

<Westbound

1.7 mi. *2.7 km* **Painted Desert Inn** (R). The inn was built by H. P. Lore in 1924, as Stone Tree House, a tourist attraction. The United States Government bought the property in 1935 and remodeled it using CCC labor from 1937-41, then turned the operation of the inn over to a concessionaire. The inn was closed 1942-1947 due to the war. In 1947 the Fred Harvey Company took over the concession and brought its famous architect, Mary Colter, out of retirement to decorate the place, which was finished in 1948 and Ms. Colter did her usual superb job. The inn was operated as a hotel until closed in 1963. Though scheduled for demolition in 1975, supporters saved it. Made a National Historic Landmark in 1987, it is now a fine place to visit, to admire the architecture, the history and the views from Kachina Point, where it is situated. There is a hiking trail going down onto the floor of the Painted Desert from the inn. As you walk out to the Kachina Viewpoint, you will find a Wilderness sign pointing to the trailhead. The trail goes to the bottom of the valley. This is not a "tame" trail like others you will find in the park. It requires planning and preparedness.

The Painted Desert Inn, a Petrified Forest landmark

2.0 mi. *3.2 km* **Chinde Point** (R). Chinde in Navajo means "spirit" or "ghost". This point looks over the Black Forest, and you must drive 0.4 miles *0.6 km* to it. There are picnic shelters and tables at the point, and a toilet.

2.6 mi. *4.2 km* **Pintado Point** (R). Requires a short walk from the parking area. Panoramic views, varied colors.

3.8 mi. *6.1 km* **Nizhoni** ("beautiful" in Navajo) **Point** (R). No walking needed, turnout to viewpoint.

4.0 mi. *6.4 km* **Whipple Point** (R). No walking required.

4.3 mi. *6.9 km* **Lacey Point** (R). No walking. You have now finished looking at the Painted Desert viewpoints and will head south, into the Petrified Forest.

5.4 mi. *8.6 km* **Route 66**. You will see another leg of Route 66 here, going to the west (R), it's lined by power poles. No asphalt remains. You can stand here and look to the east and see where the road ran across the park.

5.6 mi. *9.0 km*. You reach the **I-40 overpass**.

10.6 mi. *17.0 km* **Puerco Pueblo Indian Ruin** to your left. The paved trail through the ruins is 0.3 miles *0.5 km* long. There are about 100 rooms, many unexcavated, and it was inhabited from 1250-1380. There are some petroglyph panels. There is a toilet at the site.

11.6 mi. *18.6 km* **Newspaper Rock** is to your right. From the road you drive 0.25 miles *0.4 km* to the parking lot and make a short walk. Formerly one could hike down a trail to see and touch this rock, but so much damage was done that park officials closed the trail. Now you are limited to looking at it through a telescope.

15.3 mi. *24.5 km* **Blue Mesa** appears to your left. A 3.5 mile *5.6 km* access road takes you to the top of this mesa to see blue and white haystacks and some petrified wood. There is a 1.0 mile *1.6 km* hiking trail there. When you are finished, return to the main road. If your time is short, then skip Blue Mesa.

17.5 mi. *28.0 km* **Agate Bridge**, to your left. A paved road takes you to a high point where you will find the bridge after a short walk. There is a toilet at the site.

18.2 mi. *29.1 km* **Jasper Forest** to your right. A 0.5 mile *0.8 km* paved road takes you to the edge of a cliff from which you look down into a wood-covered valley. Years ago, this was one of the most famous sights of the park, but theft has damaged it severely. Short walk. Skip this one if time is limited.

19.9 mi. 31.8 *km* **Crystal Forest** to your left. A 0.75 mile *1.2 km* paved trail winds around this beautiful forest. Lots of color. Lots of wood. Easy trail. Recommended.

25.6 mi. *41.0 km* **Long Logs** and **Agate House** to your left. Drive 0.25 miles *0.4 km* to the parking lot. There is a good paved 0.5 mile *0.8 km* trail through Long Logs, with a 0.75 mile *1.2 km* branch going to Agate House. Recommended.

25.8 mi. *41.3 km* **Fred Harvey Building** with curio shop and fountain. A limited range of food is available in the fountain. Just south is the **Rainbow Forest Museum** run by the Park Service. Inside are a small museum, book shop and restrooms. Park information is available. Behind the museum is the **Giant Logs Trail**, which is 0.4 miles *0.6 km* long and is fun. **End of the Attractions**.

When you finish at the museum you have a decision to make. It is a drive of 26.3 mi. *42.1 km* north to return to I-40 via the park road. Many westbound motorists elect instead to go south. The south Entrance Station is 1.6 mi. *2.6 km* south of the museum. To go to Holbrook via the south, you will continue to the 28.0 mile *44.8 km* point, which is the junction with Highway 180. **Zero** here, and then turn right (W) and drive Highway 180 to the intersection of Navajo and Hopi in Holbrook, a distance of 18.3 mi. *29.3 km* from the junction. Though Highway 180 was never Route 66, it is the same kind of road that 66 was in the old days, and in many ways gives you the Route 66 feeling better than driving I-40. If you take Highway 180 you will miss the sights on Tour 3-W. There are a couple of privately owned museum-curio shops at the Highway 180 junction.

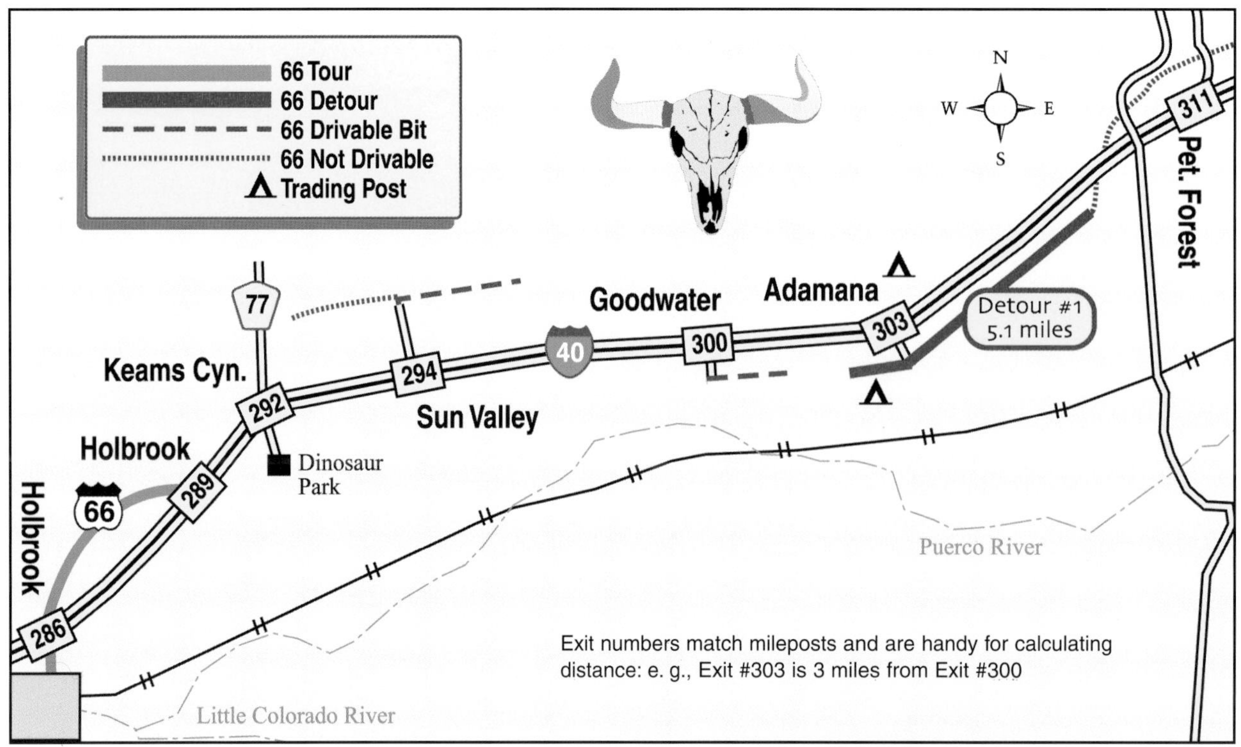

Tour 11-E Holbrook to Petrified Forest pp. 90-91

Tour 3-W Petrified Forest to Holbrook

Distance: 25.0 miles *40.0 km*
Highlights: Scenery, Petrified Forest
Driving Time: 40 minutes

Dinosaur Park

Tour 3-W. West of Exit #311-Petrified Forest, we move from Indian country into cowboy country.

We are still driving through a kind of desert known as Prairie Shortgrass. In wet years and favorable points in the climatic cycle, the grasses that grow here can be abundant, making the vast expanses of rangeland look like a sea of green. That is what it looked like to Lt. Beale and his men in 1857. The year 1885 was another time when these fields looked lush, enticing the Aztec Land and Cattle Company to invest millions of dollars (in today's money) on a huge cattle operation. They bought one million acres of land from the railroad for fifty cents an acre and imported 40,000 head of cattle. As so often happens—through ignorance and greed—they overgrazed the country and in the drought years that followed the grasses were so badly damaged that they have not yet recovered.

The Aztec company was known as the Hash Knife Outfit, celebrated in legend, the prose of Zane Grey and several Hollywood movies. Its legacy is still strong in Holbrook, as we shall see.

Exit #311—Petrified Forest
Food, Gas, Curios

There are no continuous bits of Route 66 to drive between the Petrified Forest and Holbrook. There is a detour, found at Adamana, where one can drive 5.1 miles *8.2 km* on old 66 to the site of a Route 66 roadside business, Rocky's Old Stage Station.

EXIT #303—Adamana
Trading Post, Rock Shop, Old Bridge

To get to the Painted Desert Indian Center, a trading post, take Exit #303-Adamana, go under I-40 and turn right (W). The post is 0.1 miles *0.16 km* ahead and has good merchandise, including dead pawn. 0.2 miles *0.3 km* farther west you will see (but can't cross) the old 66 bridge over Big Lithodendron Wash. Return to Exit #303. On the north side of the exit is Stewart's Petrified Wood which is like one of the old-time 66 shops. You drive up a winding road to reach it. The owners have tried every advertising gimmick, including plastic dinosaurs, old cars, mannequins, signs—even the old ploy of parking junk cars in front to make you think that it is a popular place. We liked the inside of the store, which was funky and very personal, a far cry from the formula places to the east. At Stewart's they sell petrified wood in all shapes and sizes. From Exit #303-Adamana, continue to drive I-40 west.

<Westbound

DETOUR #1
EXIT #303-Adamana
S&E
Route 66
5.1 mi. *8.2 km* one-way
Time 20 minutes

At Exit #303-Adamana, **Zero,** drive under I-40 and on the other side turn left (E) on the frontage road, which is Route 66. It runs along uneventfully for 5.1 miles *8.2 km* parallel to I-40 to a point where the paving ends. Here a gravel road turns at a right angle to the south, going to Adamana. Rocky's Old Stage Station, a former Route 66 roadside business, looking like a junkyard, is straight ahead. Please do not trespass on the premises. From the turn, backtrack to I-40.

Abandoned truck at Rocky's Old Stage Station

EXIT #300—Goodwater

No gas, No food, No lodging

The remnants of this business were torn down in 2000, so it is no longer a worthwhile detour. We recommend that you pass by this exit and keep going.

EXIT #294—Sun Valley Road

No Gas, No food, No lodging

A short stretch of Route 66 is available from Exit #294, (see map) but it is of mild interest, only for roadies, with a No Trespassing sign turning a former detour into a trip not worth making.

EXIT #292—Dinosaur Park

Sightseeing attraction

The owners of this park have spared no expense in advertising. You will see their life-size dinosaurs, petrified wood and signs for a long distance. We like this place and think that it is worth a visit. There are three attractions here: (1) International Petrified Forest, (2) Dinosaur Park, and (3) Museum of the Americas. This place is quite modern, having been opened in 1999, but is the kind of experience 66 travelers would have been glad to enjoy in the old days.

SIGHTSEEING #1
EXIT #292
Dinosaur Park
Time 1.5 hours

Take Exit #292-Dinosaur Park and follow the signs into the place. There is a ticket booth at the entrance station. The Museum of the Americas is a large building which is home to a wonderful collection of ancient Indian artifacts and a reconstruction of one of their dwellings. The museum building has a small snack bar, a gift shop and a restroom. Outside there is a very large rock shop with a huge collection of petrified wood and other stones. You can drive their private roads around some interesting purple Painted Desert haystacks through which petrified wood has been artistically scattered, about a 4.0 mile *6.4 km* loop. There are a few short hiking trails along the drive. Finally, near the entrance, there is a little park with dinosaurs for the kids to play with. Also at the entrance is a pen containing a few buffalo. As a bonus, during a June visit, we saw a Navajo weaver making a rug in the museum building. It's a three-ring circus, but tastefully done.

Dinosaur Park is only a couple of miles from Holbrook. From Exit #292-Keams Canyon get on I-40 westbound, and look for Exit #289-Holbrook, which you will take.

Exit #289—Holbrook (E. Navajo Blvd.)

Take Exit #289-Holbrook, where you will see Historic US 66 signs guiding you into the town.

TIP

If you have spent half a day at the Petrified Forest as many people do, you may decide to spend the night at Holbrook. It is a good choice, with plenty of good rooms, restaurants and things to do and see. See Page 88 for information.

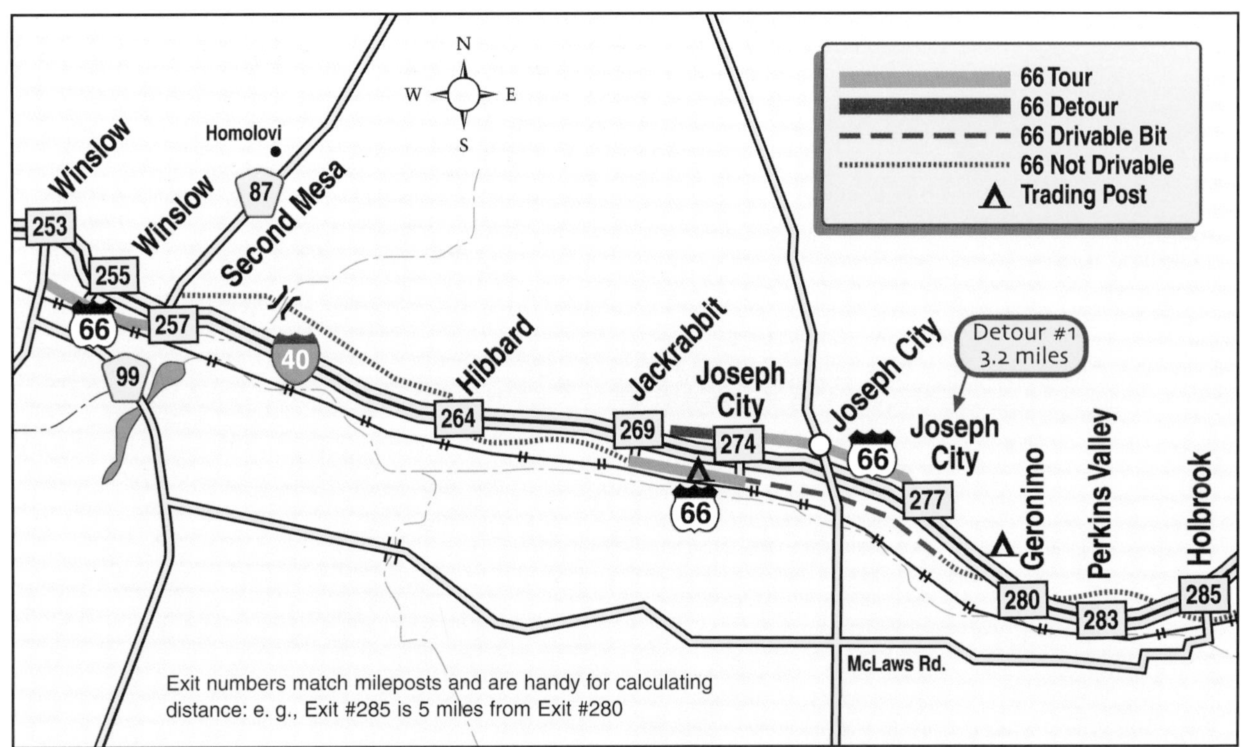

Tour 10-E Winslow to Holbrook pp. 86-89

Tour 4-W Holbrook to Winslow

Distance: 33.0 miles *53.0 km*

Highlights: Joseph City, Jack Rabbit Trading Post

Driving Time: 45 minutes

In the saddle at Jack Rabbit

Tour 4-W takes you through more flat high-desert rangeland—cowboy country—to Winslow. You will visit the 1876 Mormon town of Joseph City then go on to make a stop at a true 66 icon, the Jack Rabbit Trading Post. "Here It Is!" An optional stop is a visit to the Geronimo Trading Post, famed for having The World's Largest Petrified Log! The end of the trip will bring you into the heart of Winslow on old Route 66 where you can visit Standin' on the Corner Park, the Old Trails Museum, and other attractions. Let's go!

Downtown Holbrook

START

Start this tour at the intersection of Hopi and Navajo in downtown Holbrook, the **Zero** point. Drive west on Hopi (Route 66), which is clearly marked with Historic US 66 signs. The signs will direct you onto I-40 on the west side of town, at Exit #285-Holbrook.

As you travel west from Holbrook on I-40 you will see more of the flat grasslands that have been your companion for many miles. This is still ranching country. Coming up is an optional side-trip to Geronimo Trading Post.

EXIT #280—Geronimo (optional)

<u>Trading Post, No Gas, No Food</u>

If you want to make this stop, take Exit #280 and drive up to the trading post. The draw here is petrified wood, with a claim that they have the largest petrified tree in the world on display, and we would not dispute them. This monster weighs 80 tons and is worth seeing. The specialty here is semi-precious stones, and they have one of the largest collections of gemstones you will see on the road today. Some of their Indian jewelry is of good quality and they have dead pawn.

As you drive I-40 west of Exit #280-Geronimo, you are approaching Joseph City, one of the few Arizona 66 places where you will find farming fields. The little town was settled by Mormons in 1876 and the settlers used water from the Little Colorado River for irrigation. Nearby you will see the giant smokestacks of the Cholla power plant. The residents of Joseph City made a bargain with the devil in 1960 when the plant was built and they sold their water rights to the power company. The plant created a number of jobs for residents of the town but it also sucked up their groundwater, drying up the wells they and their grandfathers had relied on for farming.

The Jack Rabbit Trading Post's famous sign

EXIT #277—Joseph City
Gas

Take Exit #277 and **Zero** at the stop sign. Historic US 66 signs guide you through Joseph City, as the Mother Road went right down Main Street of the little burg. On your right as you enter town you will see the Old Fort Monument at 0.7 miles *1.1 km*, an interesting stop, which will only take a couple of minutes. As you drive farther you will see the sagging remains of several former road-

DETOUR #1
EXIT #277-Joseph City
Route 66 Trading Posts
3.2 mi. *5.1 km* one-way
Time 10 minutes

Zero at the stop sign. Then go through Joseph City following the Historic US 66 signs. Instead of taking the "Jct. I-40", continue to drive straight ahead on the paved road, which is is old 66. You will soon see the site of Howdy Hank's Trading Post to your right, identified by its plywood tepee. Just past it on your left is the log cabin structure of Ella's Frontier. Ella used to advertise that hers was the oldest post on Route 66, but it wasn't. Turn around at Ella's and go back to Exit #274. Cross over it and go to Jack Rabbit.

side businesses. Follow the 66 signs to "Jct. I-40" where you drive over I-40 and on the other side turn right (W), driving along the frontage road, a stretch of 66.

If you bypass Joseph City and want to see the famous Jack Rabbit Trading Post, take Exit #274-Joseph City, below.

EXIT #274—Joseph City
Food, Jack Rabbit Trading Post

At Exit #274-Joseph City, go across I-40 to its south side and turn right (W). You'll drive a paved strip of Route 66 used as a frontage road. You don't need our instructions to guide you to the Jack Rabbit, as you will see the signs that have been so effective for decades telling you where it is. In June 2000 the owners installed a new concrete driveway and apron. The bunny sits out in front just beckoning riders. Inside you will find lots of Route 66 souvenirs and a little museum. They sell a cherry cider. When you leave the post, just keep on driving west on the frontage road and get back onto the interstate at Exit #269-Jackrabbit.

The next exit, #264-Hibbard, is a disappointment. One used to be able to go north and west here and drive a great stretch of 66 to the Cottonwood Wash Bridge. No more. Access to the road is blocked by a locked gate. Pass by Exit #264-Hibbard and drive to Exit #257-Second Mesa.

EXIT #257—Second Mesa
No gas, No Food, No lodging

We reluctantly record a change in the road that occurred in the fall of 2000. Until then it was possible to take a Detour north and east of Exit #257 to visit the Cottonwood Wash Bridge. The access road is now blocked and it is no longer possible to drive to the bridge.

SIGHTSEEING #1
EXIT #257
Homolovi Ruins Park
Time 1 hour

Take Exit #257-Second Mesa, **Zero** at the stop sign, turn right, and drive north on Highway 87. At 1.2 miles *1.9 km* turn left and follow the signs into Homolovi. This is the site of an ancient Indian city and you can visit several restored ruins on roads that wander through the park. There is a visitor center with restrooms, a book store and information. A fee is charged.

Winslow

To get into Winslow, take Exit #257-Second Mesa and go south across I-40, then turn right (W). The frontage road is old 66 taking you into the historic downtown Winslow.

Where to Eat and Sleep in Winslow

Eating:
La Posada—303 E. Second St. Elegance without pretension. Moderate prices.
Port Java—At the Airport, 703 Airport Road. Informal and friendly. Inexpensive

Sleeping:
La Posada—303 E. Second St. A classic experience.

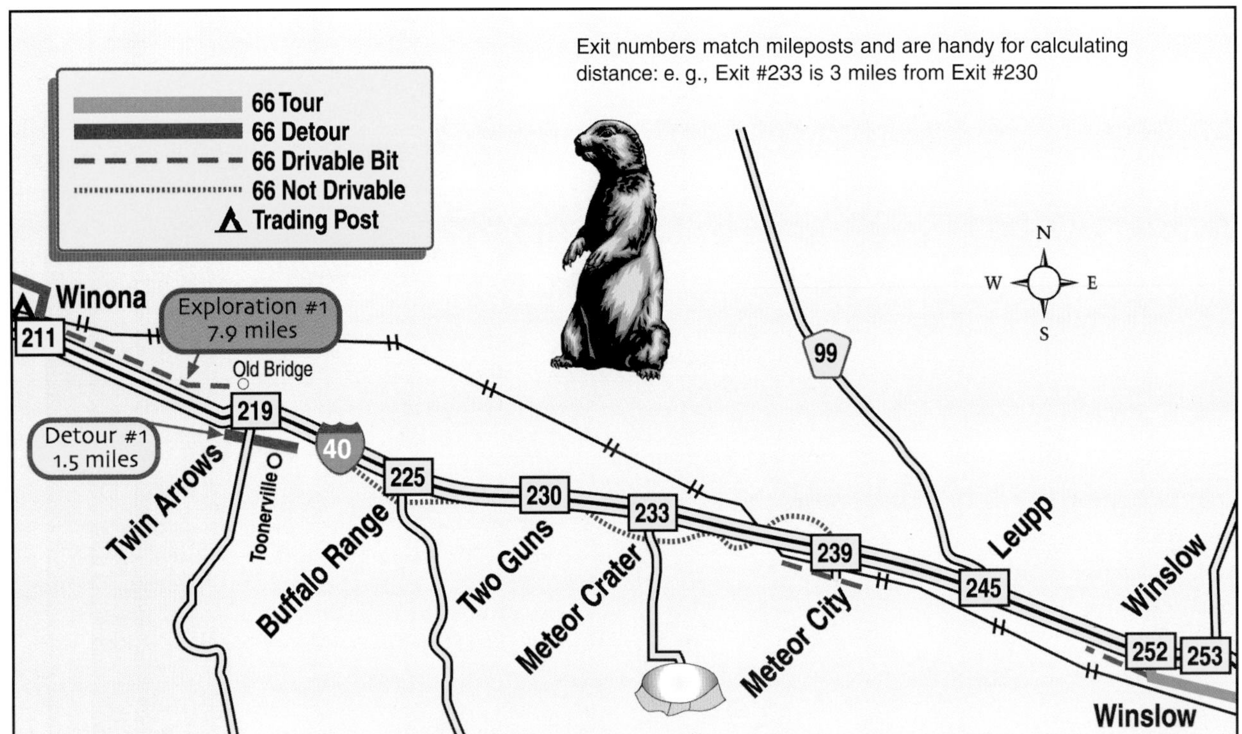

Tour 9-E Winona to Winslow pp. 82-85

Tour 5-W Winslow to Winona

Distance: 42.8 miles *68.5 km*
Highlights: Meteor Crater, Twin Arrows, Winona
Driving Time: 1 hour

Standin' on the Corner in Winslow, Arizona....

START

Tour 5-W starts at The Corner in Winslow, the **Zero** point. On this journey you will be unable to drive any parts of Route 66 on the tour, but I-40 closely parallels the Mother Road through this section and you will be able to experience virtually the same delights of this well-known stretch of highway as Route 66 travelers did. You can visit Meteor Crater, stop off at Twin Arrows for a photograph, and end the tour at—don't forget—Winona!

The Corner

Zero at The Corner, drive north on Kinsley one block to Third Street, and turn left on Third. Route 66 in Winslow was divided in 1951 so that eastbound traffic used Second Street and westbound traffic used Third Street. Until then all Route 66 traffic had been on Second Street. For this reason there were more 66 businesses on Second Street, but as you go out Third Street you will see the remains of some old roadside enterprises. At 1.0 miles *1.6 km* Second and Third streets merge at The Y. From the Y go west on the frontage road. At 1.6 miles *2.6 km* take a right turn and get onto I-40 west for "Flagstaff" at Exit #252-Winslow.

Interior view of Winslow's famous La Posada

EXIT #239—Meteor City
No gas, No Food, No lodging

Meteor City, the last of the collection of trading posts that once dotted the highway between Winslow and Winona, closed its doors on July 31, 2000, marking the end of an era. Meteor City had nothing to do with Meteor Crater, coming up. On the north side of this exit you will see a sign for Red Gap Ranch Rd. An early version of Route 66 is accessible here, but the entrance gate is locked. You can see glimpses of this old road as you drive west, until it meets I-40 at Sunshine Overpass, then even fewer glimpses of it on the south side. Pass by Exit #239-Meteor City, and get ready to take the next exit, #233, so that you can see Meteor Crater.

Meteor Crater

Rest Area

At MP 236.5, just beyond Sunshine Overpass, there is a rest area (R) with toilets, soft drinks and information.

EXIT #233—Meteor Crater
Gas, Food, No lodging, Natural Wonder

As you approach you can see a white dome south of the exit. The dome houses a modern service station, not an old Route 66 business. If you take the exit and drive up the Meteor Crater Road, at the far side of the service station you will see old 66 running east-west on both sides of the paved road where there is a *faux* cattle guard. Until recently it was possible to drive this road in either direction but today it is posted with No Trespassing signs. We lament that it is no longer possible to drive easterly to get to the old Meteor Museum. From the road you can still see the museum off in the distance with its distinctive tower.

Meteor Crater itself is a genuine natural phenomenon—no trumped up publicity was necessary to make it seem important. For years its origin baffled scientists, who argued various theories about its origin, ranging from a steam vent to a volcanic eruption, but the modern view is that it is an impact crater where a meteor struck the earth. It is such a rare phenomenon that NASA used it for training astronauts during the Apollo Program. For several decades Winslow advertised itself as The Meteor City in order to capitalize on the fame of this great crater. No Route 66 or I-40 traveler should miss it. See Sightseeing #1 for details.

SIGHTSEEING #1
EXIT #233
Meteor Crater
Time 1.5 hours

Take Exit #233-Meteor Crater and follow the signs into the place, a 6.0 mile *9.6 km* drive on paved roads. You will pass a gas station. At the far edge of the gas station Route 66 runs across the Meteor Crater road, but it is blocked by No Trespassing signs, so drive on. The road takes you up to the parking lot. You buy a ticket at the entrance and then walk up steps to a courtyard where there is an interesting display about astronauts. From there you enter the main building where you will find restrooms, a snack bar, book and gift shop including some Route 66 things, and Indian jewelry. There is a well-designed museum that tells the history of Meteor Crater, and also a theater in which programs about the crater are presented.

The main attraction is outdoors. You walk out onto the rim of the crater and are enthralled by the sight. Three observation stations have been set up, at a low, medium and high level, with lensless telescopes trained on points of interest. Signs guide you. It is not possible to walk around the entire rim unless you are escorted by a guide. Guided tours are available and are excellent.

Meteor Crater is privately owned, but the owners have done a good job developing and caring for it.

When you are finished at Meteor Crater return to I-40 headed west.

EXIT #230—Two Guns
No gas, No Food, No lodging

At Exit #230-Two Guns, on the south side of I-40 there are the remains of one of the most interesting of the old roadside attractions. In addition to the modern ruins of a gas station and a campground you will see the stone buildings of the old zoo and Canyon Lodge. Two Guns is emphatically not open to the public. If you take the exit, you will only be able to drive up to the barricade and take pictures of the place from a distance, and the sight is not very photogenic. We recommended driving past it.

EXIT #225—Buffalo Range Road
No gas, No food, No lodging

West of Two Guns you will pass Exit #225-Buffalo Range. A small buffalo herd is maintained here by the Arizona Game and Fish Commission and it is open to the public. However, don't try to go there unless you have made prior arrangements, because there are no set hours and the buffalo herd could be anywhere on the range. You need to have the keeper take you to the place where the herd is grazing, which changes from day to day. We visited the place and were lucky to find the keeper at home at his ranch house and he was willing to take us out to see the animals. The only way to make this trip is to call in advance to make an appointment, 928-774-5045.

EXIT #219—Twin Arrows

No gas, No food, No lodging, Photos

The next exit is Exit #219-Twin Arrows, where you can make a rewarding photo stop. Turn left at the stop sign, go over I-40 and turn right at the Twin Arrows sign. Drive the curving frontage road to the gas station and cafe. These are closed, so all you can do is take pictures of the arrows. This interchange has a strange design, and you cannot proceed west onto I-40. You must backtrack to Exit #219 the way you came in.

Twin Arrows

After your visit to Twin Arrows and/or Toonerville, you will return to I-40 and drive west. You will notice that trees appear on the landscape, replacing the grasslands. At first these trees are low-growing junipers, but then you see taller junipers and pinon pines. At Winona you will encounter the first ponderosa pines, tall majestic trees, of a great forest that runs from Winona to Williams and beyond.

DETOUR #1
EXIT #219-Twin Arrows S&E
Toonerville Trading Post
1.5 mi. *2.4 km* one-way
Time 10 minutes

After you visit Twin Arrows return to the I-40 onramp. Turn right at the stop sign and then take an immediate left on the old gray paving. Soon you'll see a building surrounded by a lot of junk and small buildings. This was the Toonerville Trading Post, older than Twin Arrows. In 1972 the owner, Slick McAlister, was murdered there by robbers. The old paving continues to the 1.5 mile *2.4 km* point. Return to Exit #219 and go west on I-40.

A portion of old Route 66 east of Toonerville

EXIT #211—Winona

Gas, Food

Because of the way it is treated in Bobby Troup's song, "Get Your Kicks on Route 66," many people expect to see a town when they get to Winona, but it was never a town. Today there is only a gas station and trading post at the site. Winona started as a station on the railroad. In the 1920s, as Old Trails Highway travel ran by the place, Flagstaff barber Billy Adams, who owned a ranch near the station point built a tourist court there and called it Winona. Rittenhouse in 1946 said this about Winona, "Winona Trading Post offers cafe, gas, groceries, and several cabins." The remains of the cabins are not visible.

End of Tour, Winona Trading Post

Take Exit #211 and visit the trading post. They have Route 66 souvenirs, groceries and a snack bar. In addition to tourist business the place caters to ranching families who live nearby and you may see some real Arizona cowboys here. From the store you can easily return to I-40.

The interesting Exploration #1 available from Winona is described on page 23.

Winona Trading Post

EXPLORATION #1
EXIT #211-Winona
Route 66 and 1914 bridge
7.9 mi. *12.6 km* one-way
Time 1 hour

Take Exit #211-Winona and turn right at the stop sign and then right again on the first drivable road. Go downhill on old paving—Route 66. At the bottom **Zero** at the 0 milepost sign (R). The paving lasts for 1.0 mile *1.6 km* then becomes patchy, turning into a good wide gravel road at 2.0 miles *3.2 km*. At 6.0 miles *9.6 km* there's paving again, but it's rough. At 6.6 miles *10.6 km* the road meets a wire fence. Take either dirt road to the left. At 6.8 miles *10.9 km* there's more paving to the 7.3 mi. *11.7 km* point from where you can see how the road ran in a straight line to today's I-40. Park here if you do not have high clearance; otherwise, keep driving the dirt road. At 7.7 miles *12.3 km* you are at the edge of Canyon Padre, with the I-40 bridge to your right. If you get out of your car and walk over toward the bridge, you can see the piers of the 1937 bridge under the I-40 bridge. Drive the old road down into the canyon until you reach the 1914 bridge at 7.9 miles *12.6 km*. It is very scenic for photos. Look for the faint letters "66" on the posts at the far end of the bridge. You can drive over the bridge, but the road ends at 8.8 miles *14.1 km* at a gate. Instead, hike around the old alignments. The oldest 1914 alignment went over the bridge and then made a hairpin turn, hugging the canyon wall. You will see the rock walls that supported it and it makes a good walk. A later alignment—perhaps in 1926 when Route 66 was created—blasted the side of the butte away and followed the side canyon making a wide sweeping arc to the east. On the canyon floor you will see huge chunks of paving, probably put there when I-40 replaced Route 66 in the area in the 1960s. It's a great place to explore.

In 1937 the state built a new bridge, as the old passage had become outmoded and unsafe. The route was so dangerous that there were several wrecked cars lying on the bottom of the canyon (none are visible today).

The 1937 bridge (replaced in 1952) was a steel arch 844 feet long with a 24-foot clear roadway.

Where's The Beef?

Somewhere along Route 66 west of Flagstaff was a roadside cafe selling hamburgers. The people of Flagstaff noticed that the owner came to town every week and bought 144 buns. But he never bought any meat. They wondered how he was getting his beef until they heard that a rancher near the trading post was complaining about missing a few cows.

SIGHTSEEING #2
From Flagstaff
Sunset Crater & Wupatki
Round-Trip 81.0 miles
Time 4.0 hours

From Flagstaff Visitor Center drive east on Route 66, which is combined with Highway 89. At 3.6 miles *5.8 km* Route 66 forks to the right. Go straight, on Hwy. 89. At 16.1 miles *25.8 km* turn right and go to Sunset Crater. You will soon come to a ticket booth where you pay an admission fee and will be given a map. Beyond this is the visitor center, with a museum, rest rooms and other facilities. Ask at the desk about activities. If you like hiking, then be sure to take the Lava Flow Trail, 1.6 miles *2.6 km* from the visitor center. There is a nice loop road which connects Sunset Crater National Monument and Wupatki National Monument, very scenic, with several interesting places to stop.

The Wupatki Visitor Center is 19.0 miles *30.4 km* from the one at Sunset Crater. We recommend stopping for information and to take the Wupatki Ruin Trail. From there, continue the loop, returning to Highway 89, in 13.8 miles *22.1 km*. Then turn left (south) and drive 30.5 miles *48.8 km* back to Flagstaff.

SUNSET CRATER & WUPATKI

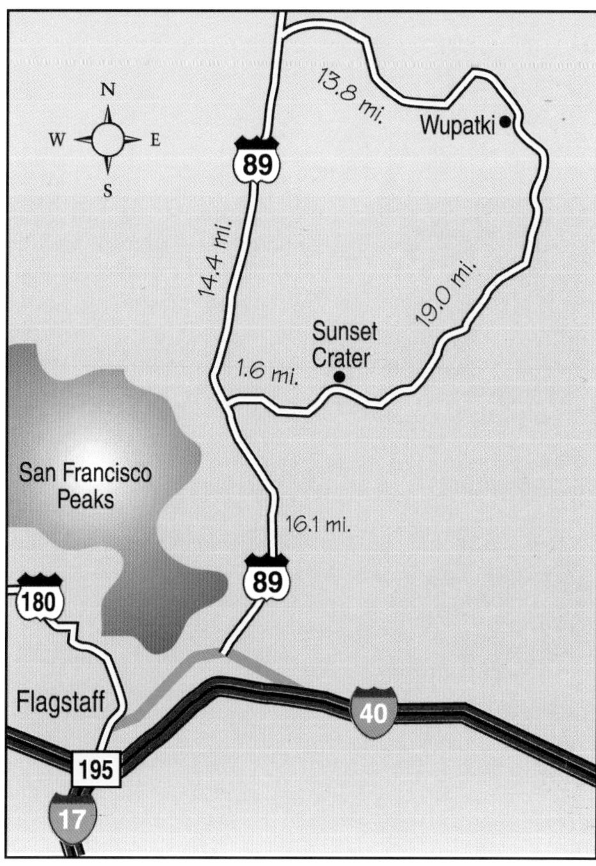

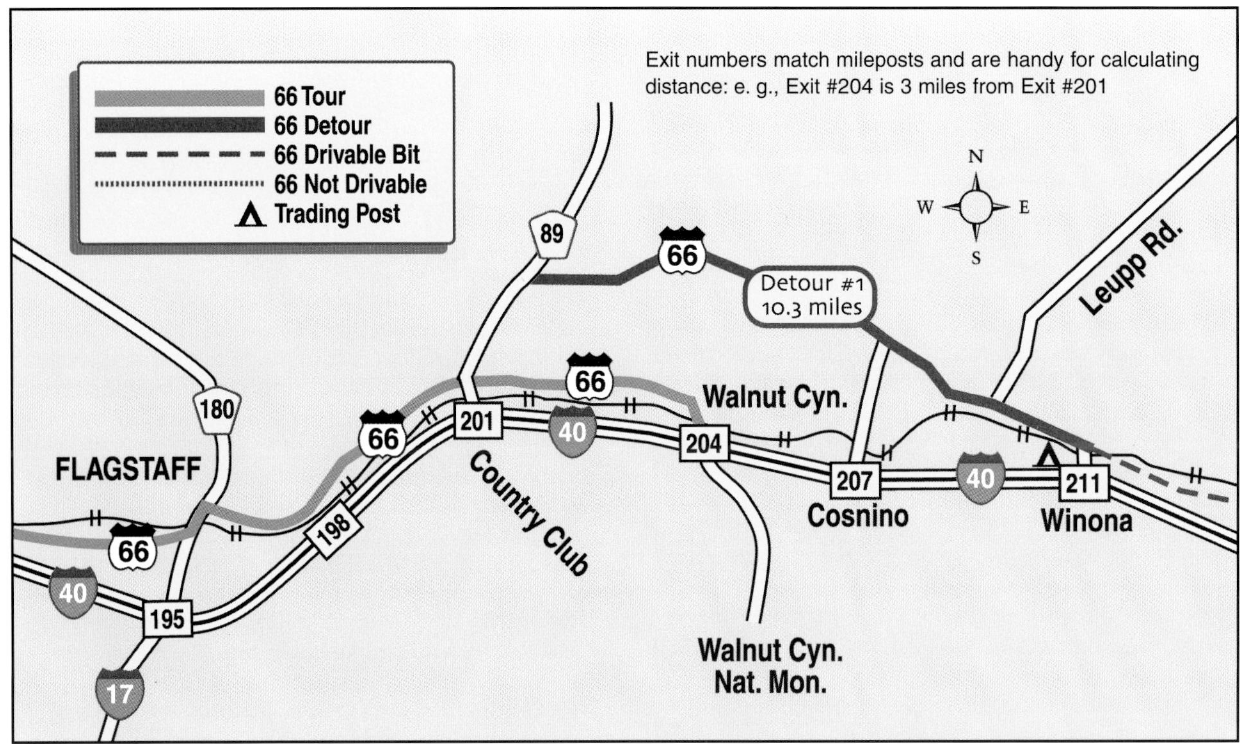

Tour 8-E Flagstaff to Winona pp. 79-81

Tour 6-W Winona to Flagstaff

Distance: 14.7 miles *23.5 km*
Highlights: Long stretch of 66, Walnut Canyon, Detour, City of Flagstaff
Driving Time: 30 minutes

Flagstaff Icon—OP

Tour 6-W takes you from Winona to Flagstaff, the largest city in northern Arizona. You will drive west from Exit #211-Winona and turn off on Exit #204-Walnut Canyon. This puts you on the alignment of Route 66 used from 1947 until 66 was bypassed in 1968. At Exit #204 you have the option of turning south to visit the wonderful Walnut Canyon National Monument.

EXIT #211—Winona

Gas, Food

START

0.0 miles *0.0 km* Start at Winona Trading Post, where you are at the eastern edge of the huge Ponderosa Pine forest through which you will pass for the next 60.0 miles *96.0 km.* Many travelers found this forested portion of Route 66 to be the most scenic on the entire highway. If you visited the Winona Trading Post, you are poised to enter I-40 easily and head west.

Detour #1 is available from Exit #211-Winona.

DETOUR #1
EXIT #211-Winona
1921-1947 Route 66
10.3 mi. ***16.5 km*** **one-way**
Time 20 minutes

At Exit #211-Winona, take the exit. **Zero** at the stop sign, turn right and take the paved road heading north. This is the first alignment of Route 66 into Flagstaff, going back to the earliest days of motor travel. It was used until 1947, when the Tour version of Route 66 that you will access at Exit #204-Walnut Canyon was opened. Just follow the red line on the map above. Along the way you will see (and photograph) the great old steel truss bridge over Walnut Creek. On both sides of the road, but mainly the right, you will see old farming fields. How the Joads must have been heartened to see cultivated land after so much desert. You will join Highway 89 at a stop light. You can turn right here and drive to the Grand Canyon (details on page 71). Turn left to come into town. Elden Pueblo, a small Indian ruin, is on your right. It's free.

EXIT #204—Walnut Canyon

No food, No gas, No lodging

6.3 miles *10.1 km* Take Exit #204-Walnut Canyon. We highly recommend a visit to Walnut Canyon, details given on the next page, under "Sightseeing #1."

<Westbound

SIGHTSEEING #1
EXIT #204
Walnut Canyon NM
Time 1.5 hours

Take Exit #204-Walnut Canyon. At the stop sign turn left and drive over I-40, then follow the signs on the other side, which lead you to the monument, 3.0 miles *4.8 km* from the exit. There is a Visitor Center containing toilets, a gift shop, and museum. The highlight of the attraction is the Island Trail, which takes you down to a butte around the rim of which are numerous cliff dwellings which you can visit. The trail is not long, only a loop of 0.8 miles *1.3 km,* but there is a steep flight of 240 stairs—easy to climb down but hell coming up. An easier path, the Rim Trail, is 0.4 miles *0.6 km* one-way, running along the edge of the scenic canyon. Special Ranger-guided tours are available from time to time. Inquire at the desk for information about these and other activities.

Historic Route 66
On the main Tour from Exit #204-Walnut Canyon the first part of this 66 segment goes through a rural area that has never been developed, so that it looks the same today as it did in 1947 when this alignment was opened. The surface is one-foot-thick (*0.3 meters*) thumpety concrete. In some places this is overlaid by asphalt, but in others the drive is over the original bare concrete.

Cosnino Overpass
At the 7.1 mile *11.4 km* point, you will drive over a railroad overpass. If you are a train buff, you may enjoy pulling over and standing on the bridge to take a photo of one of the 81 BNSF trains that pass under the bridge daily. During the days of the Mother Road, the railroad that played tag with Highway 66 all across Arizona was the Santa Fe, but the Burlington Northern bought the Santa Fe in the mid-1990s and it's now the BNSF.

Industrial Area
9.5 miles *15.2 km* You will pass through an industrial zone, something that has developed in the last twenty years.

Flagstaff Truck Center
10.4 miles *16.6 km* As you are about to drive under I-40's Exit #201-Country Club, notice the truck stop on your right. In the days of the Mother Road this was a typical filling station and motel combination. The motel was called the Tourtel, no cornier than most names picked by owners of such businesses. When I-40 was built, Exit #201 was constructed practically on top of the place. For a while after I-40 was opened the owner continued to eke out a living here. The filling station was converted into a truck stop and the truck drivers rented rooms in the motel for a while. Eventually the owners had to close the motel. The Tourtel sign hangs from the ceiling of Main Street Catering in downtown Flagstaff. The truck stop continues to do business.

Route 66—Highway 89 Junction
10.8 miles *17.3 km* As you approach this intersection, you will be driving at the rear of the Flagstaff Mall. Notice how Route 66 was blocked and a detour to meet Highway 89 was created. Turn left at the stop sign.

Museum Club
11.4 miles *18.2 km* You will see (and hopefully have time to stop at) Flagstaff's great Museum Club on your right at 3404 E. Route 66 (526-9434, www.museumclub.com). It's a must-see, soaked in Route 66 memories, with photos on the walls and a terrific atmosphere. Its owner, Martin Zanzucchi, is a leader in the Route 66 revival and was responsible for getting the Flagstaff City Council to change the name of Santa Fe Avenue to Route 66 in 1992.

Route 66 icon, the Museum Club

Flagstaff's Old Motel Row
11.6 miles *18.6 km* Beyond the Museum Club is Flagstaff's motel row. The presence of the railroad on the left side of the highway meant that all development out here was on the right side of the road, which was handy for catching westbound travelers, as it was very easy for

them to make a righthand turn off the highway into the motel, service station or cafe. You will see "Historic US 66" road signs along this stretch. Note the El Pueblo Motel at 3120 E. Route 66. It was built in 1936 by Philip Johnston, the man who invented the Navajo Code Talker program in World War Two. Many of these old places along motel row are falling apart now, some have been demolished and others are slated for demolition. Others are still in business but are very cut-rate operations. Only a few nice ones survive.

Downtown Flagstaff—Visitor Center

14.7 miles *23.5 km* you will reach a stoplight at San Francisco Street. To your left is the Visitor Center, our goal, and the endpoint of this tour. You must drive two blocks, and turn left on Beaver to access the Visitor Center because of Flagstaff's one-way street system. At the Visitor Center you will find parking, toilets, brochures, and an information desk. The Flagstaff Visitor Center won an award for the best Visitor Center in Arizona in 1999 and you will find their helpful staff to be a great aid.

Flagstaff Recommendations

THINGS TO DO:
Flagstaff is the hub of a vast scenic region full of color and interest. See page 27. Our choice of attractions:

Arizona Snowbowl, a winter ski resort. In summer the chair lift is operated as a scenic ride. Drive north 7.3 mi., then turn right on the Snow Bowl Road, which is paved, running another 6.6 mi. to the Snowbowl.

Lowell Observatory, a world-class astronomical facility. Its Steele Visitor Center and conducted tours are outstanding, not to be missed.

Museum of Northern Arizona. The Exhibition Hall is open year-round with permanent exhibits that display the region. There are many shows and special exhibits.

Pioneer Museum. Permanent displays and special exhibits tell the story of Flagstaff.

Riordan Mansion State Park. The twin mansions built by lumber barons, brothers M. J. and T. A. Riordan are a beautiful example of Craftsman architecture. Guided tours daily are a delight.

Flagstaff Historic Walks. Since 1993 the authors of this Guide, Richard and Sherry have been giving these free public tours in the summertime. Call the Visitor Center for dates and times.

Shopping and Strolling. The Flagstaff downtown historic district—centered on the attractive Heritage Square—is a diverting and rewarding place to visit. There are many interesting shops and boutiques, a welcome change for those who are jaded by cookie-cutter malls. The downtown area is loaded with good cafes and coffee houses, with prices and cuisines to suit all tastes.

WHERE TO EAT:
Top of the Line
Chez Marc, 503 N. Humphreys, 774-1343.
Cottage Place, 126 W. Cottage, 774-8431.
Down Under, Heritage Square, 6 E. Aspen, 774-6677.
Jackson's Grill, 7085 S. Highway 89A, 213-9332.

Excellent But Less Expensive
Beaver Street Brewery, 11 S. Beaver, 779-0079.
Buster's, 1800 S. Milton, 774-5155.

Genuine Route 66 Eateries
Grand Canyon Cafe, 110 E. Route 66, 774-2252.
Miz Zip's, 2924 E. Route 66, 526-0104.

Route 66 Themed
Galaxy Diner, 931 W. Route 66, 774-2466.

Chinese
Monsoon, 1551 S. Milton, 774-2266.
Szechuan, 1451 S. Milton, 774-8039.

Cowboy
Horsemen Lodge, 8500 N. Highway 89, 526-2655.

Italian
Pasto, 19 E. Aspen, 779-1937.

Mexican
Salsa Brava, 1800 S. Milton, 774-1083.

Indian
Delhi Palace, 2700 S. Woodlands Village, 556-0019.

Vegetarian
Cafe Espress, 16 N. San Francisco, 774-0541.
Macy's, 14 S. Beaver, 774-2243.

WHERE TO STAY:
Birch Tree Inn, 824 W. Birch, 774-1042. B&B in a quiet nook near city park.

Dierker House, 423 W. Cherry, 774-3249. The oldest of Flagstaff's B&B's. Small and quaint. Historic home.

Inn at 410, 410 N. Leroux, 774-0088. Primo B&B, easy walking from town. Luxury and elegance.

Little America, 2515 E. Butler, 779-7900. Wonderful hotel that has set the standard for decades.

Lynn's Inn, 614 W. Santa Fe Ave., 226-1488. Another B&B in a historic home not far from town.

Monte Vista Hotel, 100 N. San Francisco, 779-6971. Since 1927, it has hosted many movie stars and is recently renovated.

Weatherford Hotel, 23 N. Leroux, 774-2731. This historic hotel opened for business on January 1, 1900. Recently a youth hostel, the owners have converted it back into a hotel. Sample a taste of yesterday here.

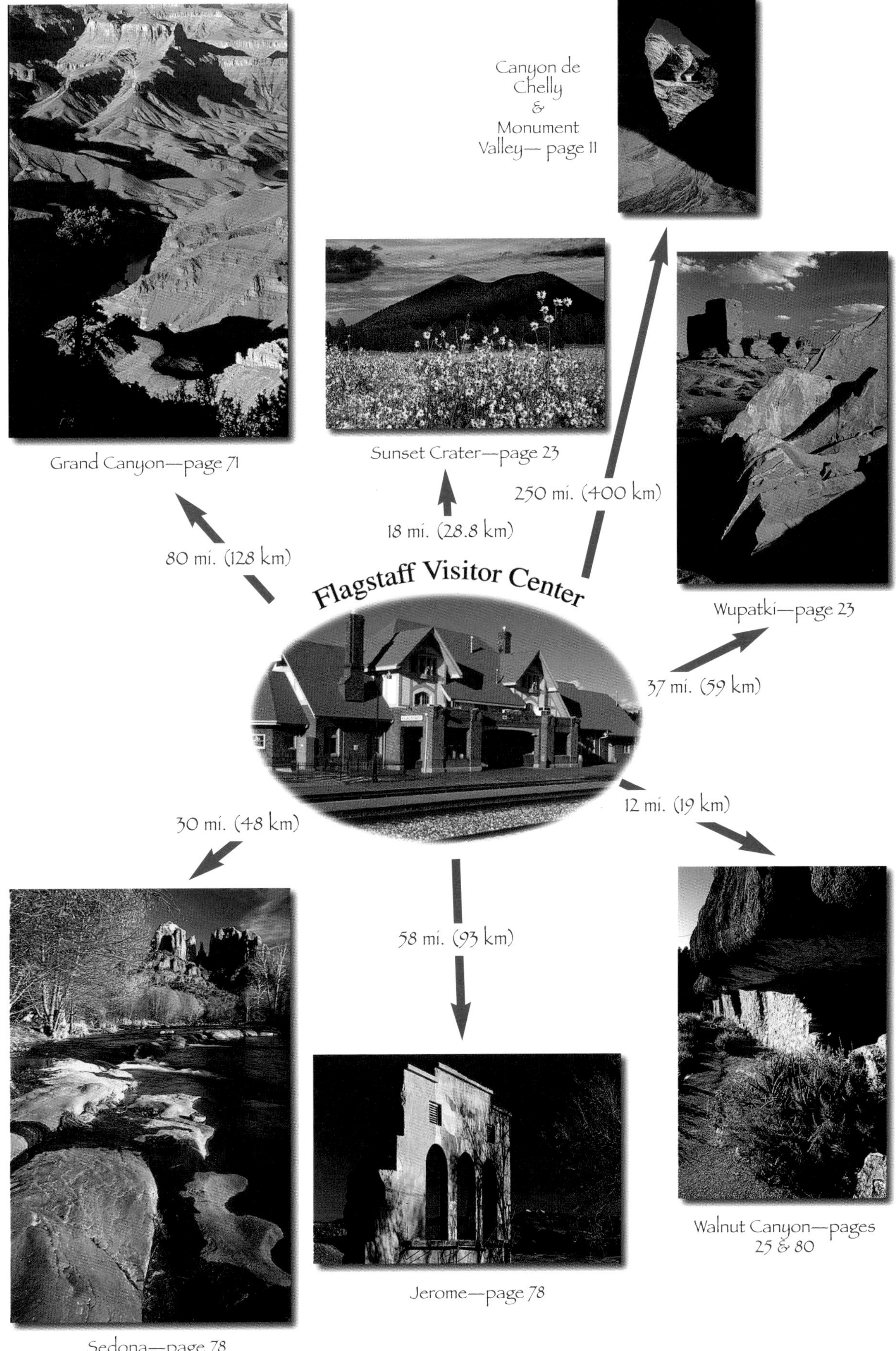

Canyon de Chelly & Monument Valley— page 11

Grand Canyon—page 71

Sunset Crater—page 23

Wupatki—page 23

Walnut Canyon—pages 25 & 80

Jerome—page 78

Sedona—page 78

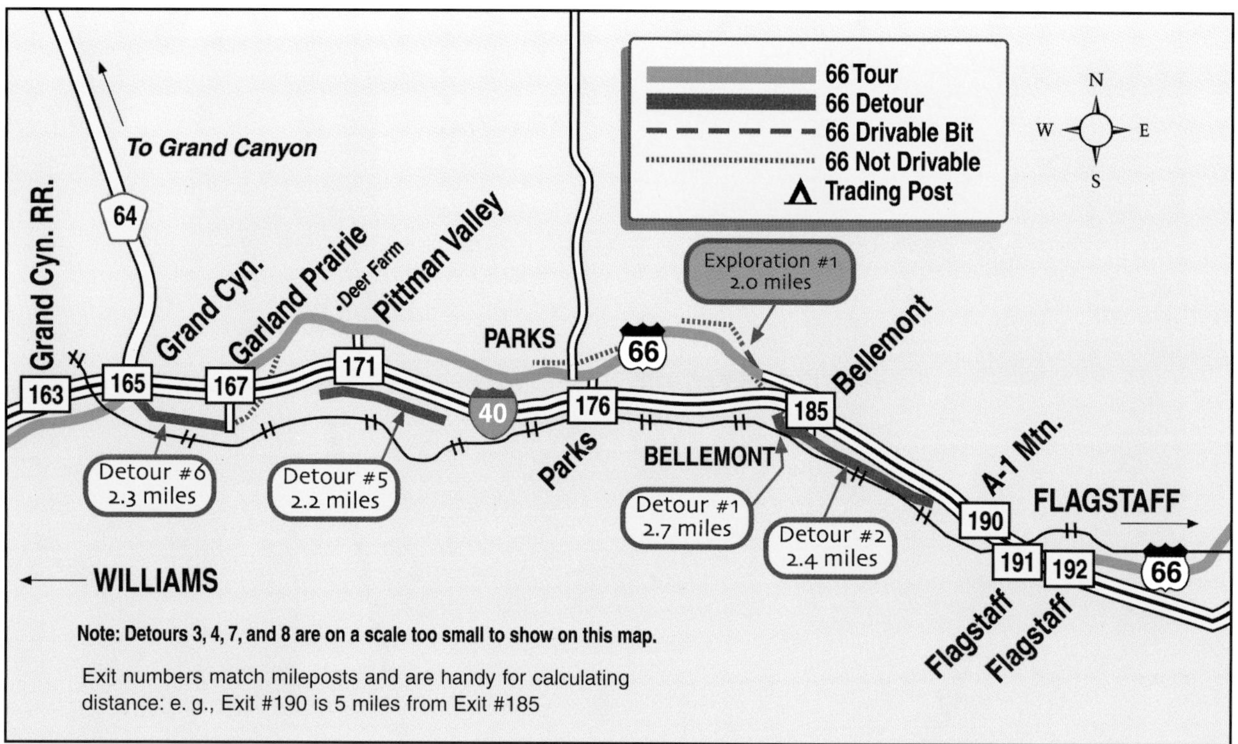

Tour 7-E Williams to Flagstaff pp. 72-77

Tour 7-W Flagstaff to Williams

Distance: 34.0 miles *54.4 km*
Highlights: Good long bits of 66, Arboretum, Deer Farm, Parks Store
Driving Time: 1 hour

Flagstaff Visitor Center

Tour 7-W starts at the Flagstaff Visitor Center, located at the train station in the center of the city. From here you will be able to drive out of town on the only alignment ever used on 66 heading west out of Flagstaff, a nice stretch of road with plenty of 66 relics along the way. Then you head west for a few miles on I-40 and detour onto an even longer piece of 66 (some bits of which are unpaved). You can visit the Arboretum and the Deer Farm, and end the tour in Williams, going into that town on more of original 66.

START

Visitor Center

Start at the Visitor Center, located on Route 66 between Beaver and San Francisco Streets. Turn left onto San Francisco Street and then left on Route 66 headed west. You will drive past City Hall and then turn under the railroad overpass, onto Milton Road. **Zero** your odometer here. South of the overpass, businesses were able to develop on both sides of 66 as the railroad no longer blocked one side, and you will see many gas stations and motels along this strip. Northern Arizona University with its nearly 20,000 students is located in this area and has a tremendous impact on Flagstaff. At 0.4 miles *0.6 km* from the overpass, turn right onto Historic US 66 (signs). You will note the Galaxy Diner, a 66-themed eatery to your left in about one block. Many of the old 66 businesses that lined the highway are closed, with most of the service stations having been converted into other uses. I-40 bypassed Flagstaff in 1968 and since then the tourist-based industries along this route have been in a steady decline.

At 2.3 miles *3.7 km* you will pass the abandoned Pine Springs Truck Stop and Motel (right). After this you leave the developed area and enter a fairly pristine forest. Sightseeing Trip #1 to the Arboretum is available here.

SIGHTSEEING #1
Arboretum at Flagstaff
Time 1.0 hour

At the 2.3 mile *3.7 km* point you will see a sign for the Arboretum (left). This is a horticultural study facility that is open to the public. If you love plants then you will want to see this place. It is 4.0 miles *6.4 km* off of Route 66, and the last 3.0 miles *4.8 km* of the road is unpaved.

Ruins of the Whiting Brothers Motel at Bellemont

Beyond Pine Springs you will pass through some nice pine forest and then be forced onto I-40 westbound. Look for Exit #185-Bellemont/Transwestern Pipeline.

EXIT #185—Bellemont

<u>Gas, Food</u>

Route 66 was realigned through this area at least three times and there are some interesting detours available. The highlight is the regular tour, which follows old 66 through the Kaibab National Forest, where Forest Service employees have developed a scenic Auto Tour. Even though portions of this road are unpaved, we think it is suitable for every traveler and include it as part of the regular tour. Two detours on the other side of I-40 are set out also, Detours #1 and #2.

Regular tour—take Exit #185-Bellemont. At the stop sign **Zero** your odometer, turn right and then left onto the frontage road. This runs west for 2.2 miles *3.5 km*, closely parallel to I-40. Then the road swings away from I-40. If you stop here and look back across I-40 you can see a path cut through the trees, where the 1931 version of Route 66 linked with the point where you are sitting. From this point you are on Route 66.

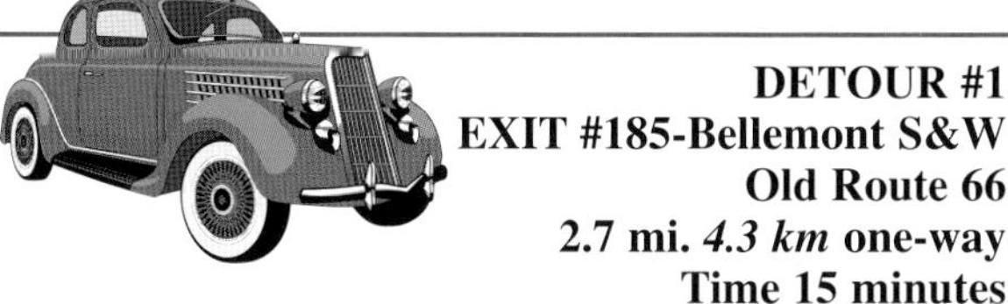

DETOUR #1
EXIT #185-Bellemont S&W
Old Route 66
2.7 mi. *4.3 km* one-way
Time 15 minutes

At Exit #185-Bellemont, turn left at the stop sign, **zero** out, and drive over I-40. On the other side, turn right on Bellemont Camp Road. As you begin to drive west look down to your left, and you will see a raised roadbed, the original Old Trails Highway alignment. The paved road you are driving replaced it in 1941. At 0.6 miles *1.0 km* is Bellemont (L). There's not much left today but a tavern and some dilapidated buildings. You can turn left on the next road and drive 0.1 miles *0.16 km* to a water tank (L) and photograph the collapsing building that fronted the 1921 road. West of this are some new industrial buildings. At 1.8 miles *2.9 km* the earlier version of the road comes in from your left and crosses your road, running about 0.2 miles *0.3 km* to your right. [For a good walk, stop here and hike along the old raised roadbed (L), which runs 0.5 miles *0.8 km* to a fence]. The paving disappears briefly west of here, so drive carefully. The paving resumes but soon ends at a wire fence. A gravel road continues west for a short distance, but it is not worth taking. Turn around and go back to Exit #185.

DETOUR #2
EXIT #185-Bellemont S&E
Old Route 66
2.4 mi. *3.8 km* one-way
Time 15 minutes

(If you are finishing Detour #1, **zero**, then go straight on East Bellemont Rd.). If starting from I-40 take Exit #185-Bellemont, turn left at the stop sign, zero out, and drive over I-40. On the other side, turn left on East Bellemont Rd. This is old 66. It runs right in front of the Harley-Davidson dealership and cafe and if you are a Hog fan you will want to stop in. The road runs along parallel to the railroad. At 1.3 miles *2.1 km* you will see the crumbling remains of a Whiting Brothers motel (left). At 1.6 miles *2.6 km* you will see the old Pine Breeze Inn and gas station (left). Rough old concrete surfacing begins here. The old highway ends at a barricade at about the 2.4 mile *3.8 km* point.

EXPLORATION #1
Old Trails Highway
2.0 mi. *3.2 km* one-way
Time 25 minutes

Take Exit #185-Bellemont. At the stop sign turn right, then left onto the frontage road. Drive west for 2.1 miles *3.4 km*, then turn right on unpaved road 9229K, which runs along a power line. **Zero** here. This is the original 1921 Old Trails Highway, which became Highway 66 in 1926. It was never paved. You must have a high-clearance vehicle and a dry road to do this. Drive along the old road for 2.0 miles *3.2 km* to a point where it starts down a grade on a raised bed. It is blocked beyond here and you must retrace your steps. Few know about this forgotten road replaced in 1931. You see this road on Detour #3 in Brannigan Park.

Auto Tour Stop #1

2.5 miles *4.0 km* The first Auto Tour sign is on your right as you enter the Kaibab Forest. Pull over and read it.

The first sign on the Auto Tour

Brannigan Park

At 3.9 miles *6.2 km* you will enter Brannigan Park, a

beautiful mountain meadow fed by springs, at a cattle guard. The paving briefly ends here. Look for the fence made of old skis on your right. **Zero** at the cattle guard.

Detour #3: If you turn right and drive up the paved road 0.6 miles *1.0 km*, you will see the 1921 road (described in Exploration #1) cutting across the paving. You can see only a bit of the grade to your right (E) but to your left (W), where there is a white gate, you can see the roadbed crossing the park. Return to the Route 66 cattle guard, **Zero**, and turn right (W).

Drive across the park on the main road, enjoying the beauty of the place. With your eye you can trace the course of the 1921 road running parallel to you out in the middle of the meadow and moving ever closer, to join your road near the high point on Fortynine Hill.

Fortynine Hill

1.6 miles *2.6 km* As you drive over a mountain pass you reach a historic point. This was the maximum elevation anywhere on the entire Route 66, at 7,410 feet *2,245 meters,* quite a bit higher than the Continental Divide (Top of the World) in New Mexico, at 7,263 feet *2200 m*.

Auto Tour Stop #2

Paving resumes at 3.1 miles *5.0 km*. At 3.5 miles *5.6 km* the second Auto Tour sign is set off from the road to your right. Drive over to it. In addition to learning more about Route 66, you have the chance here to take a hike on a 0.75 mile *1.2 km* portion of the 1931 version of 66, running downhill (blue line on map). We enjoy taking this little hike, especially if we are tired of driving. As you face the sign, if you look to your left 30 paces, you can see the raised bed of the never-paved 1921 alignment of the Old Trails Highway (which became 66 in 1926) running along between the paved road and the 1931 road.

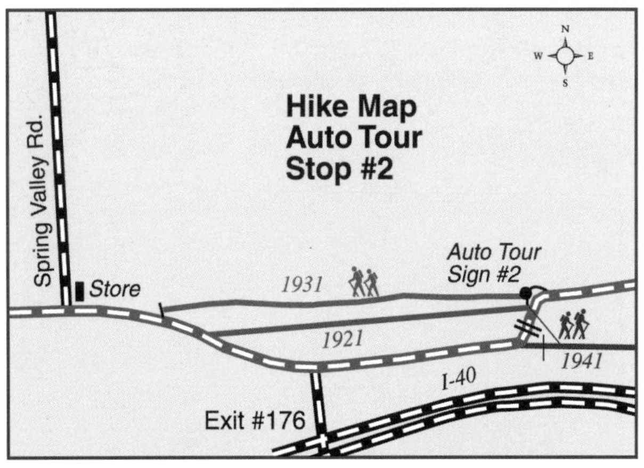

1941 Alignment

When you return to the paved road, turn right and at 3.6 miles *5.8 km* you will reach a cattle guard. To your left is a wide red gravel road, the 1941 version of Route 66, constructed to avoid Fortynine Hill. The 1941 alignment, which started at Bellemont, was used until 1964 when I-40 opened in this area, replacing it. It was then blocked off.

HIKE
1941 version of Route 66
0.4 mi. *0.6 km* one-way
Time 20 minutes

From the Auto Tour #2 sign walk south across the paved road and follow FR 097 to the point where it intersects a red gravel road (red line on map). Turn left and walk the red gravel road to its end. You will find some pieces of paving and a culvert along it. This is the Route 66 alignment used from 1941-1964 and was built to avoid the high point at 49 Hill. This bit of historical 66 ends where it bumps up against I-40. The 1941 road was replaced by I-40 in 1964.

Parks In The Pines Store

4.6 miles *7.4 km* The historic Parks Store (R). In 1921 Coconino County decided to build a road from the Old Trails Highway as the primary auto road to the Grand Canyon. They selected Maine (Parks) midway between Williams and Flagstaff as the junction. Work on the unpaved road began in March 1921 and was finished that June. Art Anderson and Don McMillan built this store and gas station at the road junction, opening for business in November 1921. A big sign supported by pyramids of stone was erected in the fall of 1921 by the Flagstaff Chamber of Commerce (seen in photo below).

Bunion Derby at the Parks Store, March 1928—KFS

Stop in at this seventy-five year old store and buy something so that the owners can keep it open, preserving the history of this charming old place. You will find all sorts of things here, including The Post Office Deli, which turns out good food. Pick up a sandwich to eat at the Garland Prairie Vista picnic area, which is just down the road.

As you drive west of the store to your right a few feet away in the trees is the 1931 road running along beside you on a raised bed. You will pass through the community of Parks, where there are a couple of former roadside businesses (L) including the Three Bears Trading Post at 5.4 miles *8.6 km*.

Garland Prairie Vista Picnic Area

7.0 miles *11.2 km* To your left is the entrance to the Garland Prairie Vista Picnic Area. This is a pleasant place to park your car and eat a meal or snack at one of the picnic tables. There is also a toilet. In the old days there was a clear view from this place to Garland Prairie (S), a vast open plain, but in the last thirty years trees have grown so tall that they block the view. One of the real treats at this place is for photographers. If you walk out onto Route 66 and face east, you will have a great shot of the old concrete-sectioned Mother Road winding through the forest with the San Francisco Peaks in the background. Many commercial photographers have made this photo.

DETOUR #4
Old Route 66
0.2 mi. *0.3 km* one-way
Time 10 minutes

From the Parks Store drive west 3.2 miles *5.1 km,* then turn left onto an unmarked gravel road. You will immediately go over a cattle guard. Drive in for 0.2 miles *0.3 km* and park by the corral. The entry road intersects another road at this point. Walk the road to your right, noticing the bits of thin old macadam paving, a sure clue that this is old 66. It ends at I-40 at 0.25 miles *0.4 km.* Old 66 went south of I-40 here and turned west, visible on Detour #5. Return to the parking place and walk the other arm of the road. We did not find any paving on this longer arm, but it is elevated and has concrete culverts, things found only on a major road. It runs 0.75 miles *1.2 km* to I-40, which has buried it. This old road forms a big curve, and near the place where you parked, in the fold of the curve, was the campground Rittenhouse described as, "A tree-shaded camping spot here (L), maintained free by the U. S. Government."

DETOUR #5
Old Route 66
2.2 mi. *3.5 km* one-way
Time 20 minutes

From Parks Store drive 4.7 miles *7.5 km,* **Zero** and turn left (S) on Sherwood Forest Rd. Drive over I-40. On the other side turn right (W) on a nameless paved road—old 66. You can see the raised bed of the unsurfaced road running the opposite direction through a ranch property, making it inaccessible. Drive the paved road and at 1.7 miles *2.7 km* turn left (W) onto paved Mountain Ranch Road at the interchange for Exit #171-Pittman Valley. Notice the raised unpaved roadbed running along to your left here. The road takes you in front of a big resort, presently called the Quality Inn. At 2.1 miles *3.4 km,* where the access road turns left into the resort, keep going straight, onto a very brief stretch of old 66 concrete, ending at a barrier at 2.2 miles *3.5 km.* With your eye you can extend it and see how I-40 merged over the top of it. Backtrack to resume the tour from the Zero point.

Pittman Valley

8.9 miles *14.2 km* From the Garland Prairie Vista you will drop down into beautiful Pittman Valley and drive along its bottom. At 10.1 miles *16.2 km* You will see the old Wagon Wheel Lodge (R), a well-known roadhouse which developed a reputation as a brothel in the World War Two era. It is now private property, so don't trespass.

Auto Tour Stop #3

10.5 miles *16.8 km* To your right is the final Auto Tour sign, and as with the others, it is worth a stop. When you leave here be sure to follow the sign marked "Deer Farm Rd." because the tour makes a funny little twist here.

Deer Farm

11.0 miles *17.6 km* To your right is the Deer Farm. See the Sightseeing #2 box for details.

SIGHTSEEING #2
Deer Farm
Time 1.0 hours

At 11.0 miles *17.6 km* you will find the Deer Farm to your right. They have restrooms, snacks, a gift shop and a petting zoo. Although they specialize in deer, having several varieties, they have other animals as well. Many of these are so tame that they will eat out of your hand, and you can buy feed for them. A paved trail winds around through the animal enclosures. Children love this place and if you are an animal lover, you will find it a treat. The owners are very nice, and on a recent visit presented us with a baby wallaby to pet. This is an old 66 business that seems to be surviving very well.

Davenport Lake

Davenport Lake

11.7 miles *18.7 km* Paving ends here. To your left you will see a large oval pasture with I-40 running across it. This is Davenport Lake. You might wonder why it is called a lake, as it usually dry, but we can assure you that we have seen it full of water. Dick remembers an occasion in high school when, as a sousaphone tooter in the Flagstaff High School band, he was traveling on the bus to a performance in Williams. One of the famous Rod's Steak House bull signs was located in the middle of Davenport Lake and the waters had risen to its knees. A girl who was not familiar with Rod's signs saw it and cried out, "Oh, that poor cow!"

14.3 miles *22.9 km* Paving resumes. The first part of this paving is great old red asphalt, colored by the red cinders in the mix. 66 took off to the left, at an angle and went across the prairie instead of curving right as the access road does today.

Exit #167—Garland Prairie Rd./Circle Pines Rd.

15.0 miles *24.0 km* Route 66 on the Auto Tour ends at I-40 Exit #167. The interesting Detour #6—a drive along old Route 66—is available on the other side of I-40.

DETOUR #6
1921 Old Trails—Route 66
2.3 mi. *3.7 km* one-way
Time 10 minutes

Drive over I-40. **Zero** at the center of the bridge. On the other side, stop at Mountain Man Trail (FR 51A)—old Route 66. To your left (E) you can see 66 but private property inhibits access. Turn right (W) and drive Mountain Man Tr., a gravel road, to a stop sign at Old Depot Rd. junction. Go straight on Mountain Man to the 1.8 miles *2.9 km* point. The 1921 road goes straight but is too rough. Go right to the 2.0 mile *3.2 km* point, and turn left on a newer version of Route 66. Drive it to the 2.3 mile *3.7 km* point, at a stop sign. Turn right and at the next stop sign, turn left, and you'll be on the road into Williams from Exit #165-Grand Canyon.

At Exit #167 If you do not take Detour #6, then you will return to I-40 at Exit #167-Garland Prairie. Turn right and drive west on I-40.

Exit #165—Williams/Grand Canyon

<u>**Gas, Food, Lodging**</u>

Take Exit #165-Williams/Grand Canyon. **Zero** out at the stop sign, and turn left.

0.6 miles *1.0 km* Railroad overpass. For Detour #7 (of interest only to die-hard roadies) see the next column.

Dave Pouquette's 50s cars in front of Twisters in Williams

DETOUR #7
1921 Old Trails-Route 66
0.3 mi. *0.5 km* one-way
Time 10 minutes

Zero at the Railroad Overpass as you drive into Williams. At 0.3 miles *0.5 km* turn left onto Echo Canyon Road. Take an immediate left over the cattle guard. **Zero**. You are now on the never-paved 1921 road that became Route 66. At 0.1 miles *0.16 km*, where the road curves, you will see a primitive road, old 66, going straight. Take it. There is an "open-arms" culvert about halfway down this road. At 0.3 miles *0.5 km* the road bumps up against a huge railroad embankment. The road continues on the other side of the railroad to link with the roads on Detour #6 from Exit #167-Garland Prairie Rd. but the railroad, realigned in 1961, blocks it. Return the way you came in.

Williams

1.8 miles *2.9 km* You enter the town of Williams. Note that the road you travel on is Railroad Avenue. Route 66 was divided in Williams in 1955 so that westbound traffic was diverted onto Railroad Avenue and eastbound traffic used Bill Williams Avenue. Bill Williams Avenue was renamed Route 66 in 1995. For most of its life all Route 66 traffic used Bill Williams Avenue, so you will find the majority of the roadside business there.

An interesting variation of the approach to Williams is to drive the earliest Route 66 into the place, Detour #8.

DETOUR #8
Original Route 66 into Williams
1.6 mi. *2.6 km* one-way
Time 10 minutes

As you enter Williams you will pass under the railroad. On the other side of the overpass, the first street to your right is Rodeo Road. **Zero**. Turn right on it, then left and follow it into town. Travel several blocks to the first stop sign, at Airport Road. Turn left onto Airport and follow it for a block, then turn right on Edison Avenue. Follow Edison for four blocks to the next stop sign, then turn left on Grand Canyon Boulevard (2d St.). Drive Grand Canyon Blvd. south for several blocks to Railroad Avenue. On the way you will see the train station to your right, with its large facilities, including a huge hotel. You will cross the railroad tracks and see the Williams Visitor Center to your right. Turn right into the parking lot. The Visitor Center has toilets, books and information.

Williams Visitor Center

2.3 miles *3.7 km* The Williams Visitor Center is to your right at the Railroad Avenue-Grand Canyon Boulevard junction. At the Visitor Center, our stopping point, you will find toilets, leaflets, books, a museum, and a helpful staff who can answer questions about Williams. For our recommendations about Williams see Page 70.

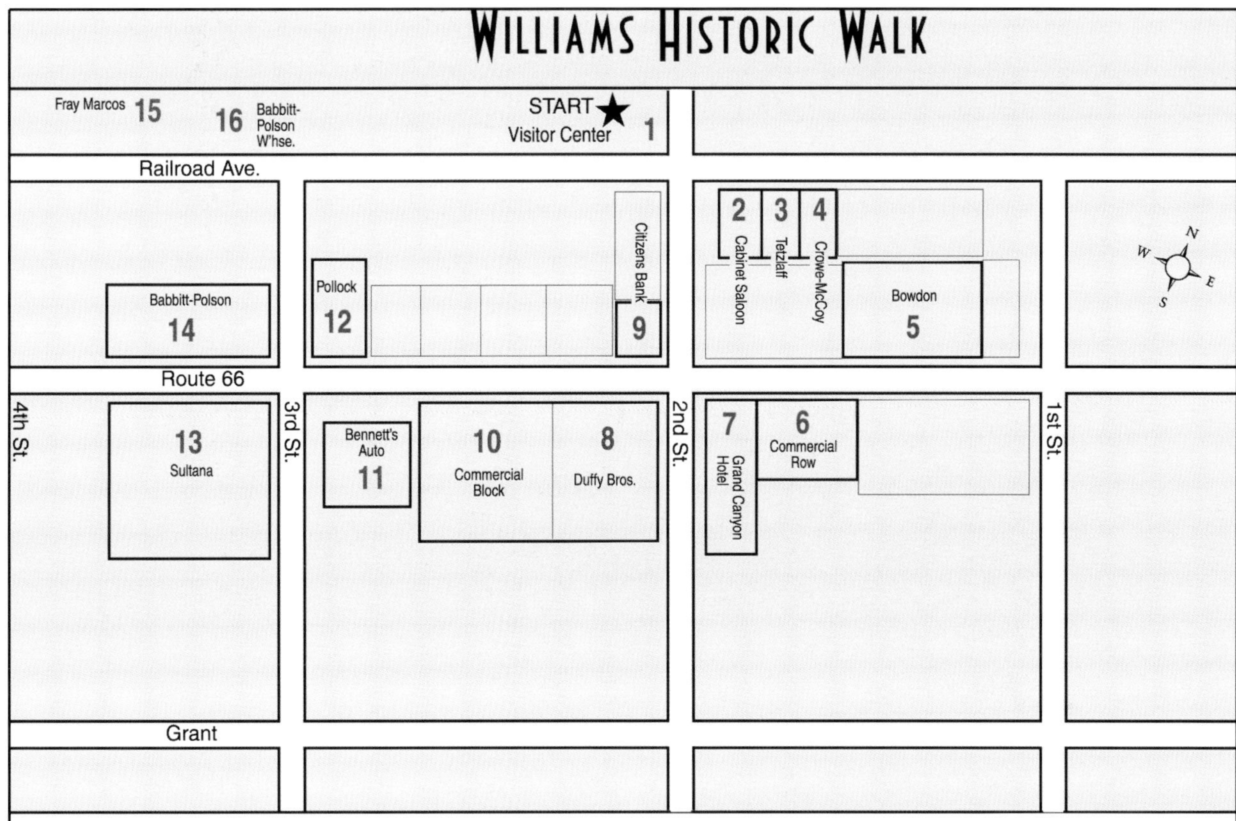

#1. Visitor Center, 1901. This was originally built by the Santa Fe Railroad as the Williams depot, at a different location. It was moved to its present site in 1914. In the back room are many names written there by hoboes, cowboys and others.

#2. Cabinet Saloon Building, 1893. This was constructed by leading citizen C. E. Boyce. Facing the railroad tracks, it picked up customers alighting from the train, and was a favorite of local characters as well.

#3. Tetzlaff Building, 1897. This was also a saloon, with a bordello on the upper floor. Note the name and date on the keystone.

#4. Crowe-McCoy Building, 1903. Another saloon with a bordello on the second floor.

As you leave Railroad Avenue and turn south on First Street and then west on Route 66, you leave the dangerous shoot-'em-up atmosphere of Saloon Row and enter the quieter, more civilized part of town, where most of the business was done.

#5. Bowdon Building, 1947. This structure features the use of flagstone on its front. There are many quarries west of Williams where this stone is taken and shipped to market. Ash Fork, about 15 miles west, calls itself the Flagstone Capital of the USA.

#6. Commercial Row, 1907. This building contains several storefronts.

#7. Grand Canyon Hotel, 1892. Another of C. E. Boyce's buildings. This was a first-class hotel, designed to appeal to travelers to the Grand Canyon.

#8. Duffy Brothers Grocery Store, 1912. C. E. Boyce also erected this building. He intended to use it as a bank, but instead it was used as a grocery store.

#9. Citizens Bank, 1918. This white brick and terra cotta building houses the town's leading bank until it closed in 1958.

#10. Commercial Block, 1910-1912. This large building has been divided into several storefronts.

#11. Bennett's Auto, 1938. A typical Art Deco gas station of the era, built to serve travelers on Route 66.

#12. Pollock Building, 1901. Originally built as a one-story edifice made of tuff, a local volcanic rock, by Flagstaff banker T. E. Pollock. A stockman himself, Pollock was sympathetic to the needs of local ranchers and businessmen. Loans from his bank were vital to the economy. The Masons bought the building in 1927 and added an upper story.

#13. Sultana, 1912. This building was once the heart of Williams social life. Its two main tenants were a saloon and a movie theater.

#14. Babbitt-Polson Building, 1901. The Babbitt brothers were pioneer merchants who came to Flagstaff in 1886 and founded a business empire. They expanded to Williams in 1905. In 1908 they merged with the Polson family and ran a large general store here.

#15. Fray Marcos de Niza Hotel, 1907-1908. The Santa Fe built this as train station, hotel, curio store, and restaurant, the latter operations being run by the Fred Harvey organization. All but the ticket office closed in 1954. In 1989 the Grand Canyon Railway took over the old building and refurbished it. It is well worth a look, and contains an interesting railroad museum.

#16. Babbitt-Polson Warehouse, circa 1905. Recently moved to this location, this corrugated metal-clad building, now coated with rust, is the survivor of many such warehouses that used to line the railroad tracks.

(FROM ORIGINAL MAP DEVELOPED BY TERI CLEELAND)

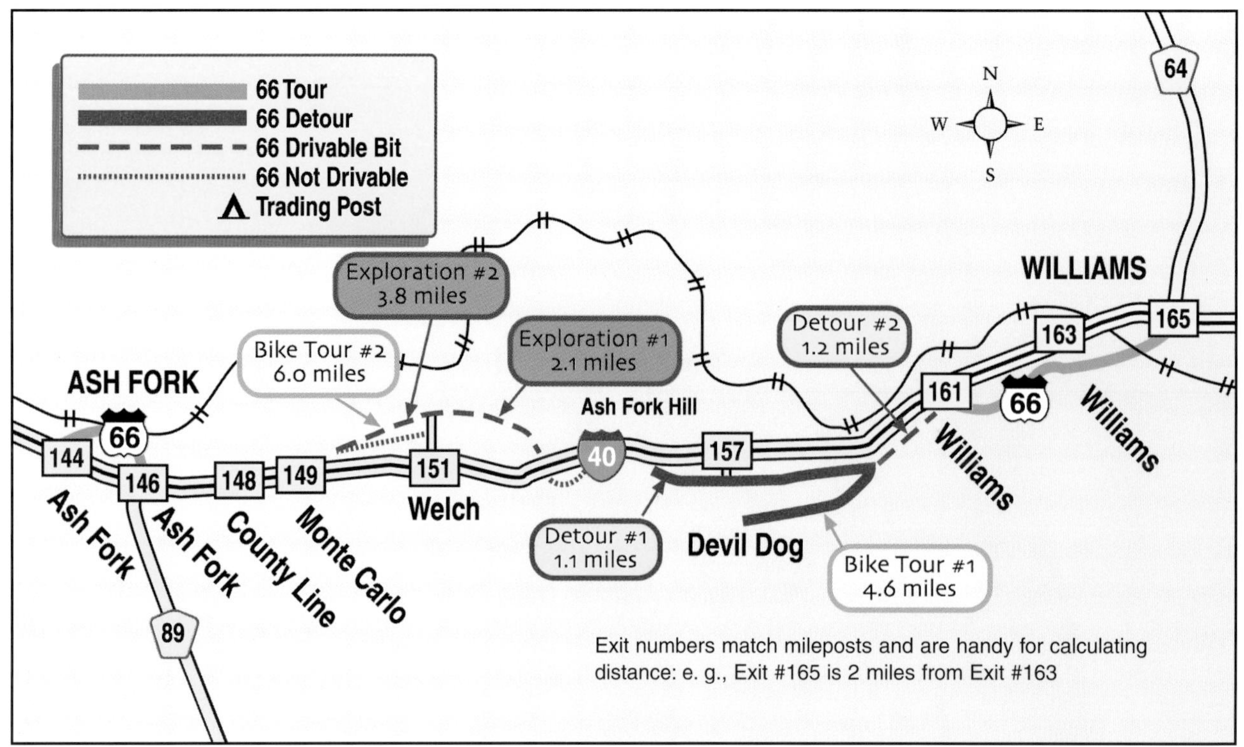

Tour 6-E Ash Fork to Williams pp. 68-70

Tour 8-W Williams to Ash Fork

Distance: 19.0 miles *30.4 km*
Highlights: Lovely forests, Ash Fork Hill
Driving Time: 30 minutes

Bill Williams

Tour 8-W takes you from the forested highlands of Williams to the flat plains of western Arizona. This segment of Route 66 includes the difficult and infamous Ash Fork Hill, a very steep grade that drops 1,700 feet *515 meters* in 12.0 miles *19.2 km*. Yesterday's roadbuilders made several attempts to find ways down this troublesome passage. Getting from Williams to the top of Ash Fork Hill was no easy matter either, as you will see. There are some interesting detours west of Williams as a result of the multitude of roads. The main tour (blue line) is confined to small scraps of Route 66 that run into and through the towns of Williams and Ash Fork. The rest is I-40 travel. But coming up just west of Ash Fork is that glorious stretch of Mother Road running all the way to California.

START

Williams Visitor Center

0.0 miles *0.0 km* **Zero** at the Visitor Center in downtown Williams. Drive west on Railroad Avenue and follow the signs to get onto I-40 at Exit #161-Williams. Route 66 does run to the west a bit, past the Forest Service camp and ends at the Ragtime Morgans ranch. There is not much to see here, but see page 69 for Detour #2 if you are interested.

The Town of Williams is located in a lovely setting

Exit #157—Devil Dog

At the upcoming Exit #157-Devil Dog, you enter an area where the early versions of the National Old Trails Highway and Route 66 have been preserved as forest roads and two of them have been marked and set aside as a mountain bike tour. The bike tour makes an excellent hike as well. If you have the time for these, they are worth exploring, and since they are far removed from I-40, you have a much better sense of going back in time than in other places.

BIKE TOUR #1
EXIT #157-Devil Dog S&E
1922 and 1932 Route 66
4.6 mile *7.4 km* loop ride

There is a special treat for mountain bikers here. The Forest Service has marked portions of the 1922 and 1932 alignments of Route 66 as the Devil Dog Bike Tour. Take Exit #157-Devil Dog and follow the loop to a stop sign. Turn right and drive under I-40. At the next road junction turn left. The paving ends at a cattle guard. **Zero** here, on FR 108. Just across the cattle guard (R) is the parking area at the trailhead, with a sign and map. You ride FR 108 for 0.4 miles *0.6 km* to a crossroad. Turn left on FR 108 (1932 version of 66) and ride to the 0.7 mile *1.1 km* point, where you will see the 1932 road going uphill. Turn right and ride to the 0.9 mile *1.4 km* point, where you turn left on FR 45 (1922 version of 66). Ride it to the 2.0 mile *3.2 km* point, where FR 45 goes right, away from Route 66. Bike straight up the old dirt road, following the power line, to the point where it meets the 1932 road, 2.5 miles *4.0 km*, then turn left and come downhill. At the bottom, 3.9 miles *6.2 km,* ride back the way you came in to return to your car.

DETOUR #1
EXIT #157-Devil Dog S&W
1932 Route 66
1.1 mi. *1.8 km* one-way
Time 15 minutes

Take Exit #157-Devil Dog and follow the loop to a stop sign. Turn right and drive under I-40. At the next road junction turn left. The paving ends at a cattle guard. **Zero** at the cattle guard. You are now on FR 108. Drive 0.4 miles *0.6 km* to a crossroad. Turn right at the stop sign on Coconino County Road #506 (the 1932 version of 66) which is paved. You can drive this fine old stretch of road (passing the 1920s Pine Springs Ranch auto campground, left) for 1.1 miles *1.8 km* to a point where it ends at an access road that goes to the right, under I-40. You will see an extension of the 1932 road going straight ahead, a gravel path running uphill. (You can walk this for about 0.2 miles *0.3 km* to a point where it ends above I-40). Turn around and drive back out the way you came in, getting onto I-40 westbound at Exit #157-Devil Dog.

Ash Fork Hill

As you drive west of Exit #157-Devil Dog on I-40 the pines begin to thin and you enter of zone of smaller trees, junipers and pinons. At MP 155.5 (Safety Pullout to the right) you reach the top of Ash Fork Hill, with sweeping views out over the countryside to the west, and you begin to descend the hill through the giant cut made in 1952, widened afterwards for I-40. Ash Fork Hill is really the western edge of the massive Mogollon Rim, which begins near Silver City, New Mexico and runs across Arizona to this point. Halfway down the hill at MP 154.5 look to your left and you can see the 1922 and 1932 road alignments winding around a basin. At MP 153.8 you can see the continuation of this road running along the side of a canyon to your right. (Drive this on Exploration #1).

1932 version of Route 66 west of Williams—Bike Tour #2

EXIT #151—Welch Rd.

No facilities

BIKE TOUR #2
EXIT #151-Welch N&W
1921-1931 Roads Detour for Bikes
6.0 mi. *9.6 km* loop
Time 1 hour

Take Exit #151-Welch. At the cattle guard **Zero** and go right (N) on FR 6. Drive it to the 0.2 mile *0.3 km* point, where you will see a pullout to your left, with a sign. This is the parking area for the Bike Tour. From here follow the markers, which will lead you downhill on the 1922 highway, then bring you back uphill on the 1932 paved version of Route 66, to loop back to the starting point.

EXPLORATION #1
EXIT #151-Welch E
Pre-1952 Route 66 segment
2.1 mi. *3.4 km* one-way
Time 15 minutes

Take Exit #151-Welch. **Zero** at the cattle guard and turn right (NE) on FR6. Drive FR6 to the 0.6 mile *1.0 km* point, and turn right on the 1932 version of Route 66, surfaced with gray gravel. You will easily distinguish this road as it is much straighter and wider than any other road in the area. You will even see bits of paving. Stay on the gray gravel road. Do not turn left on FR6 where it leaves Route 66. The road runs over to the base of Ash Fork Hill and then begins to climb it, ending at a fence at the margin of I-40. You can see how it went across I-40 and kept climbing. We believe that this bit of road was used from 1922 or even earlier. It was not abandoned until 1952. Backtrack 1.5 mi. *2.4 km* and go straight for Exploration #2, below.

EXPLORATION #2
EXIT #151-Welch W
1932-1952 Route 66
3.8 mi. *6.1 km* one-way
Time 30 minutes

Take Exit #151-Welch. **Zero** out at the cattle guard and turn right (NE) on FR6. Drive FR6 to the 0.6 mile *1.0 km* point, where you intersect 1932 Route 66. Exploration #1 turned right here. This time, turn left (W) instead. You will find thin old gray macadam paving, cracked and full of potholes, taking you downhill. Drive it slowly and carefully. We love this quiet old road, which really gives the feel of what it must have been like to drive 66 in the old days. At the bottom you go through a fence and come out onto the parking lot for the Monte Carlo Truck Stop. You can follow the 1932 version of Route 66 right past the door of the truck stop and beyond for a short distance. From the parking area for the truck stop return to I-40 westbound at Exit #149-Monte Carlo.

EXIT #149—Monte Carlo

At the Monte Carlo exit you are pretty well at the bottom of Ash Fork Hill, thoroughly out of the pines and back into range grass country.

EXIT #146—Ash Fork

Gas, Food, Lodging

Because Ash Fork was a Route 66 town, you will find Historic US 66 signs guiding you in from Exit #146. At the entrance to the little community you will find a sign reading, "Ash Fork Elevation 5144, Founded 1882." Route 66 was divided in Ash Fork, and you will drive in on westbound Lewis Avenue. (The eastbound traffic is carried by Park Avenue). Lewis is lined with service stations and motels on both sides, as it had all the Route 66 traffic before the one-way street system was created. Many of the old roadside businesses are in sad condition, with the majority of them being closed.

Sign on Ash Fork post office

The Town of Ash Fork

Ash Fork has a history very similar to its neighbor to the west, Seligman. Both were created as railroad towns and had comparable populations. In fact, Ash Fork was always a little larger than Seligman in the old days. Both were located on the Atlantic & Pacific Railroad (which became the Santa Fe). The railroad ran east and west. A branch line running south to Prescott was needed and both towns competed for the prize. Seligman won it in 1886, but the railroad that was built was so poorly financed and managed that in 1892 a second railroad to Prescott was built, this time with Ash Fork as its terminus. It was a success, later purchased by the Santa Fe. In addition to the railroad, ranching was Ash Fork's life blood. Since the 1950s the flagstone industry has been its mainstay.

When Route 66 was created in 1926, it followed the route of the Old Trails Highway through Ash Fork, and the little town eagerly embraced its new industry, tourism. As time went on, tourism became its primary industry, and Ash Fork took a terrible hit when I-40 bypassed it. You can see the sad results as you drive through town.

We feel bad about what has happened to Ash Fork and do not want to be unkind to the little town, but today it does not have much to offer, and most motorists will simply want to pass through it.

In the old days some travelers were attracted to Cathedral Caves, but today the road to the caves, which are on private property, is barred.

Tour's End, Lewis & 5th

We end this tour at the intersection of Lewis Avenue and Fifth Street, our **Zero** point at 19.0 miles *30.4 km*. The White House Hotel is located on the east side of Fifth Street and the Fire Station is located on the west side.

Where to Eat & Sleep in Ash Fork

Although there are a few restaurants and motels in Ash Fork, we have tried them and were disappointed with them. As a result, we do not recommend any places to eat or stay here.

El Escalante Hotel, a Harvey House. This was the pride of Ash Fork for decades. When passenger travel declined in the 1960s, the Santa Fe tore down this grand old building. What a shame!
—OP

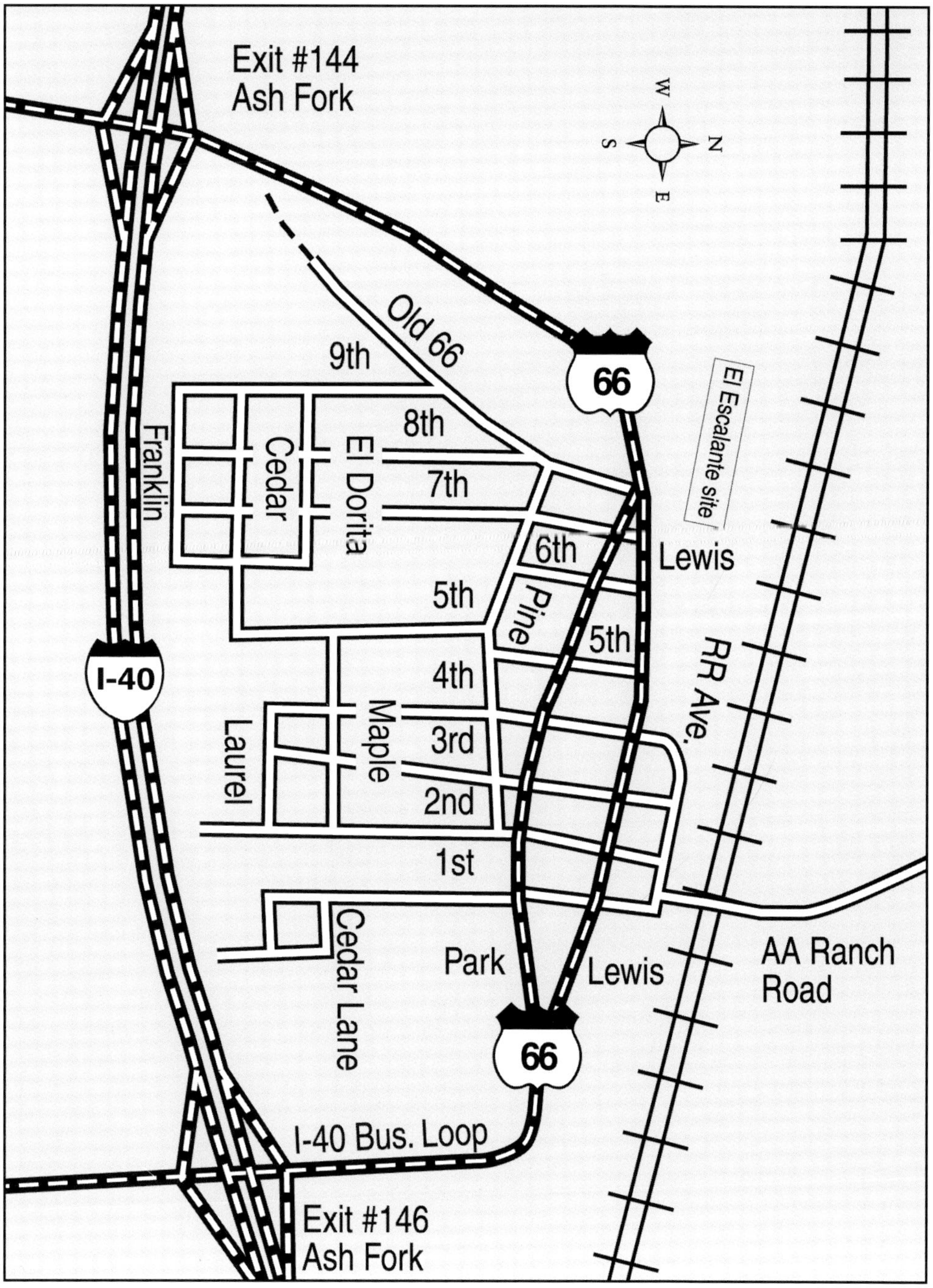

Map of Ash Fork

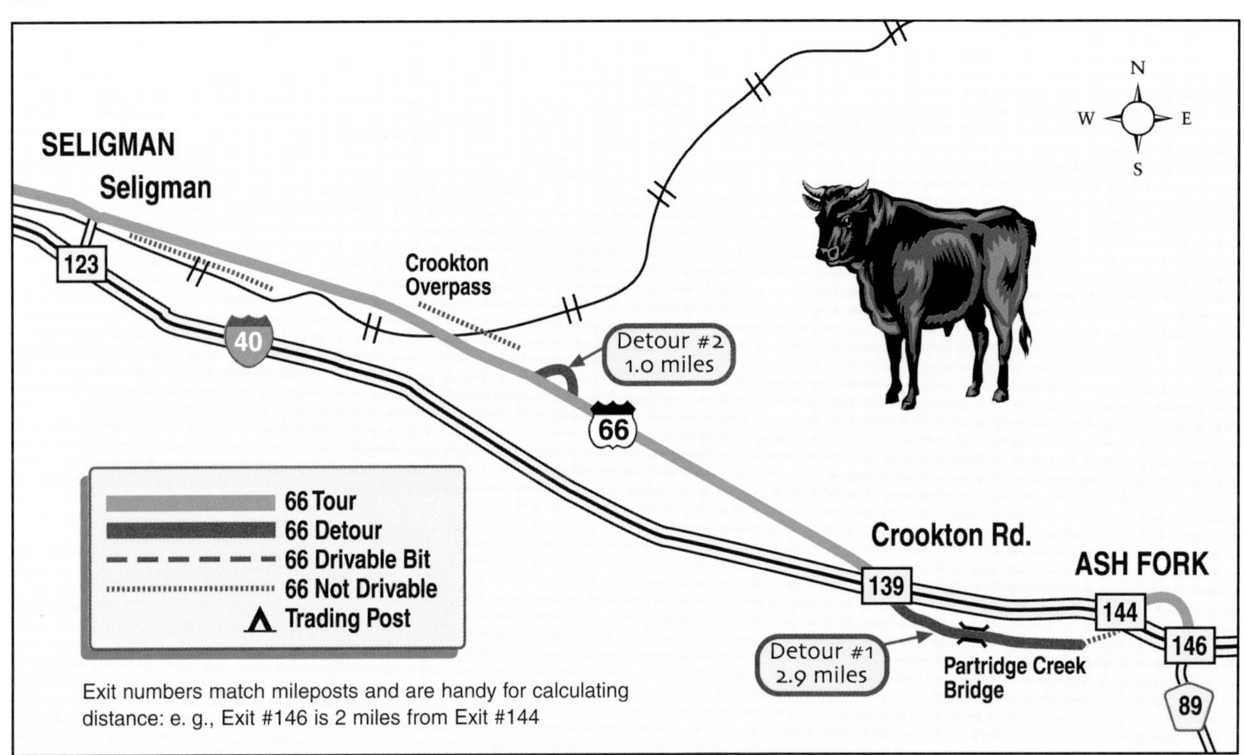

Tour 5-E Seligman to Ash Fork pp. 66-67

Tour 9-W Ash Fork to Seligman

Distance: 23.1 miles *37.0 km*

Highlights: Crookton Overpass, Long section of pure Route 66

Driving Time: 30 minutes

Ash Fork Welcoming Sign

Tour 9-W takes you west of Ash Fork through grasslands and rolling prairies to the Crookton Exit on I-40 where you turn off of the freeway and begin the long drive on pure Route 66. Throw your I-40 maps away at Crookton Exit, and from that point on kick back and enjoy the true 66 experience as you roll down the one and only Mother Road.

START

Ash Fork

Start this tour at the corner of Lewis and Fifth in Ash Fork. Drive west on Lewis which will take you back onto I-40 west at Exit #144-Ash Fork. At the west end of town you will see the flagstone yards, where extensive stacks of this flat stone await shipment to customers.

EXIT #144—Ash Fork

Once you are on I-40, from milepost 143 you will see some large, long old grades to your right, but they are railroad embankments, not Route 66. The railroad underwent some extensive rerouting in this area in the 1960s and you will see portions of the abandoned grades as you travel.

EXIT #139—Crookton Rd.

Take Exit #139-Crookton Road. The Arizona Highway Department recently improved the road between this exit and Seligman and it is now included on the Historic US 66 roster in Arizona, so you will see 66 signs at the exit. Although you may be itching to roll your wheels down the longest unbroken piece of Route 66 in the country, the nice Detour #1 is available at this exit.

DETOUR #1
EXIT #139-Crookton S&E
Old Route 66, Bridge
2.9 mi. *4.6 km* one-way
Time 10 minutes

Zero at the stop sign, turn left and drive over I-40, turning left on the other side on the frontage road. Drive 1.25 miles *2.0 km* on good paving to a road junction where the main road makes a big curve to the right. Go straight ahead on the old red paving, which is rough and broken, so go slowly. It moves along to the east, running parallel to I-40. At the 2.9 mile *4.6 km* point you will come to the fine Partridge Creek Bridge, built in the 1920s. The bridge is still in sound condition and you may drive across it without fear...

(Continued on page 39)

even though a fairly large cottonwood tree is growing out of the west end. Down in the creek bottom on the north side of the bridge you can see a low concrete curb where there was an old crossing used before the bridge was built; in other words, they drove across the creekbed. You can see the old grade going uphill. These crossings were impassable when the creek was in flood and motorists could be stranded for days waiting for the water to drop. Stop driving at the bridge. Beyond the bridge the old red paving (it got its color from red cinders mixed in with the asphalt) continues for 1.3 miles *2.1 km* east, then ends—not worth taking. Double back the way you came.

After you take Exit #139-Crookton, you will come to a stop sign. **Zero** your odometer here. Turn right and—ahh! you're on it at last. No more hunting for 66. This piece of Mother Road is just as authentic as the famous leg from Seligman to Topock, and is a very welcome addition to Historic Route 66 in Arizona. It is an 18-mile supplement to the road already billed as the longest surviving stretch of 66 in America, and we think it deserves the same fame as the Seligman to Topock section. As you drive Crookton Road you will see old grade to your right, which is an old railroad bed, not 66. The posted speed limit is 55 mph, which seems unnaturally slow, as the road is paved and in excellent condition. It is also fenced on both sides so that livestock will not wander out into the right-of-way. As you drive, you will see a long line of large rocks running parallel to the roadway (L). These are stones that were dug up when a pipeline was installed and have nothing to do with Route 66. Farther left there is another obvious cut that looks like a road, but is a natural gas pipeline. The country through which you will drive is high rangeland, with scanty grasses growing for miles over a rolling landscape.

DETOUR #2
Crookton Hill Detour
Old Route 66
1.0 mi. *1.6 km* one-way
Time 5 minutes

At 6.8 miles *10.9 km*, as you are beginning to climb a hill, you will see a gray gravel road to your right. Turn onto this road and drive it uphill. It is an older version of Route 66, forgotten, but in good condition. There are patches of old asphalt showing on its surface. Note a little campground to the left at 7.1 miles *11.4 km*. The road winds around to the top of the hill and meets the modern pavement at MP 151, where there is a sign reading "Elevation 5700 feet" at the 7.8 mile *12.5 km* point. On the other side of the road is a hilltop on which a transmitter tower is located. Turn right here and continue your 66 journey.

Crookton Overpass

At 9.5 miles *15.2 km* you reach a most interesting point on this tour, the Crookton Overpass. This is a great place, worth a stop for photos. The newer alignment is still in use, while an older bridge to the right has been blocked.

Have a chair at Delgadillo's Snow Cap in Seligman

The old bridge is perfectly safe for walking. It is thrilling to see a train pass underneath while you are on the bridge—a great photo. Look below and you will see older 66 grades. One old unpaved ramp ran up to the older bridge. You can see a raised roadbed part of which is lined with concrete curbing for several feet, similar to that used at the old creek crossing at the Partridge Creek Bridge. The concrete was used to hold the roadfill in place so that it would not wash out. These old alignments are all on private ranch land, so all you can do is look at them.

As you drive west of the overpass, you will see an older version of Route 66 to your left, running between the road you are driving and the railroad. You will have glimpses of this older road almost all the way into Seligman.

At 15.5 miles *24.8 km* you approach Seligman, and can see how it sits in a valley surrounded by a line of ridges.

Entering Seligman

At 17.3 miles *27.7 km* you're in the outskirts of Seligman at the "Welcome to Seligman" sign. You curve right beyond this and then reach a stop sign. Turn left (W). The street you are traveling is labeled Historic Route 66.

The Town of Seligman

At 17.9 miles *28.6 km* you are in town. Immediately beyond this point you will see the famous **Delgadillo's Snow-Cap** to your left—a must stop. We have been here many times and always enjoy it. Beyond the Snow-Cap, on the same side of the street, you will see **Angel Delgadillo's Route 66 Visitor Center.** Angel no longer cuts hair, but he is usually hanging around the Visitor Center and will be happy to talk to you and pose for pictures. This is another place that you must see. A bit farther down the road you will come to the Main Street crossroad. This is our **Zero** point in Seligman at 18.0 miles *28.8 km*. The Copper Cart is located here, and is a good place to stop and have a meal. (Adding the 18.0 miles to the 5.1 miles from Ash Fork to the Crookton Exit gives a total of 23.1 miles for this Tour).

Where to Eat and Sleep in Seligman

There are good cafes and motels here. Our choices are:

Food

Copper Cart Cafe. American Food in a Route 66 standout that was opened in 1950. Good solid food, properly cooked, and lots of it. Modest prices.
Westside Lilo's. Built after the town was bypassed. Lilo is a German, who adds bits of her native cuisine to the menu. Good tasty food at a reasonable price.
Roadkill Cafe. A grill-your-own steakhouse. Rather barnlike interior, but good food at a fair price.

Lodging

Route 66 Motel. This place was in business before the bypass and the rooms are named after famous people who stayed there. It is showing its age, but the rooms are clean, large and have nice amenities. Low prices.

Seligman Historic Walk

Italics—building destroyed by fire or other causes
See map on the next page
Start—Snow Cap

1. D&M Garage (1946) & Delgadillo Grocery
2. Delgadillo's Barber Shop & Route 66 Visitor Center (1916)
3. Store
4. Deluxe Motel (1932)
5. Gas Station & Bus Stop (closed 1985)
6. Miller's Dry Cleaning (1935), then Rainbow Cafe
7. Thunderbird Indian Store
8. *Corner Bar & Hotel (1928) (Demolished 1962)*
9. *H&J Cafe (fire 1974)*
10. *Bowling Alley (fire 1974)*
11. *Shorty's Magazines (fire 1974)*
12. *Bar & Town Tavern*
13. *Barber & Beauty Shop*
14. *Hotel, Drug Store, Casino & Brothel (1903-1952)*
15. *Chinese Restaurant*
16. *John King's Barber Shop*
17. *Clothing Store*
18. *Camilo Arduno's Restaurant*
19. *Gambling Hall & Brothel*
20. Original Delgadillo Barber & Pool Hall
21. Old Seligman Garage & Bus Stop
22. *Frank Smith's Gas & Groceries*
23. Home
24. Delgadillo Home (1920)
25. Standard Oil Bulk Plant (1920)
26. *Rental cabins for sheepherders*
27-28. *Cribs for prostitution (1920s-1930s)*
29. *Warehouse for store at Main & Historic 66*
30. *Ice Storage House (original burned 1930)*
31. *East Train Supply Room*
32. *Santa Fe Bull Lawman Office & Hobo Jail*
33. *Car (RR cars & wheels) Inspector's Shack*
34. *Home Supply Commissary*
35. *Rest Rooms for RR employees*
36. *Dispatcher's Office*
37. *Loading Dock for Autos/Warehouse*
38. *Crewmen's Office*
39. *Passenger Train Ticket Office*
40. Fred Harvey Hotel & Cafe (1900-1954)
41. Copper Cart Cafe
42. Central Commercial Department Store
43. Hotel
44. *Chinese Restaurant*
45. Chevrolet Garage (1933)
46. *Frank Smith's Groceries #2 (moved from #22)*
47-48. Homes
49. Donovan's Garage (1933)
50. White Horse Cafe

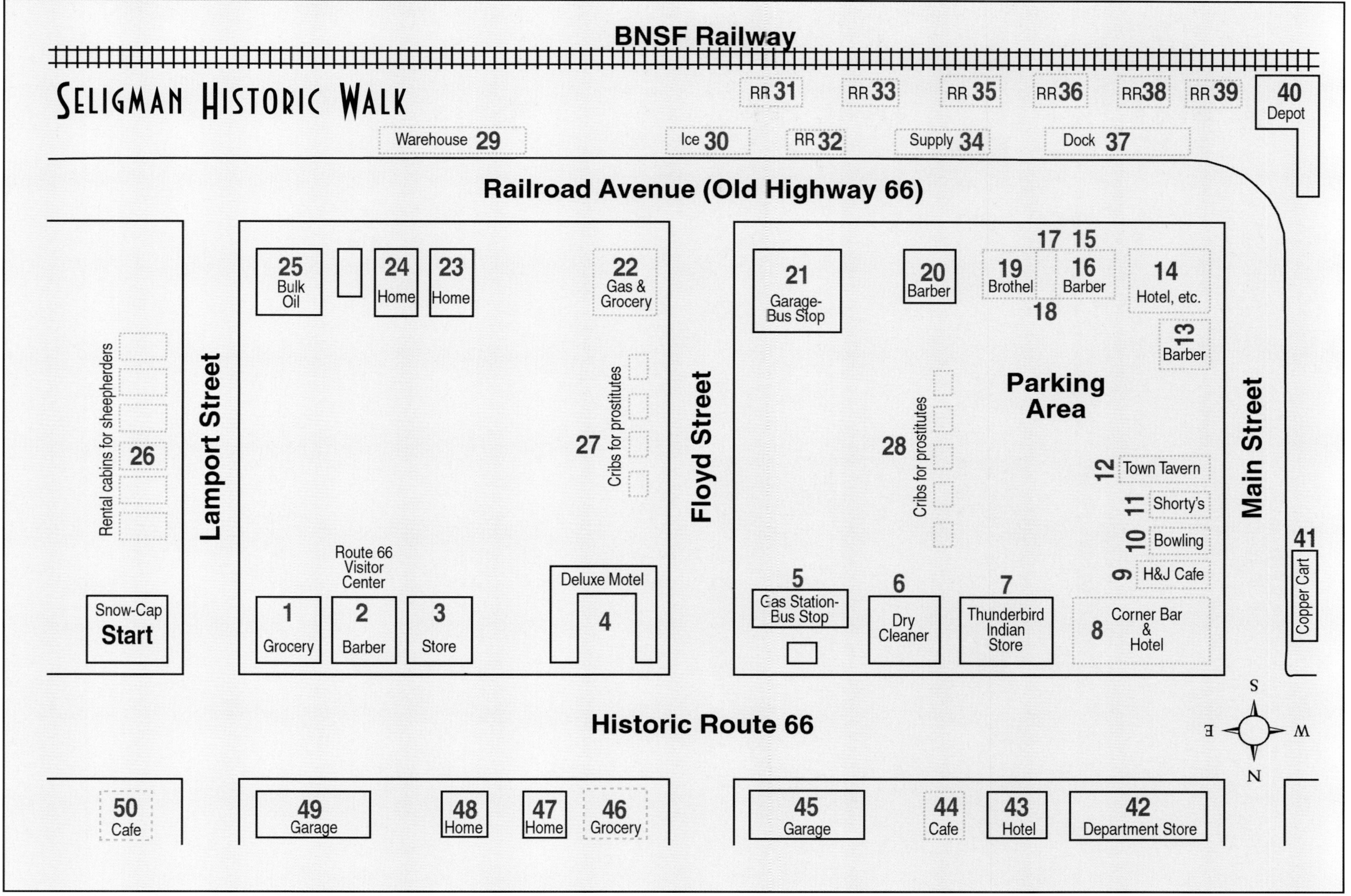
BNSF Railway
Seligman Historic Walk
RR 31
RR 33
RR 35
RR 36
RR 38
RR 39
40 Depot
Warehouse 29
Ice 30
RR 32
Supply 34
Dock 37
Railroad Avenue (Old Highway 66)
25 Bulk Oil
24 Home
23 Home
22 Gas & Grocery
21 Garage-Bus Stop
20 Barber
17 15
19 Brothel
16 Barber
14 Hotel, etc.
18
13 Barber
Rental cabins for sheepherders
26
Lamport Street
27 Cribs for prostitutes
Floyd Street
28 Cribs for prostitutes
Parking Area
Main Street
12 Town Tavern
11 Shorty's
10 Bowling
9 H&J Cafe
41 Copper Cart
Route 66 Visitor Center
Snow-Cap Start
1 Grocery
2 Barber
3 Store
Deluxe Motel 4
5 Gas Station-Bus Stop
6 Dry Cleaner
7 Thunderbird Indian Store
8 Corner Bar & Hotel
Historic Route 66
S E W N
50 Cafe
49 Garage
48 Home
47 Home
46 Grocery
45 Garage
44 Cafe
43 Hotel
42 Department Store

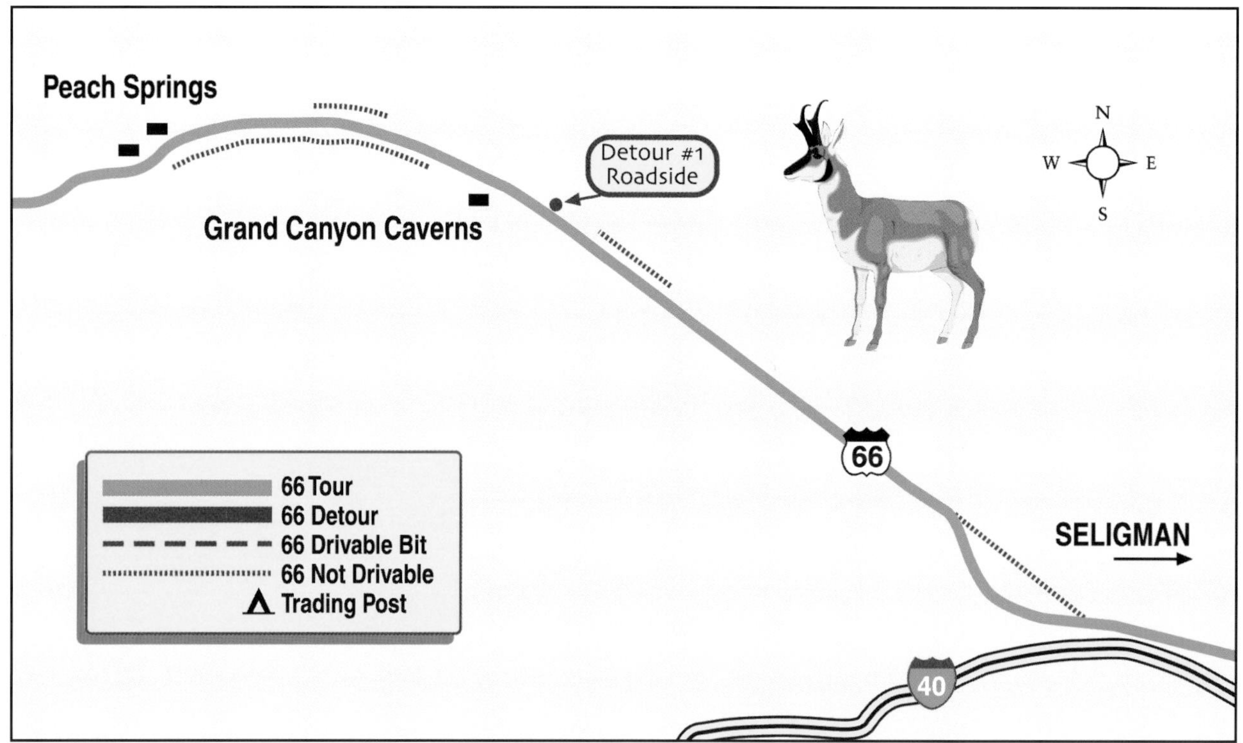

Tour 4-E Peach Springs to Seligman pp. 64-65

Tour 10-W Seligman to Peach Springs

Distance: 37.2 miles *59.5 km*
Highlights: Pure Route 66, Grand Canyon Caverns
Driving Time: 45 minutes

Delgadillo's

Tour 10-W takes you from the center of Seligman to the small community of Peach Springs, a historic railroad town that's now the headquarters of the Hualapai Indian Tribe. You will pass through more of the flat ranchland that characterizes so much of northern Arizona, driving pure Route 66 all the way. One detour is available, and there is a sightseeing trip to Grand Canyon Caverns, a roadside wonder.

START

Seligman

Start this tour at the junction of Historic Route 66 and Main Street in Seligman (Copper Cart Cafe). **Zero** out here. Drive out Route 66 to the west. Blessedly we will not have to mention any I-40 exits, because I-40 is far to the south and we will be on Mother Road all the way.

As you leave town you will see the access road to I-40 to the right. Pass by it, going straight west, following the Historic Route 66 signs, and that's the last you'll see of I-40 until you get to Kingman.

The Rusty Bolt in Seligman

Beale Road (maybe)

At 1.1 miles *1.8 km* you will pass Big Chino Wash (R). Writer Norman Wallace in a 1955 *Arizona Highways* article said Beale Road wagon tracks going to a spring were visible here. Are the tracks still visible? One can see tracks there. In any event, the Beale Road of 1857 came right through this area, and was followed by Route 66.

Chino Point

At 4.4 miles *7.0 km* as you go past Chino Point (R), you will see a raised bed to the right (N), this is an earlier version of 66, and is 3.0 miles *4.8 km* long. It is located on the Big Boquillas Ranch, a huge historic cattle operation now owned by the Navajo Nation. A sign on every access road gate to this bit of older Route 66 advises that entry is granted by signing in at Pica Camp at MP123.2 or at Hoffman Camp at MP141.5. The grade can't be driven, but can be walked, with permission.

Aubrey Valley

At 6.3 miles *10.1 km* you enter the Aubrey Valley, a very large level plain lined by cliffs and ridges. You will make a curve and then drive a long straight section of highway. As you drive this road, you will see little traffic and will gratefully be aware of the absence of big vehicles, especially the 18-wheelers. The road surface is excellent. There was no need to tinker with the path of Route 66 here; engineers ran it dead straight across the valley.

At 18.7 miles *29.9 km* there is a cluster of church buildings (L) which was formerly the Deer Park Motel, owned and operated by the man who owned the Grand Canyon Caverns.

Hyde Park Ruins

At 23.6 miles *37.8 km* you will find the interesting remains of the old roadside business known as Hyde Park to your right. This was a solid business that existed for many years and was even shown on road maps. It was intended primarily to house visitors to the Grand Canyon Caverns and was quite a bit nearer to the site than the Deer Park.

DETOUR #1
Milepost 117
Ruins of Hyde Park
Time 10 minutes

As you approach this site, going west from Seligman, you are climbing a hill. You see a transmitter looking like a golf ball on a tee to the left. There is a sign "Hyde Park Road" to the right. Just beyond the sign is the turn to the right, on a hilltop, just a pullout at the side of the road. No travel is necessary. The site of Hyde Park is a large one, and in the past you could enter it. Now the access gate is locked, as the Arizona Game and Fish Department is conducting a black-footed ferret reintroduction program on the premises. There are extensive ruins here; Hyde Park must have been a big operation. The surprise that greets you as you walk along the fence looking at the ruins is the old swimming pool on the east end. The operator of this business had a famous slogan, "Park your hide at Hyde Park tonight." See a photo of the sign at page 65.

At 24.3 miles *38.9 km* as you are going uphill, there's a short section of older road to the right in a cut.

Grand Canyon Caverns

At 25.3 miles *40.5 km* you reach the turnoff into Grand Canyon Caverns (L). Route 66 is divided here for about 0.5 miles *0.8 km* to make a safer turn situation.

SIGHTSEEING #1
Grand Canyon Caverns
Time 1.5 hours

When you pull in, you will see a motel and store. The caverns are not here. Look for the sign to the caverns and drive over to them. They are on a paved road about 1.0 mile *1.6 km* from the highway.

At the cavern office, a fairly large place in good condition, there is a curio store and restaurant. The cafe is simple, just serving hamburgers and the like. Nearby is an RV park.

To see the caverns you buy a ticket and are given a token, then wait for the next tour (given every half hour).

You reach the caverns via an elevator, going down with a guide. The descent is about 200 feet *60 meters*, from 5,700 feet *1727 meters* at the surface to 5,500 feet *1666 meters* below. The cavern is a nice one. Visitors walk through the caverns on concrete sidewalks lined with handrails, listening to the guide.

There are two main chambers of the cavern. There are no stunning stalactites, etc. as in some famous caves, but there are some interesting features. The cave smells fresh—with no dankness. It is very dry, averaging 10% humidity.

The tour is about 0.75 miles *1.2 km* long and proceeds at a leisurely pace, so that it is not physically demanding.

Hualapai Reservation

At 28.5 miles *45.6 km* you enter the Hualapai Nation.

At 30.6 miles *49.0 km* you will see older 66 to your left (S), a raised bed that runs alongside for miles.

Peach Springs

At 36.3 miles *58.1 km* you reach the outskirts of Peach Springs. Peach Springs, which used to be one little community, is now spread out. The part you see first is called the east end. Soon you will be in the main part, where you will find the tribe's modern Hualapai Lodge (L) our **Zero** point at 37.2 miles *59.5 km* MP 103.4. Here you can obtain lodging and good food.

Arizona commercial license plate—author's collection

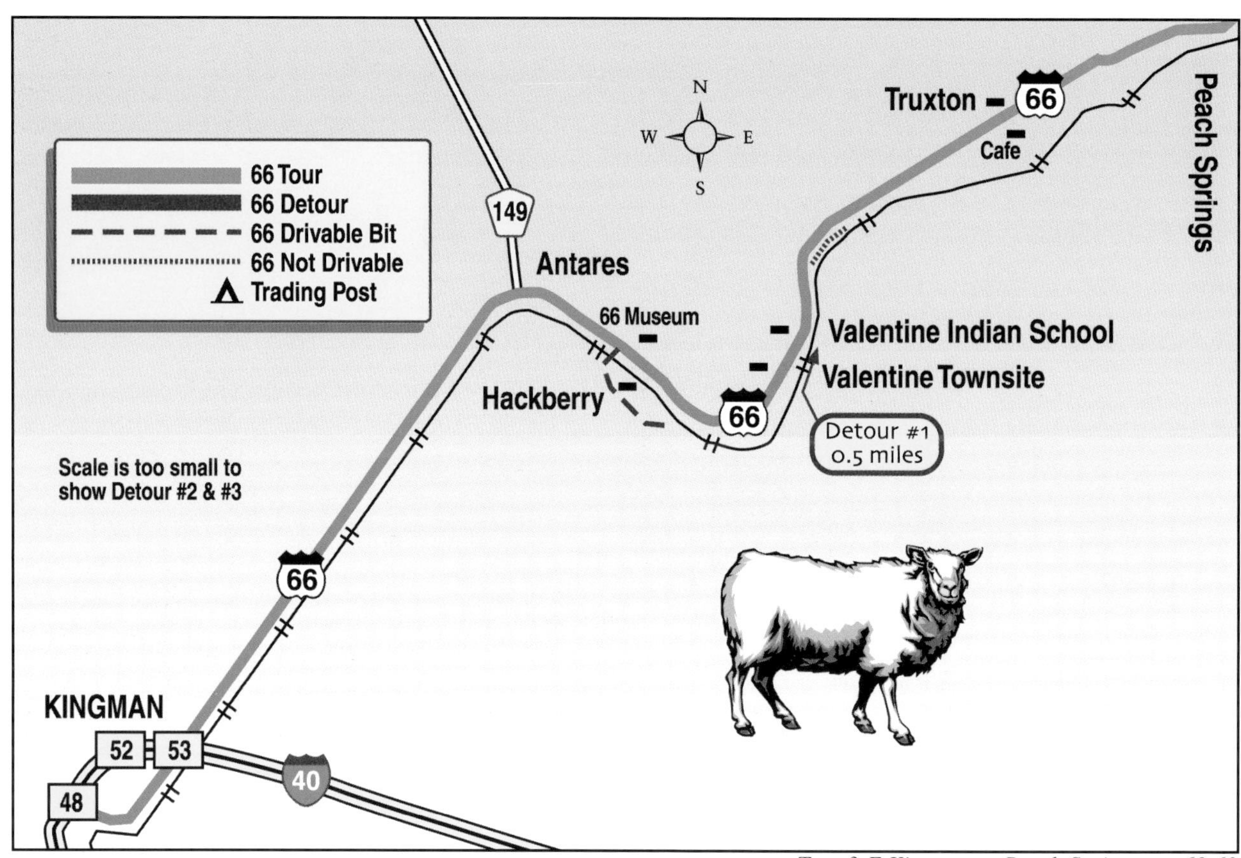

Tour 3-E Kingman to Peach Springs pp. 60-63

Tour 11-W Peach Springs to Kingman

Distance: 50.5 miles *80.8 km*

Highlights: Truxton, Valentine, Hackberry, Route 66 Museum

Driving Time: 1 hour

Arizona Historic 66 Sign

Tour 11-W, still on the long old wonderful strip of uninterrupted Route 66, takes you from Peach Springs to Kingman. Along the way you will stop at the Frontier Cafe at Truxton for a snack, take a photo or two at Valentine, wallow in Route 66 memorabilia at Hackberry, and follow the historic road into the bustling town of Kingman, which—after Flagstaff—is the largest AZ town on the Mother Road.

Peach Springs

START

Start at the Hualapai Lodge at Peach Springs, where we ended the last tour. **Zero** here. Leaving town is dead easy, just head west on Route 66.

At 2.1 miles *3.4 km* you will see a short segment of older 66 to the right, then it crosses to the left.

At 2.8 miles *4.5 km* you will see Buck and Doe Road (R). The Hualapai Nation is beginning to develop Grand Canyon tourism, as the lower or western part of the canyon is within their reservation boundaries. This road is designed to give access for their tours. Part of it is paved, and the tribe hopes to have all of it paved soon. A collection of newer homes has built up around this area, which is called the west side of Peach Springs.

At 4.4 miles *7.0 km* you see jagged mountain ranges ahead; you will soon be driving around them.

At 6.2 miles *9.9 km* is the modern Music Mountain Indian School (L), a far cry from the old schools at Valentine, which you will see soon.

At 7.4 miles *11.8 km* you leave the Hualapai Reservation.

At 7.7 miles *12.3 km* notice the Beale Road sign (R) below the faded "Welcome to Truxton" sign.

Truxton

At 8.4 miles *13.4 km* you enter the little settlement of Truxton. Here you cross a bridge over a wash. The Frontier Motel and Café, Route 66 institutions, are still open (L). Mildred Barker, owner of the Frontier Cafe, told us that she had been working in the café since 1955. Stop in and enjoy a burger and pick up a souvenir in their little gift shop. There is a Beale Wagon Road sign on the front of the motel.

At 13.6 miles *21.8 km* a short bit of the older 66 is visible to the left.

Old tourist cabins in Crozier Canyon

Crozier Canyon

At 14.5 miles *23.2 km* MP 89 the historic sector of Crozier Canyon including the bridge (L) where the last bit of paving of Route 66 in America was laid in 1937 is now marked with No Trespassing signs. You can see the bridge as you drive by but since the late summer of 2000 you can no longer drive it. The oldest version of the road ran down the canyon bottom but a huge flood in 1939 wiped out the road and it was moved uphill, away from the water.

DETOUR #1
Valentine Anglo School
0.5 mi. *0.8 km* one-way
Time 10 minutes

At 17.2 miles *27.5 km* (MP87.7) you will reach the Valentine School for non-Indians (L). To reach the building, turn left off of 66 here, go under the railroad bridge and you will see the school to your immediate right. You can drive over to it. This was a school for the non-Indian children who were forbidden by law to attend the Valentine Indian School, which you will pass farther to the west.

Old 66 business Site

At 16.5 miles *26.4 km* are the ruins of a couple of roadside businesses to the right.

Valentine Indian School Site

At 18.1 miles *29.0 km* there is a cluster of buildings marked Valentine (R). Today this is the site of a federal agency for the Hualapai Nation. The government built a big two-story red brick schoolhouse here in 1901, used as an Indian school, adding other buildings to the campus later. Students were Apaches, Havasupais, Hopis, Mohaves, Navajos and Papagos, as boarders, and Hualapais as day students. By 1937, the year the school closed, it had 200 resident students. You can turn off of Route 66 onto the parking lot for a closer look.

The old Valentine School for non-Indians

Valentine Townsite

At 20.0 miles *32.0 km* you will see a handful of buildings including Ernie's Country Dancing and the Chief's Motel ruin (R). Across 66 here was the Valentine Post Office, famous for its heart-shaped cancellation stamp, which brought hundreds of visitors to the place each Valentine's Day. Before the I-40 bypass hit Valentine in September 1978, some 200 lived in the settlement. Jacqueline Ann Griggs, the last postmistress, was murdered by a robber here on August 15, 1990, causing her grieving husband to raze the building. Most of Valentine's other buildings have been torn down as well.

At 22.3 miles *35.7 km* you can see an interesting old building, the Hackberry School, down in the valley (L). Ask the folks at the Hackberry General Store and Route 66 Museum for directions if you'd like to see it.

Hackberry General Store & Route 66 Museum

At 22.8 miles *36.5 km* is the Hackberry General Store and Route 66 Museum (R). This is a must stop. A 5-star attraction. Originally this was a true general store built to service the residents of Hackberry, who lived on the other side of the railroad track, down in the flat. Hackberry began life as a mining town, and the site of the original mine can be seen, a shiny building surrounded by green trees, high on the mountainside. After the railroad arrived in 1882, Hackberry became an important cattle shipping point. At its peak, it annually shipped the third largest volume of cattle in Arizona. When Route 66 arrived on the scene, the

Hackberry General Store & Museum

general store began to serve the traveling public as well as the locals. After the I-40 bypass went into effect, the general store languished and was eventually closed. Bob Waldmire bought the property and made it into a Route 66 museum. In late 1998 John and Kerry Pritchard bought it from Waldmire, and they are devoted to increasing the allure of this place for the roadie. It is absolutely fascinating and getting better all the time. If the Pritchards are able to carry out even half of their plans for improvements, this will be roadie Disneyland. Even if you have only a couple of minutes to spare, stop in and buy something to help these people turn their dream into a reality.

The Big Curve

At 26.5 miles *42.4 km* you have now passed through Crozier Canyon, and enter a big plain. Here you begin the longest continuous curve on Route 66, 7.0 miles *11.2 km,* as Route 66 carves a path around the north tip of the Peacock Mountain range and enters Hualapai Valley, flanked by the Cerbat Mountain Range on the west and the Peacock Mountains on the east. These mountains are full of valuable minerals.

Antares

At 28.5 miles *45.6 km* you reach Antares (R). Closed business. There is an important road junction there, with a highway going to Grand Canyon West and other points.

Valle Vista

At 31.6 miles *50.6 km* the curve straightens out and you enter a dead-straight stretch that continues for miles. Valle Vista, a desert development, is to the right. Picture yourself here in the old days, knowing that California lay beyond the mountains in the distance, your pulse quickening as you realize you are getting near.

At 41.8 miles *66.9 km* the Kingman Airport and Industrial Park is to your left. Here 66 becomes divided, with two-lanes each way. You are entering Kingman's outskirts.

Kingman

At 46.8 miles *74.9 km* you reach a road junction where Route 66 goes under the freeway. There is an Historic US 66 sign here. Drive under I-40. On the other side (W) of the underpass, you approach the old downtown. You are now on Andy Devine Avenue, and will continue to see Historic US 66 signs marking it. Andy Devine was a popular Hollywood actor. Although born in Flagstaff, his family moved to Kingman when he was very young and he considered Kingman to be his home town. Some purists believe that this piece of road cannot be called Route 66 because its name was changed to Andy Devine. We think that is being nitpicky and do not hesitate to consider it part of 66. There are lots of new and old motels along here. El Trovatore (L), one of the older ones, is on a hilltop. You now drop down into old Kingman.

Downtown Kingman

At 50.1 miles *80.2 km* you will see a gigantic water tower (L) by the railroad with a huge sign painted on it: "Historic US 66. Welcome to Kingman. Heart of Historic US 66."

At 50.3 miles *80.5 km* you reach the intersection with Fourth Street. The historic Beale Hotel is to your right. This crossroads is the heart of the historic downtown Kingman.

DETOUR#2
Chadwick Road Detour
Old Route 66
0.25 mi. *0.4 km* one-way
Time 5 minutes

At 49.2 miles *78.7 km* at the hilltop, just before the road enters a big cut, you'll find Maple Street. Pass it and take the next street to the right, Chadwick Road. This is a short paved road that curves around the hilltop, and is about 0.25 miles *0.4 km* long. It rejoins 66 at the bottom of the cut. We like this little road because it is very instructive about roadbuilding practices. In the earliest days, the builders lacked money and equipment. They had to follow the contour of the land. When they approached a hill, they would curve around the top. Later, with more money and more powerful equipment, they would cut the road through the hilltop. You can see the difference very clearly by taking this little drive.

Powerhouse and Route 66 Museum

At 50.5 miles *80.8 km* is a large building to your left, the Powerhouse. Pull in here. This is our **Zero** point in Kingman. In the Powerhouse is the Visitor Center, with food, toilets, and information, including the office of the Historic Route 66 Association of Arizona. Here you can get information and buy Route 66 souvenirs (and join the association). The Route 66 Museum opened on May 5, 2001, and we are happy to report that it is first-class, something that every Route 66 traveler in Arizona should see.

Advertising the National Old Trails Highway, one of the fine exhibits in Kingman's outstanding Route 66 Museum—MMHA

DETOUR #3
Old Trails Highway
2.8 mi. *4.5 km* one-way
Time 10 minutes

This was the alignment of Route 66 from Old Trails Highway days until 1939. From the junction of Andy Devine Avenue and Fourth Street (train station), **Zero** and turn south on Fourth Street. Drive over the railroad tracks. The road curves, and is easy to follow, as it is the main paved road going through the neighborhood, and the only one with striping. It leaves the residential area and goes into a narrow rocky canyon. There is a large exposed metal pipeline to your right, which carries sewage to treatment ponds. At 0.8 miles *1.3 km* you pass under a railroad bridge and the road curves left to run parallel with Route 66 and the railroad, both of which are to the right of the Old Trails Road. A higher railroad track is above you to your left. At 1.2 miles *1.9 km* there is a Kingman City Limits sign. Here you see (and smell) sewage treatment lagoons to your right. The center stripe disappears (eaten by the fumes?) though the road is still well paved. At 2.2 miles *3.5 km* there is a high railroad bridge to your left acting like a picture frame for a scenic canyon behind the bridge. At 2.8 miles *4.5 km* the paving ends at a grandstand for a racetrack. You can see where the old road went from here to join the present alignment, but you cannot drive it any farther. Turn around and retrace your path.

Kingman Recommendations

Sightseeing

Mohave Museum of History & Arts, 400 W. Beale. Phone 928-753-3195. Website: www.ctaz.com/~mocohist/museum/index.htm.

Beale Park and Locomotive Park, side-by-side north of the Powerhouse. A pleasant place to visit, especially if you are a train buff, in which case you will really enjoy the huge historic locomotive there.

Bonelli House, 430 E. Spring St.

Route 66 Museum, At the Powerhouse.

Eating

Mister D'z Route 66 Diner, 105 W. Andy Devine. Real Route 66 atmosphere, shakes and burgers. Inexpensive.

Ristorante Italiano, 2215 Hualapai Mtn. Rd. Ste. A, 753-0542. Good Italian food with reasonable prices.

Sleeping

Wayfarer's Inn, 2815 E. Andy Devine, Kingman, AZ 86401. Reservations: 1-800-548-5695

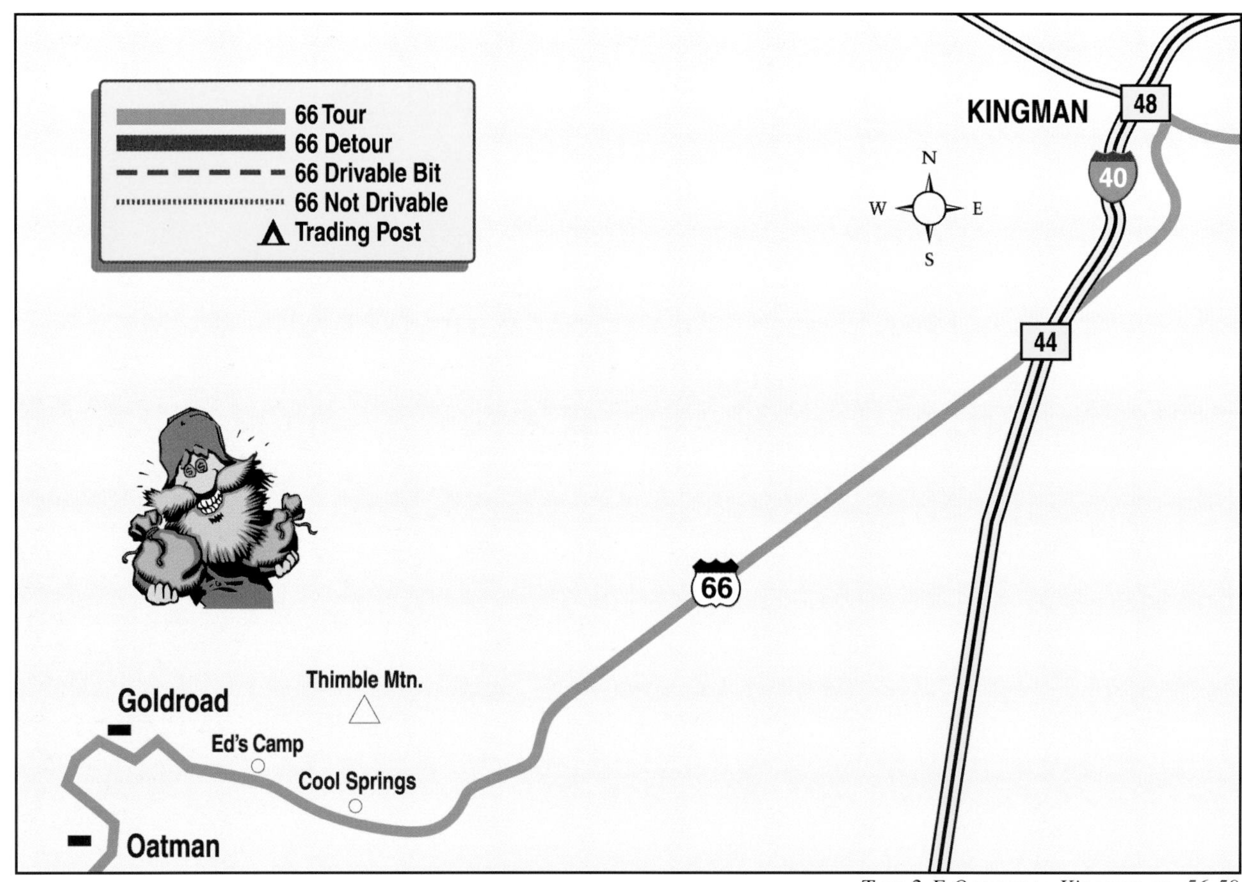

Tour 2-E Oatman to Kingman pp. 56-59

Tour 12-W Kingman to Oatman

Distance: 28.4 miles *45.4 km*

Highlights: Great bit of Route 66 winding up over Sitgreaves Pass, Ghost Towns

Driving Time: 1.5 hours

Kingman Water Tower

Tour 12-W is one of our favorites and is a lot of fun. In addition to passing through districts rich in history and mineral wealth, you will see some breathtaking scenery and drive up Oatman Hill over Sitgreaves Pass, the famous steep twisty road that posed the most difficult problem on Route 66 in Arizona. The road has been resurfaced recently so that it is in excellent condition, but it is still narrow, steep and twisting—a thrill to drive.

START

Powerhouse in Kingman

Start at the Visitor Center in Kingman, located in the Powerhouse. This is the **Zero** point. Turn left and drive west on Andy Devine Avenue.

0.2 miles *0.3 km* The Oatman Road junction is to your left. Turn left here. You will notice that the road heads toward a canyon pass through which giant cuts have been made (this is Kingman Canyon). The railroad is to your left. You will see the Old Trails Road (See Detour #3 Tour 11-W) going under a railroad bridge to your left, then running along below the railroad grade.

At 1.0 miles *1.6 km* you will see two large ponds below to your left. These are sewage treatment lagoons for the Town of Kingman. The stinky fumes that they give off have caused the locals to nickname this place Perfume Pass.

At 2.8 miles *4.5 km* Route 66 becomes the frontage road for I-40, running alongside it, just a few feet away. Both are headed toward Exit #44-Oatman on I-40.

McConnico

At 3.8 miles *6.1 km* you have driven out of the Kingman suburbs and are out in the country here. This place is on the maps as McConnico, though you can't see any distinct community. McConnico was significant in the past because it was the place where the shortline railroad to Chloride, the Arizona and Utah, met the Santa Fe. The railroad was called the CB&F (Chloride Back & Forth) by residents.

The ruins of Cool Springs Camp with Thimble Mountain in the background

At 5.2 miles *8.3 km* is a stop sign. Turn right. There's a big sign reading *Historic US 66, Oatman Highway* here. Drive under I-40. Don't take the frontage road on the other side; instead drive ahead to the 5.6 mi. *9.0 km* point.

Oatman Highway

At 5.6 miles *9.0 km* turn left on the Oatman Highway. The road to Oatman is well marked with historic US 66 signs, and also by Back Country Byway road signs. You are now down on the desert floor. The dominant plant on this landscape is chaparral, with lots of yucca mixed in. As you drive across the valley you are headed toward the Black Mountains. Almost every mountain range in the world has a break, called a pass, through which a road can be built, and that is the case here with Sitgreaves Pass.

At 19.3 miles *30.9 km* is the Back Country Byway Interpretive Site to your right. There is an information kiosk here with helpful information on both sides of the signboard. From this point you will begin a steep twisting climb up to the top of the pass. The scenery is amazing but keep your eyes on the road.

Cool Springs Camp

At 19.8 miles *31.7 km* are the ruins of Cool Springs Camp (R). You will see two stone pillars and some other ruins of the tourist camp that was operated here for many years before it burned in 1964. This is a good place to stop for photos, with the very scenic Thimble Mountain in the background. We enjoyed seeing this ruin modified by Hollywood technicians for a scene in the movie filmed here in 1991 and released in 1992, *Universal Soldier,* starring Jean-Claude Van Damme and Dolph Lundgren.

Ed's Camp

At 20.9 miles *33.4 km* is Ed's Camp (R). As you approach this place you will see the name "Ed's Camp" spelled out with white stones on the face of a hill. The camp, to your right, is a fascinating jumble of buildings and other structures, but is on private property and visitors are unwelcome. In this area you will see unpaved roads all over the hills—those old prospectors and miners covered every inch of these mineral-rich mountains. They left some of their burros behind them, and the animals have learned how to survive. Bands of them roam the area, so watch out for them. We came around a curve one evening and almost slammed into a group of six burros standing in the middle

Unique traffic sign—watch out for wild burros

of the road.

Little Meadows

At 21.7 miles *34.7 km* you will see a tiny settlement to your right called Little Meadows. This was the site of a pumping station, where water was taken out of this valley and pumped over Sitgreaves Pass for use in the mine at Goldroad. The rusty pumphouse remains.

Shaffer's Fish Bowl

At 23.3 miles *37.3 km* is the Shaffer's Fish Bowl Spring (L). The road makes a climbing curve to the right here and there is a little apron on the left side of the road where you can park. You can climb 35 steps to reach the fish bowl, which collects water from a seep, a spring from which water slowly drips through seams in the stone. You can see the drip marks on the face of the hill. The bowl holds water and is a pleasant place to visit, though we have never seen fish here. There is a memorial plaque to Shaffer. Look down into the canyon from the road where you parked and you will see the rock walls of an earlier wagon road.

Sitgreaves Pass Summit

At 24.0 miles *38.4 km* just before you reach the summit of the pass there is a pullout to the right where you will see some iron railings. This was the site of the Summit Ice Cream stand. It is a great viewpoint and worth a stop. Just beyond this is a sign reading, *Sitgreaves Pass Elevation 3550'* at the crest. (3550 feet is *1075 meters*). On the other side of the pass is another pulloff where a different business was located to the left. Here you will find some old concrete footings and a short flight of stairs that goes down to nothing.

Tri-State Lookout

At 24.2 miles *38.7 km* is the Tri-State Lookout (R), at a curve where you will see a gravel road going out to a point. Don't try to drive to the tip. Park in the big wide area and walk out to the end. The three states you can see from here are California, Nevada and Arizona.

Onetto Spring

At 24.5 miles *39.2 km* is Onetto Spring (L), in an alcove with a little tunnel and a green tree, an important source of pure water for early travelers. From here you can see below to a flat barren area, which was a leach field from the Goldroad mine. Cyanide used in the leaching process was poisonous to plants, causing these old fields to be toxic and growth-free for decades.

Onetto Spring (where car is parked)

Goldroad

At 25.0 miles *40.0 km* you can see an old road below and the ruins of Goldroad, a once-mighty gold mining town. It was a large operation until gold and gold mining were declared non-strategic in World War Two, and the mine was shut down. The modern Addwest mine has since been built, but is now idled until gold prices rise.

At 25.5 miles *40.8 km* to your right is the entrance to Addwest's Goldroad mine, where you can take the Mine Tour, which we recommend.

Everywhere you will see ruins of the mine and town of Goldroad, on both sides of Route 66. We were fascinated to see a 1938 photo of the place in the mine tour office showing that 66 ran under one of the mine structures.

SIGHTSEEING #1
Goldroad Mine Tour
Time 1.5 hours

Although it is the oldest mine in the entire Oatman district, the Goldroad mine is still in operation, or was until the price of gold dropped so low in July 1998 that operations were suspended, waiting a return of the gold price to $325 per ounce. In the meantime, a portion of the mine is open to the public for a mining tour. We took this and loved it. The basic tour takes about one hour, and there is a modest cost (in 2000) of $12 per adult and $6 per child. Open from 10 am to 5 pm except Wednesday. Snacks, drinks and light lunches available. After buying a ticket you are issued a hard hat and taken to a drift at an upper level of the mine by an authentic hardrock miner. He takes you into the mine pointing out the geological formations, the timbering used to support the tunnels, the fact that miners always want to cut into the veins upwards, etc. The tour is very well thought out and conducted and we came away with lots of knowledge, wanting to know more. There are two gift shops on the premises where you can buy souvenirs, books and so on. The mine recently began to offer a 4-hour tour, and we can hardly wait to take it. Reservations are a must for the long tour. For the ordinary tour, just drop in. These folks are very friendly and made us feel that we had experienced a real slice of history. Goldroad has always been treated as if it were Oatman's little cousin, but after taking this tour, we now realize the importance of Goldroad. There is still a ten-year supply of paydirt in the mountain, and if prices rise, the old mine will run again. Oh, yes, we almost forgot to mention: you will be given a free sample of real gold ore from the mine, a perfect souvenir.

Oatman

At 27.9 miles *44.6 km* Oatman comes into view. There is a large tailings dump at the side of the road from the old United Eastern Mine. In gold mining, the ore came from the mines in large chunks of hard rock. These were crushed and ground until a fine powder about the consistency of sand was produced. Water and chemicals were mixed with the powder to make slurry from which the gold and silver could be separated. At the end of the process, the remains of the wet slurry were poured out into ponds. The water settled out and left dry lakebeds of rather pinkish toxic sand in which no plant can grow. Beyond the tailings dumps, you will see the mountains that surround the town, dominated by the eye-catching Elephant's Tooth. The mountain peaks here are very jagged needles. Oatman is squeezed into this picturesque setting, leaving room for only one narrow main street. Both sides of the street are lined with buildings, some old, some new. The new ones have usually been built to resemble the old, so it is hard to tell them apart. Oatman is a tourist town, and it seems that every business is tourist oriented. Ask a business owner when the burros will appear. There is a small band that wanders in daily. You can buy carrots to feed them, which is great fun.

Oatman Community Hall

At 28.4 miles *45.4 km* you are in the heart of Oatman and will find the Oatman Community Hall to your right. This is the end of this tour, the **Zero** point.

What To Do and See in Oatman

Oatman is a tourist town and makes its living from the visitors who line its crowded streets. During peak season and on holidays a group of local history re-enactors dress up in colorful Western clothing and stage mock gunfights on the streets. Ask in the stores for times. Another Oatman specialty is feeding the wild burros. A small band of these sturdy animals comes into Oatman regularly, a jack leading the jennies and youngsters. You can buy carrots to feed them, which is great fun. Otherwise, you will enjoy wandering through the town, shopping and enjoying its history. We have noticed quite a turnover in restaurants in Oatman. You will probably find a few of them open when you visit. The most dependable seems to be the one in the hotel. The hotel has a couple of rooms, but we don't recommend Oatman as a place to sleep.

Photo of Oatman—about 1920 (OP)

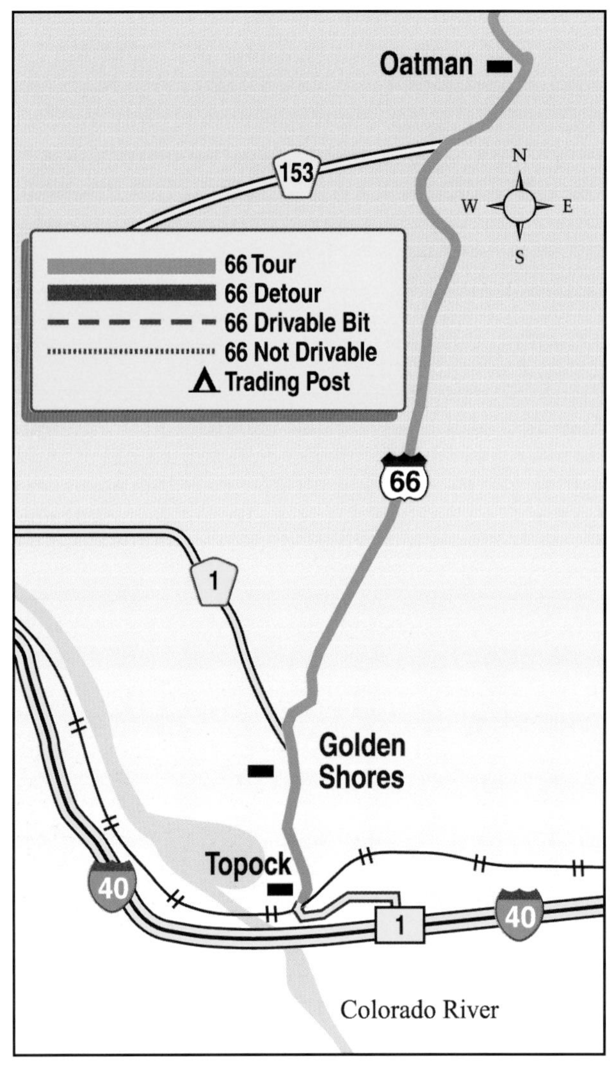

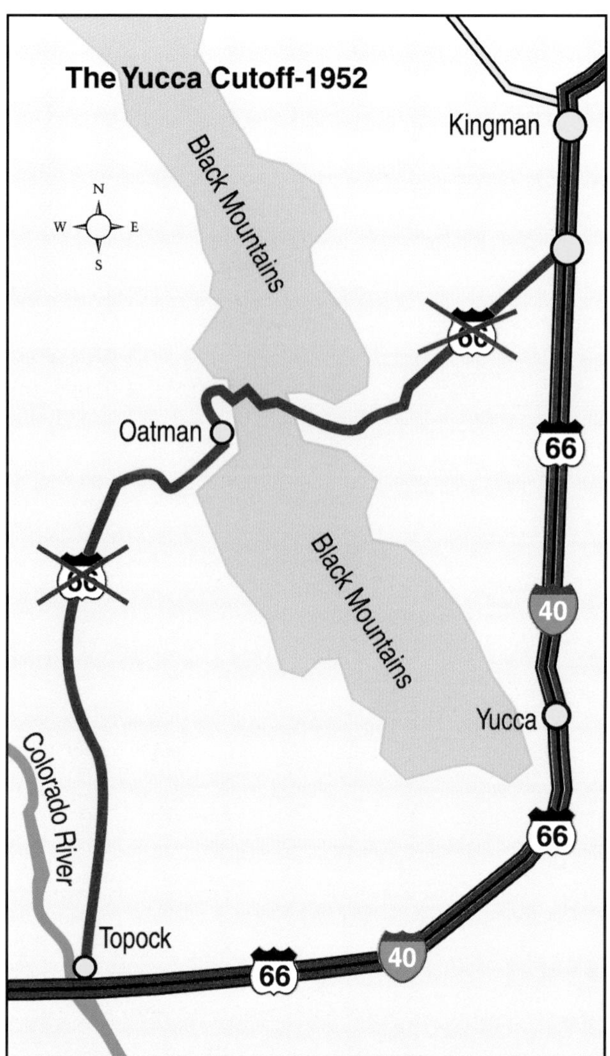

Tour 1-E Topock to Oatman pp. 54-55

Tour 13-W Oatman to Topock

Distance: 24.5 miles *39.2 km*
Highlights: Colorado River, Old bridge
Driving Time: 45 minutes

Tour 13-W is your last tour westward through Arizona, as it takes you from the relative high point of Oatman to the low desert at the Colorado River, where motorists cross the river on a bridge to get into California, as the river is the boundary between the two states. We don't like this barren sun blasted country much, but it is something to see and it does complete the journey as Route 66 travelers of old made it. When you get to the Colorado River you will see the old bridge that was used for decades by Route 66 travelers, a graceful arch, now carrying a pipeline.

START

Oatman Community Center

Start this tour at the Oatman Community Center.

0.0 miles *0.0 km* **Zero** at Oatman Community Center. From here you are on a continuous downgrade to the Colorado River.

At 0.1 miles *0.16 km* as you leave town, you see mining ruins, and another huge tailings dump (L), this one from the Tom Reed Mine, Oatman's most productive venture. All around are old dumps, mines, and the ruins of mining structures.

Old Trails

At 1.0 miles *1.6 km* is Old Trails (R). This is a tiny but distinct community that appears to have been founded in the early 1920s when the National Old Trails Highway (the

LOST 66—The Yucca Cutoff
On October 1, 1952, the Yucca Cutoff was opened, (see map) going around the Black Mountains rather than over them through Oatman. When I-40 was built, it went right on top of the 1952 alignment of 66. Today there is nothing worthwhile to see of Route 66 while driving I-40 west from Kingman. So, the 1952 alignment is seldom mentioned today.

predecessor to Route 66) was created, running through the area. Today there isn't much to see, just a few homes and some attempts at roadside businesses.

Road Junction
At 2.3 miles *3.7 km* is a road fork. Go left, following the Historic US 66 signs. Mine ruins have disappeared by now, but you still see roads all over the hills leading to mines and prospects. The Boundary Cone, a big volcanic needle, now appears (L).

Cholla Forest
At 4.4 miles *7.0 km* stark and forbidding desert begins. Sparse vegetation. Lots of tall Cholla, the infamous Jumping Cactus. It does not actually jump, but got its name because the cactus pads are so loosely attached that if you brush against the plant even slightly, the spines cling to you and pull the head loose, so that it seems that the cactus pad has jumped onto you. Soon even these cacti disappear. The ground is stony and burnt looking. The landscape is monotonous.

Riverside Court
At 6.4 miles *10.2 km* is the site of the long-abandoned Riverside Court (L). You will see a turnout to a large level clearing. There was a motor court, gas station, etc. here in the old days. The operator was either a crook or had a mean sense of humor. Calling this place "riverside" was definitely a misnomer, as it is at least 17.0 miles *27.2 km* from the river. One can imagine the comments made by indignant guests when they found out where the court was actually located.

Power Line
At 12.6 miles *20.2 km* you cross under a big power line carrying electricity from Davis Dam to Phoenix. You now see mountains in the distance. These are in California across the Colorado River. The river is in the valley in front of the mountains and you can't see the water yet.

Backcountry Kiosk
At 16.8 miles *26.9 km* there is a Byways Backcountry information kiosk (L). There is a pullout where you can go to read the information on the sign.

At 17.0 miles *27.2 km* you see large sand dunes (R) crisscrossed by dune buggy tracks.

At 18.6 miles *29.8 km* you can see the Colorado River.

Golden Shores
At 18.8 miles *30.1 km* you enter Golden Shores. This is a subdivision, where some palm trees have been planted.

At 19.8 miles *31.7 km* you pass through the commercial area of Golden Shores, with scattered businesses, and where the Topock Post Office (L) is located.

At 20.0 miles *32.0 km* is a stop sign. Go straight here. You see a sign "Topock 5." The desert gets even bleaker.

Topock
At 22.3 miles *35.7 km* you can see Topock Bay (R). This is not the flowing river itself, but a bay where there is a marina. We don't really "get" Topock, as it is not a town and there is nothing to see there. In fact, the Topock post office is located in Golden Shores.

The old bridge at Topock, no longer used by automobiles

Railroad Overpass—End of Tour
At 24.5 miles *39.2 km* you reach a railroad underpass. We end the tour here at this convenient marker. In the distance you can see bridges over the Colorado River. The graceful white arch shown above was built in 1916 and used for 66 travel. Today it is only a support for a pipe line. The earlier Red Rock Bridge built by the railroad has been removed. The present I-40 bridge, which you will drive in a few moments, has none of the charm or beauty of the old bridges.

Well, that's the end of Route 66 in Arizona. We hope you have enjoyed it. You will have to use I-40 to get across the river into California, but in the Golden State there are many more miles of Route 66 to drive and savor.

On the other side of the underpass the road curves left and steers travelers onto I-40 at Exit #1-Topock. You will see a sign reading "Los Angeles." Follow it and get onto I-40 headed west.

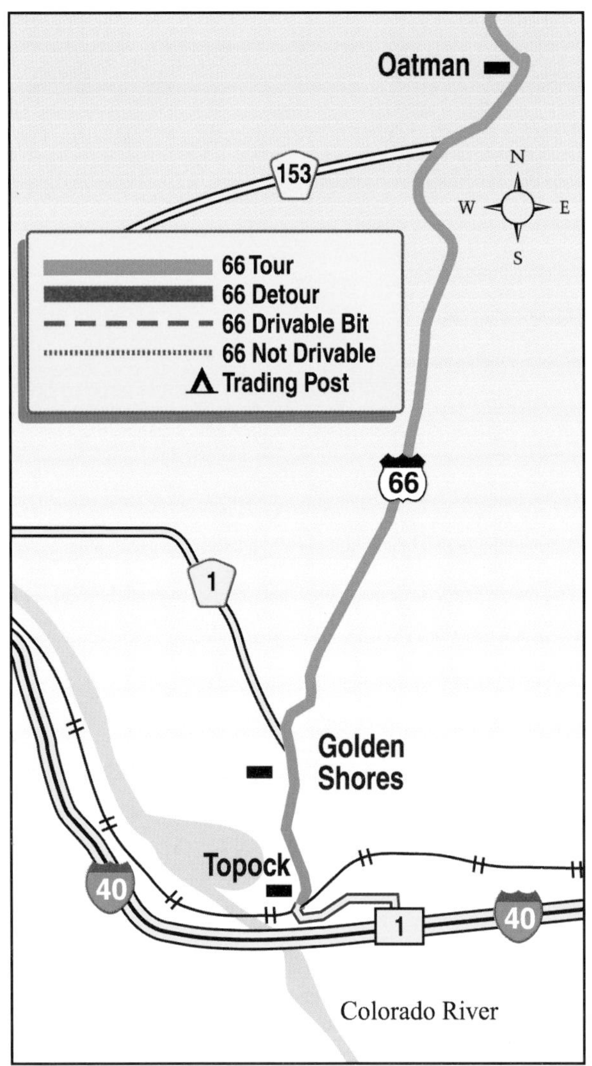

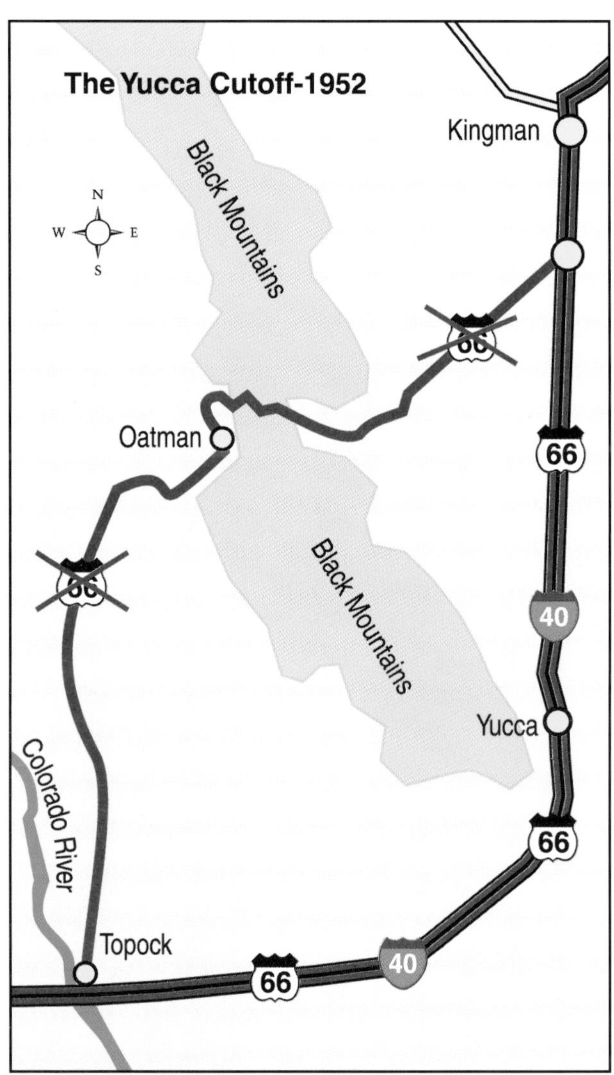

Tour 13-W Oatman to Topock pp. 52-53

Tour 1-E Topock to Oatman

Distance: 24.5 miles *39.2 km*
Highlights: Colorado River, Desert Landscape
Driving Time: 45 minutes

LOST 66—The Yucca Cutoff
On October 1, 1952, the Yucca cutoff was opened, (see map) going around the Black Mountains rather than over them through Oatman. When I-40 was built, it went on the top of the 1952 alignment of 66. Today there is nothing worthwhile to see of Route 66 while driving I-40 west from Kingman. So, the 1952 alignment is seldom mentioned today.

Tour 1-E begins as you enter Arizona from California on I-40. The numbering of the freeway exits starts at the state line, which is in the middle of the Colorado River, so the first exit you will see is Exit #1-Topock. You want to take Exit #1-Topock. If you turn right at the stop sign and right again on the frontage road, you will run a short distance along the river to the yard of Pacific Gas & Electric. Don't trespass on their property, but you can park nearby and look out at the river, where you will see one of the old bridges used by Route 66 to cross the river. It is the large white bridge, now just used to support a pipeline.

START

Topock

Start Tour 1-E at Exit #1-Topock. At the stop sign, turn left and drive over I-40. You are now traveling the fabled Route 66 and will be able to do so for miles.

The country over which you first pass is the same kind of hard desert that you found on the California side, sunblasted and bleak. We must confess that we are not fans of this desert and find it forbidding. It does have a certain kind of spare and austere beauty, though.

Topock is not a town. You will not find any kind of village near the river, so don't spend time looking for Topock, because you won't find it. You will immediately come to the railroad bridge, where the tracks pass high over your head. This is our **Zero** point.

Sign seen at Topock for many years—OP

Railroad Overpass

At 0.0 miles *0.0 km* you drive under the railroad overpass. The railroad has built the embankment very high here, probably to allow plenty of headroom for the highway underneath, and perhaps to protect it from the massive floods that hit the region periodically.

At 2.1 miles *3.4 km* the desert begins. You have been driving along the river area, where vegetation is thick because of the availability of water to the plants. The dominant riverbank species is tamarisk, an exotic that was introduced years ago to control erosion. It loved this habitat and has taken over, spreading to all the desert rivers of Arizona, where it is often an unwelcome pest. You now leave the river riparian area and enter into the desert, vegetation disappears and sand dunes take over.

Golden Shores

At 3.9 miles *6.2 km* you will see a sign notifying you that you are entering Golden Shores, a desert community. You will find scattered homes and businesses along here, all quite new, and will see the Topock Post Office. Riverside communities have become popular with retired people since air conditioning made life comfortable in the desert.

At 4.5 miles *7.2 km* you reach a highway fork. Go straight. The road to the left goes to Bullhead City.

At 5.5 miles *8.8 km* you will see a sign saying, "Begin Historic US 66 (R)."

At 7.4 miles *11.8 km* you have clear views of the Black Mountain range ahead of you. Notice how sharp and jagged they look. Oatman is located in the heart of these mountains.

Back Country Kiosk

At 7.5 miles *12.0 km* there is a Back Country Byway kiosk to your right. You can pull into the parking lot and read the informative signs. You are now climbing steadily, and will note that the appearance of the desert changes with the elevation.

Eastbound>

Power Line

At 11.8 miles *18.9 km* you pass under a huge power line that carries electricity generated at Davis Dam on the Colorado River to Phoenix.

Riverside Court

At 18.1 miles *29.0 km* to your right, on a hillcrest, is a pullout to a flat pad. It doesn't look like anything if you just drive by but if you get out and investigate you will see that some large structures were located here in the past. These are the ruins of Riverside Court. What a joke to call this place Riverside, because you can hardly even see the Colorado River from here, as it is 17 miles *27 km* away. This deceptive name must have outraged guests who booked rooms without having seen the place.

Cholla Forest

At 18.5 miles *29.6 km* take a look at the desert and you will see that a change in the plant life begins here. You will now see countless acres of a tall spindly cactus, the Teddy Bear Cholla. This is the infamous Jumping Cactus. It doesn't actually jump, but seems to because if you walk through a patch of it you will find some of the pads stuck to your clothing no matter how carefully you tried to avoid contact with them. The Boundary Cone, a tall volcanic needle, towers above. Early surveyors thought this cone was right on the 35th parallel, though later studies showed that it is south of it about a mile.

At 20.1 miles *32.2 km* look down to the left, and ahead and you will see a tailings dump, remains of a small mining operation. The hills are full of these old dumps.

At 22.2 miles *35.5 km* you will reach a road junction. Go straight.

Old Trails

At 23.5 miles *37.6 km* you will pass through Old Trails, a community. There are only a couple of buildings here, where owners struggle to operate a little business. There is a sign "This is Old Trails." The place took its name from the Old Trails Highway built through here in 1922.

At 23.6 miles *37.7 km* you will see an enormous pink tailings dump (R) from the Tom Reed Gold Mine, one of the Oatman's largest. See page 108 for a photo of this operation in its heyday. You turn a corner, and you are in the outskirts of Oatman.

At 24.3 miles *38.9 km* mine ruins appear, then homes. You are almost in Oatman, just around a curve.

Oatman

At 24.5 miles *39.2 km* is the Oatman Community Hall (L). Our **Zero** point. Park wherever you can find parking nearby (it is scarce) and get out of your car so that you can walk around Oatman.

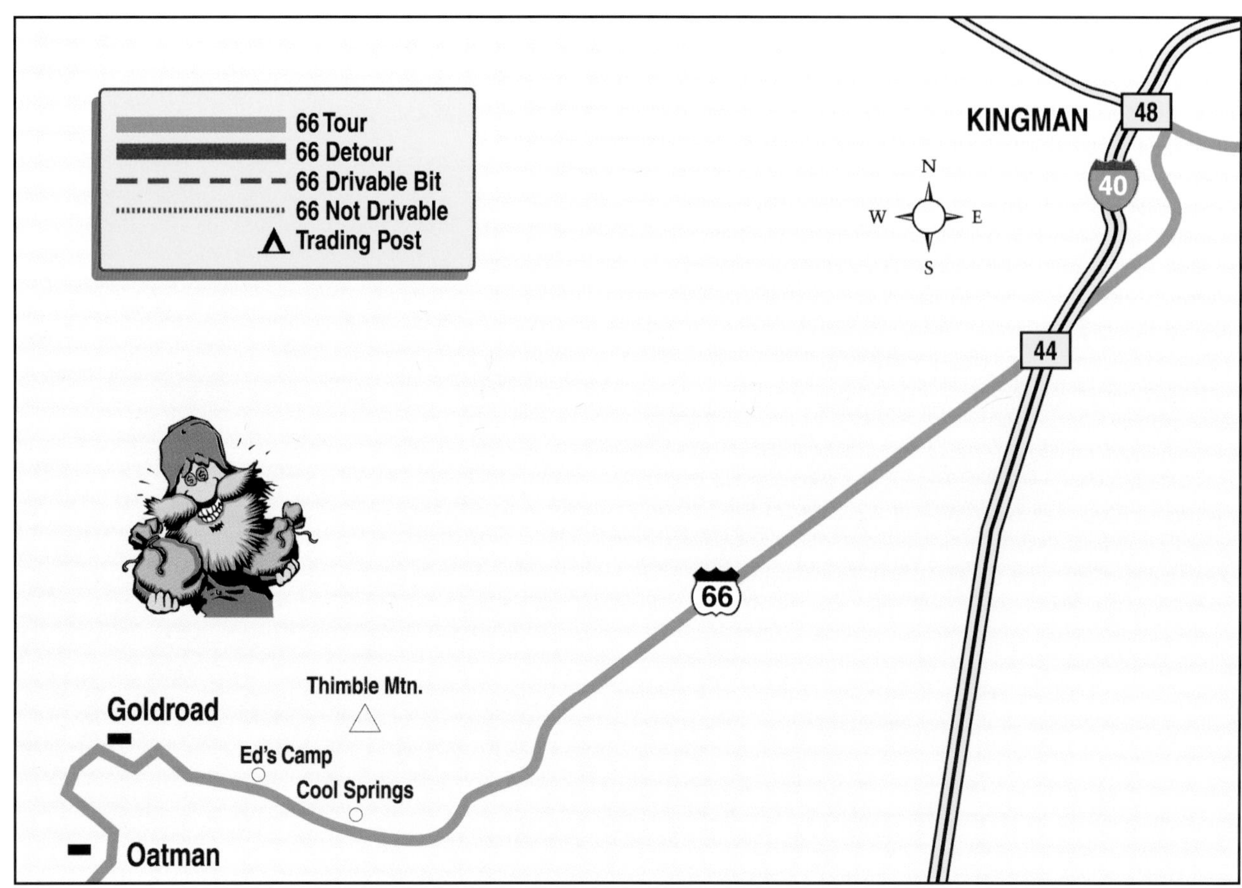

Tour 12-W Kingman to Oatman pp. 48-51

Tour 2-E Oatman to Kingman

Distance: 28.4 miles *45.4 km*

Highlights: Thrilling road, Oatman & Gold Road, Ed's Camp, Cool Springs, Route 66 Museum

Driving Time: 1.5 hours

Historic Oatman Hotel

Tour 2-E takes 66 travelers from Oatman into Kingman over one of the most thrilling parts of Route 66. In modern cars, we don't hesitate to drive the steep winding roads such as this, but in the old days when vehicles were not so reliable, drivers had good reason to fear breakdowns from overheating and other mechanical problems. Many of the old cars did not have enough power to handle roads like this, and as late as 1946 Jack Rittenhouse reported in his Route 66 guide that a service station in Gold Road offered to tow motorists over Sitgreaves Pass for $3.50.

The highway has been worked over extensively in the past few years and is in excellent shape. It is still steep and narrow and winds back and forth, so if you are not used to this kind of driving, be sure to pay attention to the road.

START

Oatman Community Center

Zero at the Community Center. As you leave town at 0.3 miles *0.5 km* you'll see a big tailings dump at the side of the road (R). In the old gold mining process, the ore came from the mines in large chunks of hard rock. These were crushed and ground until a fine powder about the consistency of sand was produced. Water and chemicals were mixed with the powder to make slurry from which the gold and silver could be separated by chemicals, primarily cyanide. At the end of the process, the slurry was poured out into ponds. The water settled out and left dry lakebeds of rather pinkish toxic sand in which no plant can grow.

At 1.0 miles *1.6 km* is the Silver Creek Road (L), an unpaved road going to Bullhead City. Stay on the paving, which is a narrow twisting road.

Goldroad

At 2.7 miles *4.3 km* Goldroad, a former gold mining town. There is a modern mine there today, with metal buildings. They conduct a worthwhile daily tour. Entrance to the left.

SIGHTSEEING #1
Goldroad Mine Tour
Time 1.5 hours

Although it is the oldest mine in the Oatman district, the Goldroad mine is still in operation, or was until the price of gold dropped so low in July 1998 that operations were suspended, waiting a return of the gold price to $325 per ounce. Meanwhile, a portion of the mine is open to the public on a mining tour. We took this and loved it. The basic tour takes about one hour, and costs (in 2000) $12 per adult and $6 per child. The tour is open from 10 am to 5 pm except Wednesday. Snacks, drinks and light lunches are available. After buying a ticket you are issued a hard hat and taken to one of the drifts at an upper level of the mine by an authentic hardrock miner. He takes you into the mine pointing out the geological formations, the timbering used to support the tunnels, the fact that miners always want to cut into veins upwards, etc. The tour is very well thought out and conducted and we came away with lots of knowledge, wanting to know more. There are two gift shops on the premises where you can buy souvenirs, books, etc. The mine recently began to offer a 4-hour tour, and we can hardly wait to take it. Reservations are a must for the long tour. For the ordinary tour, just drop in. These folks are very friendly and made us feel that we had experienced a real slice of history. Goldroad has often been treated like Oatman's little cousin, but after taking this tour, we realize the importance of Goldroad. There is still a ten-year supply of paydirt in the mountain, and if prices rise, the old mine will run again. Oh, yeah, we almost forgot to mention: you will be given a free sample of real gold ore from the mine, a perfect souvenir.

You will note ruins all around the Goldroad area. Going up from the mining tour entrance, the road does a triple switchback, an amazing thing to see.

At 3.4 miles *5.4 km* the ruins end. There are old roads into the mountains everywhere, made in the days when gold-crazy miners left no stone unturned. You are near the top of Sitgreaves Pass. Note the old rock-walled road up high to the right.

Onetto Spring

At 4.0 miles *6.4 km* there is a little alcove on the right side of the road where there is a small tunnel, a tree and the plants are especially green. This is Onetto Spring.

Sitgreaves Pass Summit

At 4.4 miles *7.0 km* is the crest. On your side there is a wide area to the right, the site of an old business. This is a very fine viewpoint, worth a stop. We inspected the area and found a few concrete footings and a short flight of stairs going down to nowhere. On the other side of the crest to the left are some iron railings at a widened site. This was The Summit ice cream store. The crest itself is marked *Sitgreaves Pass, Elevation 3,550' (1,075 meters).*

Eastbound>

Inside the Goldroad Mine, on the tour. Dick is standing at a point that is 500 feet directly below Route 66

On the way down the other side you will find the same narrow twisting kind of road for about 4.5 miles *7.2 km*.

Shaffer's Fish Bowl

At 5.2 miles *8.3 km* is Shaffer's Fish Bowl (R). This is hard to see and there are no signs. The road makes a hard turn to the left here. There is a small parking apron to the right if you want to see the bowl. From the parking area you walk a short distance back uphill and then climb a flight of about 35 home-made stairs. The bowl is made of native rock and concrete to catch the water from a seep. The bowl has been full of water every time we examined it, but we never saw any fish. It is a pleasant and unexpected little grotto, a nice place to visit.

Little Meadows

At 6.6 miles *10.6 km* is Little Meadows (L), where there are some buildings, including some old rusted industrial buildings, including an old pumphouse, with giant pipes sticking out of a shed. This site was a pumping station. Water was taken from nearby springs and pumped uphill over Sitgreaves Pass and down to the mine at Goldroad.

Ed's Camp

At 7.3 miles *11.7 km* is Ed's Camp (L). Westbound travelers can see a big sign spelling out the name of Ed's Camp with white rocks on the hillside behind you and to your right, but you will come upon this site blindly. The camp is a fascinating jumble of buildings and other structures on the left, but is on private property and visitors are unwelcome. In this area you will see unpaved roads all over the hills—those miners were incredible. Note the rare saguaro cacti at Ed's.

Route 66 to Oatman, near Shaffer's Fish Bowl

Ruins of Cool Springs Camp

At 8.5 miles *13.6 km* is Cool Springs Camp (L). This is a good place to stop for photos, with Thimble Mountain, a tall, scenic volcanic needle, in the background. In 1991 a movie company filmed a scene here for *Universal Soldier*, a 1992 release starring Jean-Claude Van Damme and Dolph Lundgren. The scene lasts for only a few minutes, but the Hollywood special effects people did a fine job of recreating an old-time desert service station built around these ruins. As you would expect in an action film of this type, the scene ends with the fiery destruction of the set, though it seems that the ruins were left undisturbed.

Kiosk

At 8.9 miles *14.2 km* is the Back Country Byways kiosk (L) with a turnout for parking. The big sign here gives interesting information and is worth a stop.

At 22.8 miles *36.5 km* is a stop sign. Follow the sign reading, "To I-40." Turn right (E). Drive under I-40, then turn left on the Frontage Road, which is old 66, at 23.3 miles *37.3 km.*

McConnico

At 24.4 miles *39.0 km* MP 45 is McConnico (R). McConnico is one of those places that doesn't look like a place. It appears as McConnico on old maps and was a distinct settlement when it served as the terminus for a short haul mining railroad that ran north to the mining town of Chloride. Although it was officially the Arizona & Utah RR, locals called it the CB&F, the Chloride Back and Forth. It has been decades since the line stopped running and McConnico is now undistinguished, just a grubby industrial area on the outskirts of town.

Perfume Pass

At 27.1 miles *43.4 km* is Perfume Pass (R). Older 66 is seen as a paved road running along the bottom of the pass between two ponds and the upper and lower railroad grades. See Detour #1, page 60. The ponds are sewage treatment lagoons.

At 28.2 miles *45.1 km* is a stop sign. Turn right. Across the street is Locomotive Park containing a huge old Santa Fe railroad engine and the Beale Monument.

Kingman, the Powerhouse, & Route 66 Museum

At 28.4 miles *45.4 km* turn right and drive into the Powerhouse (R) parking lot. The Powerhouse is the end of this tour. Inside the building you will find toilets, cafes, shops and the headquarters of the Arizona Route 66 Association, which has an office and a gift shop selling Route 66 souvenirs. There is also an information desk. where you can get directions and find out what is happening in town and the surrounding area.

On May 4, 2001, the **Arizona Route 66 Museum** opened in the building. We are tickled to death with this museum, which is a fine one, and we thoroughly enjoyed our visits. The exhibits are comprehensive and professionally done, tell the story of 66 well, and are a credit to the State of Arizona and to the Mother Road. Be sure to visit this fine attraction, which has become an instant "must-see."

Note: On page 47, Kingman westbound, we have a brief mention of our recommended places to eat and sleep.

Kingman Downtown Area

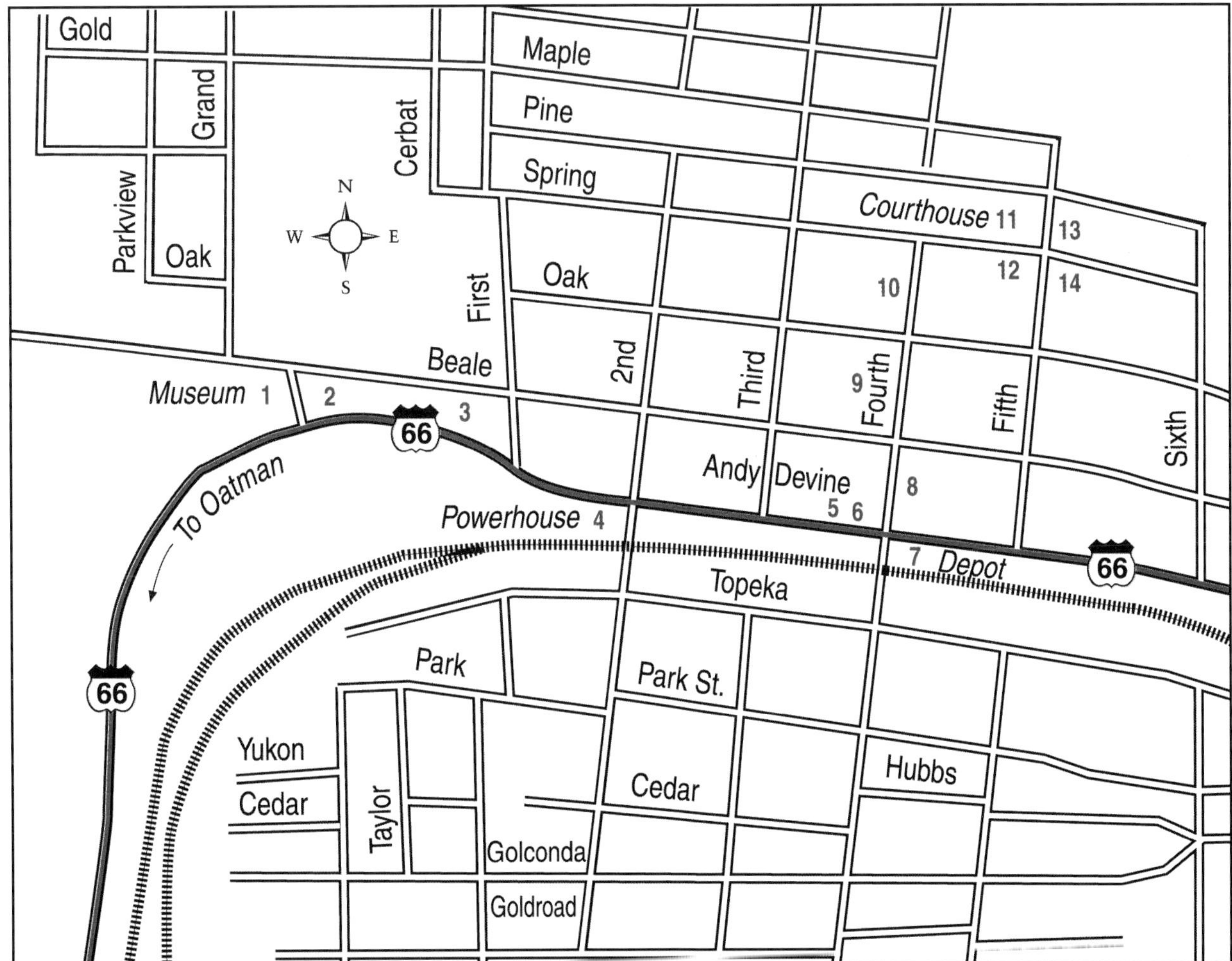

Kingman has two areas of interest for the Route 66 traveler who wants to get out and see the town on foot. The first is in the western area, around the Mohave Museum of History and Arts, including the **Museum** itself (1), the **Beale Monument and Beale Park** (2), the **Locomotive in Locomotive Park** (3), and the **Powerhouse** (4). You can park at the Powerhouse, where we end our tour into Kingman and then see the other places on foot.

The other area of interest is the historic downtown district, which is centered on Fourth Street, from the train depot to the courthouse. Buildings of interest in this district are these:

5. **Brunswick Hotel**, 1909. Once a grand hotel it has been partially renovated and rents rooms. Restaurant.

6. **Beale Hotel**, 1901. This was the major hotel in Kingman and for many years was managed by Thomas Devine, the father of movie actor Andy Devine. Andy grew up here. From time to time someone announces plans to renovate this large building but so far no one has.

7. **Depot**, circa 1900. We are intrigued by this building, with its mission style. The Santa Fe borrowed the style and grafted it onto the depot at Holbrook in a funky juxtaposition. There are plans afoot to renovate the old Kingman depot and we hope that they are successful.

8. **Central Commercial Company**, 1917. Once a great department store, outfitting the mines and ranches around Kingman, one could buy anything under the sun here. It closed in 1978.

9. **Little Red Schoolhouse**, 1896. Pioneer building. Many a Kingman resident learned the ABCs here.

10. **Elks Lodge**, 1906. For many years this was the social center of Kingman, with a vigorous membership.

11. **Mohave County Courthouse**, 1915. From its high point, the old building has a commanding presence looking down Fourth Street.

12. **Bonelli House**, 1915. This home was donated to the City of Kingman and is open for visitation.

13. **Blakely House**, 1887. A real old-timer, but not open for visits.

14. **Methodist Church**, 1917. This large old church was built to last and is still an impressive structure. Clark Gable and Carole Lombard were married here in 1939. It is no longer a church, and now contains county offices.

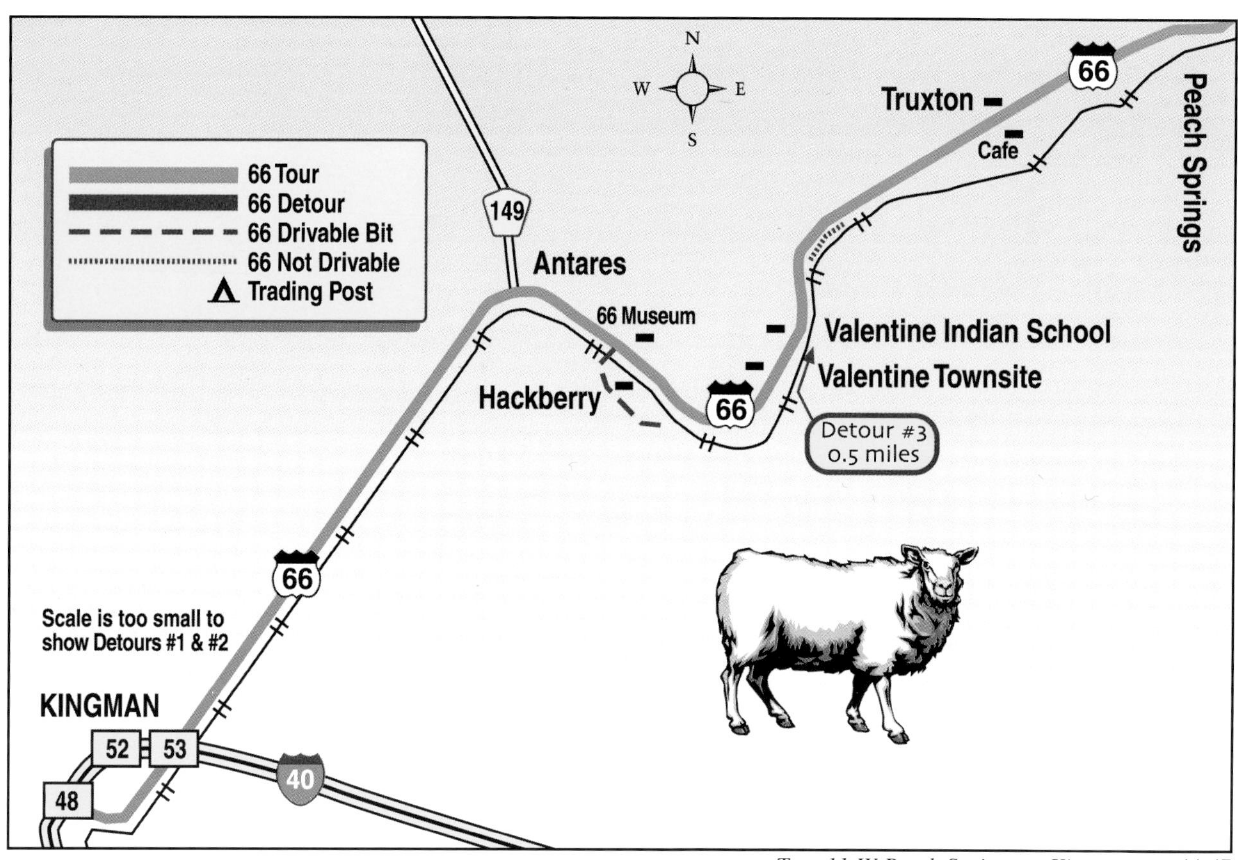

Tour 11-W Peach Springs to Kingman pp. 44-47

Tour 3-E Kingman to Peach Springs

Distance: 50.5 miles *80.8 km*

Highlights: Hackberry 66 Museum, Valentine, Crozier, Truxton

Driving Time: 1 hour

Hackberry

Tour 3-E takes you from the heart of historic downtown Kingman and out on the road, where you will drive through a long valley and then wind around several mountain ranges. You will enjoy one of the main attractions of Route 66, the General Store and Museum at Hackberry, then continue to move east as you see what remains of Valentine and stop in for a snack at Truxton. Finally the tour will end at Peach Springs, the capital of the Hualapai Tribe.

START

Powerhouse in Kingman

0.0 miles *0.0 km* Start at the Powerhouse. **Zero** out at the point where the driveway out of the parking lot meets Andy Devine Avenue. At the stop sign, turn right and drive east on Andy Devine Avenue.

DETOUR #1
Old Trails Highway
2.8 mi. *4.5 km* one-way
Time 10 minutes

From the junction of Andy Devine Ave. and 4th Street, **Zero** and turn south on 4th Street. Drive over the railroad tracks, staying on the main paved road, the only one with striping. It leaves town and goes into a narrow rocky canyon where there is a large metal pipeline to your right carrying sewage to treatment ponds. At 0.8 miles *1.3 km* you pass under a railroad bridge and the road curves left to run parallel with Route 66 and the railroad, both to the right. A higher railroad track is above you to your left. At 1.2 miles *1.9 km* there is a Kingman City Limits sign. Here you see (and smell) sewage treatment lagoons to your right. The center stripe disappears (eaten by the fumes?) though the road is still well paved. At 2.2 miles *3.5 km* there is a high railroad bridge to your left acting like a picture frame for a scenic canyon behind the bridge. At 2.8 miles *4.5 km* the paving ends at a racetrack. You can see where the old road went from here but cannot drive it any farther. Turn around and retrace your path.

Mohave Museum of History and Arts

At 0.25 miles *0.4 km* is the Fourth Street intersection. On your right is the old train station.

Beale Hotel

To the left near Andy Devine and 4th Street is the Beale Hotel. At the top of Fourth Street, left, is the 1915 Mohave County Courthouse. This corner was the heart of Kingman in the days of the Mother Road.

As you drive east on Andy Devine Avenue, you will see many old 66 businesses on the left, but none on the right for some distance as there is no room between 66 and the railroad. The highway veers away from the railroad and goes through a deep cut on Trovatore Hill. Note the historic old El Trovatore Motel (R) at 1.5 miles *2.4 km*.

DETOUR #2
Chadwick Road Detour
Old Route 66
0.25 mi. *0.4 km* one-way
Time 5 minutes

At 1.0 mi. *1.6 km* near the top of Trovatore Hill, just before the road enters a big cut, is Chadwick Road to your left. Turn left and drive Chadwick, a short paved road that curves around the hilltop, and is about 0.25 miles *0.4 km* long. It rejoins 66 at the top of the cut. We like this little road because it is very instructive about roadbuilding practices. In the earliest days, the builders lacked money and equipment and had to follow the contours of the land. When they approached a hill, they would curve around its top. Later, when they had more money and more powerful equipment, they would cut the road through a hilltop. You can see the difference very clearly by taking this little drive.

Eastbound>

Beyond El Trovatore there are old 66 businesses on both sides for a mile until they thin out at 1.9 miles *3.0 km*. You will pass Lewis Kingman Park (the town is named for him) at 2.2 miles *3.5 km* (L). Then a buildup of businesses resumes as you approach the I-40 interchange.

At 3.7 miles *5.9 km* you come to Exit #53-Kingman. Drive under the freeway, and then follow the sign reading, "66 East Peach Springs." Beyond the underpass are post-66 buildings all the way to the airport.

At 4.2 miles *6.7 km* Route 66 divides into two two-lane roads.

At 5.7 miles *9.1 km* the roadside businesses thin out and disappear.

Kingman Airport

At 8.5 miles *13.6 km* is the Kingman Airport and Industrial Park (R). The airport seems much larger than a town of Kingman's size would need. This is because it was built as a huge air base during World War Two. After the war, whole fleets of planes were mothballed there, and thousands of them lay gleaming in the sun.

Beyond the airport, the desert takes over as you enter Hualapai Valley, a vast open plain between mountain ranges.

Valle Vista

At 17.6 miles *28.2 km* is Valle Vista (L). This is a large desert subdivision with a golf course.

Antares Curve

At 20.5 miles *32.8 km* you begin the 7-mile long Antares Curve, which takes Route 66 between the Peacock Mountains to your right and the Music Mountains to the north. This was regarded as the longest single curve on the entire length of Route 66.

Hackberry General Store & Route 66 Museum

At 27.7 miles *44.3 km* is Hackberry. The location of Hackberry can be confusing, as there is more than one place labeled with the name "Hackberry" on many maps. The Hackberry General Store-Route 66 Museum, a must-see attraction, is to your left. Be sure to stop by there and check it out. It is a fascinating place to see and the owners are very nice. The townsite of Hackberry is to your right, though there isn't much to see there. Ask for directions at the store if you are interested.

Valentine Townsite

At 30.3 miles *48.5 km* a few old roadside businesses remain, such as Ernie's Country Dancing (L) and the ruins of the Chief's Motel. Across 66 here was the Valentine Post Office, famous for its heart-shaped postmark, which brought hundreds of visitors to the place each Valentine's Day. Before the I-40 bypass hit Valentine in September 1978, 200 souls lived in the settlement. Jacqueline Ann Griggs, the last postmistress, was murdered by a robber here on August 15, 1990, causing her grieving husband to raze the building. Most of Valentine's other buildings have been torn down as well.

Valentine Indian School Site

At 32.3 miles *51.7 km* is a group of buildings marked Valentine (L). The government built a big two-story red brick schoolhouse here in 1901, used as an Indian school, adding other buildings to the campus later. Students were Apaches, Havasupais, Hopis, Mohaves, Navajos and Papagos, as boarders, and Hualapais as day students. By 1937, the year the school closed, it had 200 resident students. You can make a brief detour to see the place by pulling into the school's parking lot. It makes a good photo. A bit farther east you can take Detour #3 to the right to see the old abandoned school that was built for non-Indian students, another good photo opportunity.

DETOUR #3
Valentine Anglo School
0.5 mi. *0.8 km* one-way
Time 10 minutes

At 33.4 miles *53.4 km* you will find the road to the Valentine School (R) on the other side of the high railroad embankment. To reach the building, turn off of 66, go under the railroad bridge and you will see the school to your immediate right. You can drive right over to it. This was a school for the non-Indian children who were forbidden by law to attend the Valentine Indian School farther west.

Hackberry General Store, interior view

Crozier Canyon

At 35.7 miles *57.1 km* you enter Crozier Canyon and can look down (R) and see lush vegetation along a river bottom. There is a two-story home here and a series of tourist cabins. This was the V-Bar Ranch, which started as a dude ranch resort and became a roadside business. The highway ran down on the bottom. A huge flood in 1939 wiped out the road and many of the tourist buildings.

Teacher's residence at Valentine Indian School

At 36.0 miles *57.6 km* you are at an historic place on Route 66, as it was here, where you will see a concrete bridge to your right, that the last bit of Route 66 in America was paved in 1937. Alas! you can no longer drive over this bridge. In the late summer of 2000 No Trespassing signs were posted on it.

At 37.2 miles *59.5 km* as you emerge out of Crozier Canyon you can see a big plain ahead, and juniper trees appear.

Truxton

At 41.5 miles *66.4 km* you enter the community of Truxton. Like so many places on the map of old Route 66, Truxton does not look like a town, just a little settlement. You can see the ghosts of roadside businesses on both sides of the highway.

At 41.8 miles *66.9 km* is one of the remaining active businesses in Truxton, the Frontier Motel and Café (R). This has been a fixture on the Mother Road since the early 1950s, and Mildred Barker has been waiting tables there since 1955. Stop in and have a burger or a cup of coffee and enjoy the ambiance. As you drive east from here you will see a few derelict roadside businesses to the left.

At 43.3 miles *69.3 km* you will see the roadbed for an older version of Route 66 to the right just as you enter the Hualapai Indian Reservation. There is no access to this old road.

At 44.1 miles *70.6 km* is the modern Music Mountain Indian School to your right, a far cry from the old school buildings at Valentine. Older 66 is still running along to the right along here, and you will see it from time to time.

West End of Peach Springs

At 47.7 miles *76.3 km* you have come to the west end of Peach Springs, where you will find a collection of newer buildings. The Buck and Doe Road meets Route 66 here. The Hualapai Nation is developing Grand Canyon tourism and this road will be the primary access road to the West Grand Canyon, on the Hualapai Reservation.

Peach Springs

At 50.1 miles *80.2 km* you reach the central part of Peach Springs, the place that Route 66 travelers of old would have referred to when they mentioned or thought of Peach Springs. There were roadside businesses there.

Hualapai Lodge

At 50.5 miles *80.8 km* the tribe's Hualapai Lodge and Café is located to your right. This large, attractive modern building fills a long-felt need. This is the end of this tour.

In 1929, the era of zany stunts such as flagpole-sitting, the men in the middle, Happy Lou Phillips, Jr., and Lucky Jimmy Parker, decided to roller-skate across country, quite a feat on unpaved Route 66. Here they are in Peach Springs—MMHA

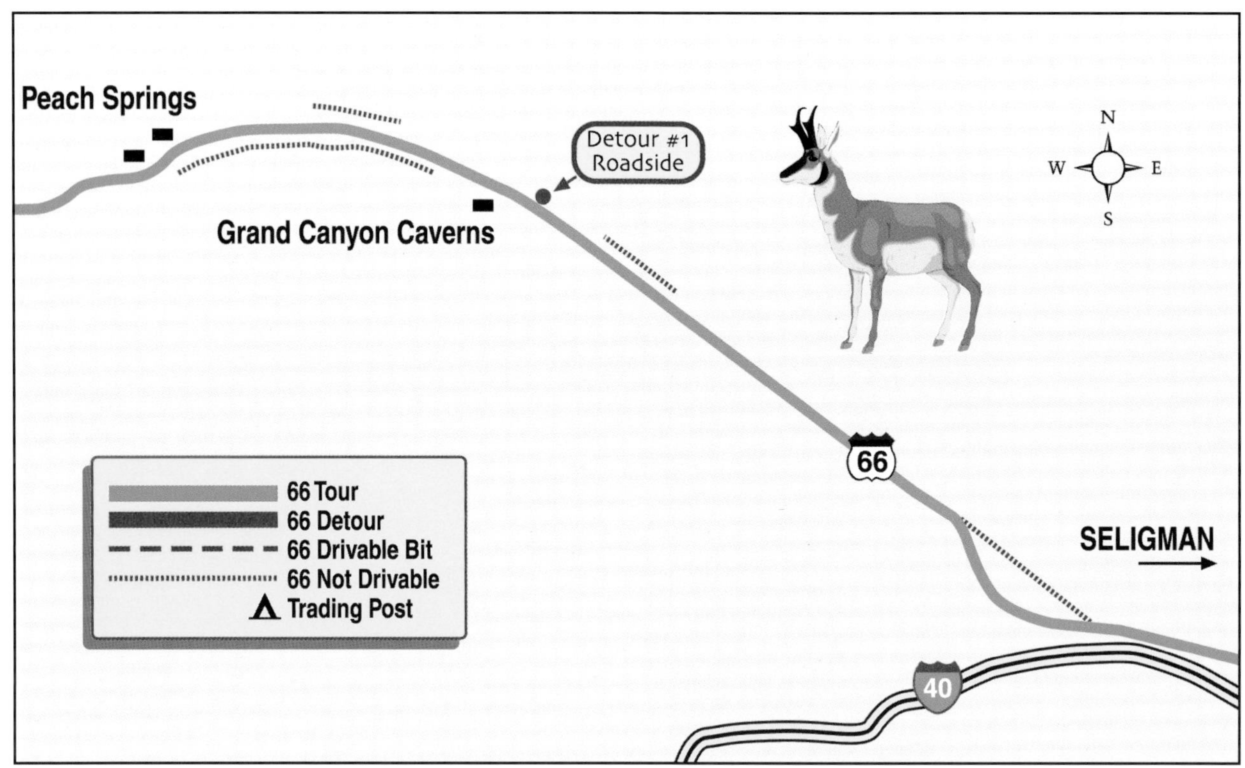

Tour 10-W Seligman to Peach Springs pp. 42-43

Tour 4-E Peach Springs to Seligman

Distance: 37.2 miles *59.5 km*
Highlights: Grand Canyon Caverns, Aubrey Valley
Driving Time: 45 minutes

Delgadillo's

Tour 4-E takes you from Peach Springs, the capital of the Hualapai Nation, across rolling scanty rangelands to Seligman. Along the way you will have a chance to visit the Grand Canyon Caverns, a natural wonder, and then proceed to Seligman, where Arizona's Route 66 revival was started in 1984 by Angel and Juan Delgadillo. Juan still runs the Snow-Cap and Angel still runs his souvenir store-museum next to his barber shop, though he has laid down his clippers.

START

Start at the Hualapai Lodge in Peach Springs, the **Zero** point.

Peach Springs

0.0 miles *0.0 km* **Zero** at the Hualapai Lodge and Café As you drive east from the lodge, at MP 104 you will see a newer part of the community. You begin a noticeable climb east of Peach Springs. As the road goes through a cut at 1.9 miles *3.0 km* notice two old road alignments above and to the right. At 2.7 miles *4.3 km* the older paved road is seen (R). At 4.0 miles *6.4 km* you finish your climb and level out on a plateau, where older 66 is often visible to the right.

Peach Springs Trading Post circa 1920—MMHA

At 5.6 miles *9.0 km* you can see a nice old 66 bridge to the right on an old alignment. At 6.2 miles *9.9 km* the older road merges with the present one.

At 7.1 miles *11.4 km* you reach the junction of Indian Road 18, which goes to Supai and Frazier Well (L).

At 8.8 miles *14.1 km* you leave the Hualapai Nation.

Grand Canyon Caverns

At 11.9 miles *19.0 km* you reach the entry point for Grand Canyon Caverns (R). The road divides here briefly to provide convenient access to the caverns.

SIGHTSEEING #1
Grand Canyon Caverns
Time 1.5 hours

When you pull in, you will see a motel and service station. The caverns are not here. Look for the sign to the caverns and drive over to them. They are on a paved road about 1.0 mile *1.6 km* from the highway.

At the cavern office there is a curio store and restaurant, a fairly large place in good condition. The cafe is simple, just hamburgers and the like.

You buy a ticket and are given a token. There is an elevator to the left of the ticket counter. Tours are given every half hour, so after you buy your token, you wait for the next departure.

The elevator holds about 12 people, and the guide takes you down. The descent is about 200 feet *60 meters*, from 5,700 feet *1727 meters* at the surface to 5,500 feet *1666 meters* below. The cavern is a nice one. Visitors walk through the caverns on concrete sidewalks lined with handrails.

There are two main chambers of the cavern. The caves have no stunning stalactites, etc. as in Carlsbad Caverns, but there are some interesting features. The cave smells fresh—no dankness. It is very dry, averaging 10% humidity and the caverns are always cool, which can be an attraction in itself on a hot day.

The tour is about 0.75 miles *1.2 km* long and will take about an hour and a half.

Hyde Park

At 13.6 miles *21.8 km* MP 117 are the ruins of Hyde Park (L) at a hilltop. Before the present tourist facilities were developed at Grand Canyon Caverns, Hyde Park was the nearest place for visitors to stay.

Old photo showing Hyde Park's famous slogan, "Park Your Hide At Hyde Park"—MMHA

DETOUR #1
Milepost 117
Ruins of Hyde Park
Time 10 minutes

To the left, on a hilltop, there is a paved driveway going up to a fence where there is a wide parking area. Drive up to the fence and park, and then get out and walk along the outside of the fence, looking over at the ruins. The site of Hyde Park is a large one, and in the past you could enter it. Now the access gate is locked, as the Arizona Game and Fish Dept. is conducting a black-footed ferret reintroduction program on the grounds. There are extensive ruins here; Hyde Park must have been a big operation. The surprise you see as you walk along the fence looking at the ruins is the old swimming pool on the east end. The operator of this business had a famous slogan, "Park your hide at Hyde Park tonight," see the photo on this page.

Deer Park

At 18.3 miles *29.3 km* is a group of church buildings, the former Deer Park Motel (R).

At 29.7 miles *47.5 km* older 66 goes straight ahead at a point where the paved road curves to the right. Power poles running along its right side outline the old road. This old alignment is located on the Big Boquillas Ranch, now owned by the Navajo Nation, and permission from the tribe is necessary before one can enter this land. A sign on every access road's gate advises that entry is granted by signing in at Pica Camp at MP 123.2 or at Hoffman Camp at MP 141.5. The grade can't be driven, but can be walked or biked if you have permission.

At 32.6 miles *52.2 km* the older alignment joins the road you are driving, moving in from your left.

At 36.3 miles *58.1 km* you drive underneath the I-40 interchange. Drive straight ahead into Seligman.

Entering Seligman

At 36.5 miles *58.4 km* you will see a "Welcome to Seligman" sign and enter the town.

[Note: Old guidebooks say that the Pacific Time Zone Line runs through Seligman and that everything west of Seligman is in the Pacific Time Zone. This was changed in 1950. The Time Zone line is now the Colorado River].

Seligman

As you drive into Seligman you will find roadside businesses on both sides of the street. Route 66 was never divided in Seligman, just widened. This makes it nice for cruising.

End of Tour

At 37.2 miles *59.5 km* Route 66 intersects Main Street. The famous old Copper Cart Café is to your right. This tour ends here at our **Zero** point. See page 40 for our recommendations, where to eat and sleep in Seligman.

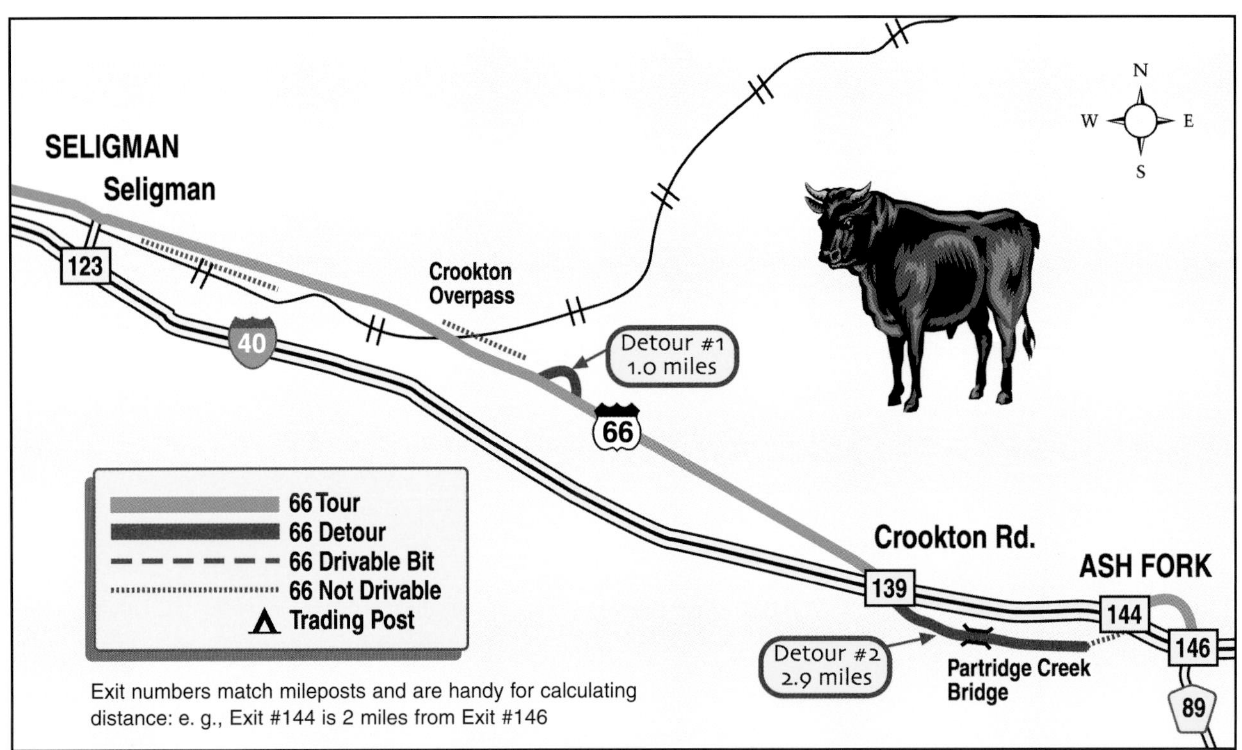

Tour 9-W Ash Fork to Seligman pp. 38-41

Tour 5-E Seligman to Ash Fork

Distance: 23.9 miles *38.2 km*

Highlights: Unspoiled stretch of Route 66, Crookton Overpass

Driving Time: 30 minutes

Angel Delgadillo

Tour 5-E takes you from Seligman through more rangelands, to the town of Ash Fork. The entire trip from Seligman to Exit #139-Crookton Road, is on Route 66, a wonderful unspoiled 18-mile *28.8 km* strip of 66. This is a lonely stretch of road even today and as we drive it we wonder what tourists of old must have thought as they traveled it.

Seligman

START

0.0 miles *0.0 km* **Zero** point is at the intersection of Route 66 and Main Street in Seligman (Copper Cart Cafe). Drive east on Route 66.

At 0.3 miles *0.5 km* you reach a road fork. Turn right on Crookton Road following 66 sign. There is another sign at 0.6 mi. *1.0 km* reading, "Reconstructed Historic Route 66."

Older Versions of Route 66

At 4.0 miles *6.4 km* you can see an older paved version of Route 66 running along to your right between you and the railroad in this area. We think that this dates back to the early 1930s. At 4.3 miles *6.9 km* you will see the interesting remains of an old stone bridge to your left. This was on the 1920s unpaved alignment of Route 66, and if you look as you drive through this area you will see more of the raised bed of the unpaved road in several places. These older alignments of Route 66 will be your companion for miles. The paved 1930s version (R) merges with the road you are driving at 8.1 miles *13.0 km,* at a hillcrest. The unpaved 1920s road is glimpsed all the way to the Crookton Overpass and beyond.

Fun Runners at the Rusty Bolt, Seligman

Crookton Overpass

At 8.4 miles *13.4 km* you come to a most interesting place on this tour, the Crookton Overpass, where the highway goes over the BNSF railroad tracks. There are two bridges here, side by side. The older one, which is blocked to vehicles, is to the east (L). Below, down on the valley floor, to the east, you can see older road alignments. One of these is an unpaved ramp leading up to the blocked bridge. The other, looking more interesting, is a grade crossing, which ran across the railroad. This road had low concrete walls or curbs for several yards to prevent the roadfill from washing out. All of these roads are on private ranch land. Older 66 runs along to the left as you drive east of the overpass. The overpass is a great place to stop and take pictures. If you are lucky a train will come thundering through as you are standing there and you can get a great action shot.

DETOUR #1
10.4 miles *16.6 km*
Crookton Hill, Old Route 66
1.0 mi. *1.6 km* one-way

As you approach this detour, you are going uphill, and will see a transmission tower on a hilltop to the right. Pass through a big cut, and on the other side to your left, at MP 151, where there is a stop sign, turn left on an unpaved road, which is an older alignment of 66. Now you can make an interesting trip downhill to the 11.4 miles *18.2 km* point. You will see patches of old paving on this forgotten roadway, and the road surface overall is in good condition, suitable for any vehicle. Near the bottom on your right is an old camping ground. You will join the paved road again, where you turn left (E).

At 12.4 miles *19.8 km* you can see Bill Williams Mountain, the highest on the horizon, to the NE. Note how the mountains that you see in this area are smoother and not as jagged as the mountains you saw around the Colorado River and Oatman.

The Great Wall

At 13.5 miles *21.6 km* you will see substantial rock walls to the right. A major pipeline was installed in this area years ago. The lines of rock running parallel to the road mark pipelines, not highways. Some of the residents asked for the rocks dug up and cast aside by the pipeline crews, which they used to make fences and corrals, resulting in the "Great Wall of Crookton."

At 16.8 miles *26.9 km* you will see a big raised roadbed to your left. It is an old railroad grade, and not a bit of old 66.

Exit #139—Crookton Rd.

At 18.0 miles *28.8 km* you reach I-40, at Exit #139-Crookton Road. This is the end of the wonderful long stretch of Route 66 that you have driven all the way from the California border. From now on your tour will consist of driving long stretches of I-40 interspersed with Route 66 hopping. There are only short bits of 66 to enjoy from now on. To get to Ash Fork, drive onto the on-ramp, and follow the signs to "Flagstaff," taking I-40 east.

DETOUR #2
EXIT #139-Crookton S&E
Old Route 66, Bridge
2.9 mi. *4.6 km* one-way
Time 10 minutes

Zero at the start of the I-40 overpass, turning left on the other side on the frontage road. Drive 1.25 miles *2.0 km* on good paving to a road junction where the main road makes a big curve to the right. Go straight ahead on the old red paving, which is rough and broken, so go slowly. It moves east parallel to I-40. At 2.9 miles *4.6 km* you will come to the fine old Partridge Creek Bridge, built in the 1920s. The bridge is still in sound condition and you may drive across it without fear even though a fairly large cottonwood tree is growing out of the west end. Down in the creek bottom on the north side of the bridge you can see a low concrete curb, like the one at the Crookton Overpass, where there was an old crossing used before the bridge was built; in other words, they drove across the creekbed. You can see the old grade going uphill from the curbed road. These creek crossings were impassable when the creek was in flood and motorists could be stranded for days waiting for the water to drop. Stop at the bridge. Beyond the bridge the old red paving (it got its color from red cinders mixed in with the asphalt) continues for 1.3 miles *2.1 km* east, then ends, becoming a dirt track. Don't try to drive out the east end on the dirt roads, because it is not worth the trouble. Double back the way you came.

Exit #144—Ash Fork

Take Exit #144-Ash Fork and turn left at the stop sign, and then follow the "Historic US 66" road signs into Ash Fork. The towns of Seligman and Ash Fork are sister cities with a similar history, but where Seligman has interesting things for the Route 66 traveler to see and do, Ash Fork is disappointing, and we think a quick look suffices.

Town of Ash Fork

As you enter town eastbound, you see a sign reading "Flagstone Capital of the USA," and pass the flagstone yards. Flagstone is sandstone that formed in layers and is broken out in sheets about two inches thick. There are stacks of it on both sides of the road. Route 66 in Ash Fork is divided. You will drive eastbound on Park Avenue. Before the street division all traffic had come through town on Lewis Avenue, which is now for westbound only. As a result, Park Avenue did not have much time to develop for the tourist trade, and you will see few old businesses along it. To end this tour, **Zero** at the Ash Fork post office, which you will find to your right, at the corner of Park Avenue and Fifth Street at 23.9 miles *38.2 km*.

We are sorry to say that we do not recommend any restaurants or motels in Ash Fork.

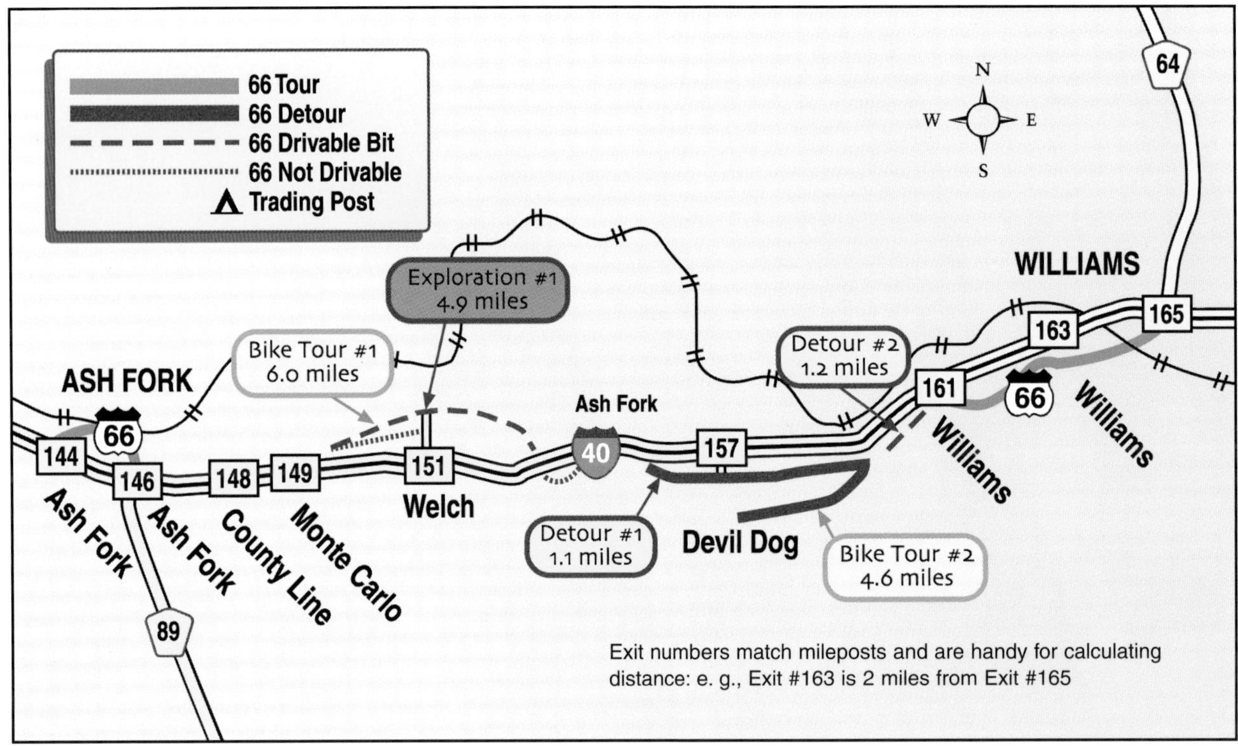

Tour 8-W Williams to Ash Fork pp. 34-37

Tour 6-E Ash Fork to Williams

Distance: 19.0 miles *30.4 km*
Highlights: Ash Fork Hill, Forests, Williams
Driving Time: 30 minutes

Rod's Steak House sign, Route 66 icon in Williams

Tour 6-E takes you from the sleepy town of Ash Fork out onto I-40. Here you will be at the foot of the feared Ash Fork Hill, one of the steepest and most daunting uphill grades for drivers on Route 66. At the top of the hill you will enter a beautiful Ponderosa pine forest, which stretches for miles, to Flagstaff and beyond. The town of Williams at the end of this tour is an interesting place to visit, with lots of Route 66 souvenirs and items of interest. It is the home of *Route 66 Magazine*, and owners Paul and Sandi Taylor run a top-notch Route 66 store at 401 W. Railroad Ave. Another don't-miss business is Twisters at 417 E. Route 66.

START

Ash Fork

0.0 miles *0.0 km* **Zero** for this tour at the Ash Fork post office at Park and 5th. Drive east on Park Avenue.

Exit #146—Ash Fork

At 0.5 miles *0.8 km* you have reached the end of town. Use the I-40 interchange at Exit #146 to go eastbound, toward Flagstaff.

Ash Fork Hill

At Exit #149 Monte Carlo Road you begin climbing Ash Fork Hill. You will have glimpses of old 66 to your left (N) as you ascend. To see part of this old road take Exploration #1, if you are in a high-clearance vehicle.

EXPLORATION #1
EXIT #149-Monte Carlo E
1932-1952 Route 66
4.9 mi. *7.8 km* one-way
Time 45 minutes

Take Exit #149-Monte Carlo. **Zero** at stop sign and turn left (N), going under I-40. Turn left at the next stop sign and drive into the truck stop, heading for the cafe. At the cafe (closed) you will see old 66 going NE into the trees. Follow it. Once through the fence you are on old gray paving. It's in bad shape so drive carefully. At 3.4 miles *5.4 km* FR6 comes from your right at an angle. The paving ends here. Stay on the gray gravel road, which takes you to the base of Ash Fork Hill and begins to climb it. The road ends at a fence at 4.9 miles *7.8 km* where you have great views. **Zero.** Drive back 1.5 miles *2.4 km* and turn left on FR6, following it out to the interchange at Exit #151-Welch. Get onto I-40 eastbound at this interchange.

Exit #151—Welch Rd.

No facilities

Exit #151 Welch Road. Mountain Bike Tour #1 is available here.

BIKE TOUR #1
EXIT #151-Welch N&W
1921-1931 Roads for Bikes
6.0 mi. *9.6 km* loop
Time 1 hour

Take Exit #151-Welch. Loop around and go under I-40 to the stop sign. Turn left. On the other side **Zero** at the cattle guard and turn right (NE) on FR6. Drive it to the 0.2 mile *0.3 km* point, where you will see a pullout to your left. This is the parking area for the Bike Tour. From here follow the signs, which will lead you downhill on the 1922 highway, then bring you back uphill on the 1932 paved version of Route 66, to loop back to the starting point.

Pre-1952 Ash Fork Hill Road

At MP 153.7 look to your left and you can see the 1932-1952 road on the hillside. At MP 154.3 you will see a bowl to your right, with lava cliffs at its top. Look carefully and you will see 1932-1952 road grades in this bowl, climbing to the top of the cliffs. This version of Route 66 going up Ash Fork Hill was used until 1952.

Top of Ash Fork Hill

At MP 155.5 you have reached the top of Ash Fork Hill and will find yourself in a Ponderosa pine forest.

Exit #157—Devil Dog

Detour #1 and Bike Tour #2 are available here.

DETOUR #1
EXIT #157-Devil Dog S&W
1932 Route 66
1.1 mi. *1.8 km* one-way
Time 15 minutes

Take Exit #157-Devil Dog. As you come off the interchange the paving ends at a cattle guard. Turn your odometer to **Zero** here. You are now on FR 108. Drive 0.4 miles *0.6 km* to a crossroad. Turn right at the stop sign onto Coconino County Road #506 (the 1932 version of 66) which is paved. You can drive this fine old stretch of road (past the 1920s Pine Spring Ranch Auto Campground, left) for 1.1 miles *1.8 km* to a point where it ends at a right turn to an access road going under I-40. You'll see an extension of the 1932 road straight ahead, a gravel path running uphill. You can walk this for about 0.2 miles *0.3 km* to a point where it ends above I-40. Turn around and drive back out the way you came. When you get to the interchange for Exit #157-Devil Dog, follow the signs to get onto I-40 headed east, toward Flagstaff and Williams.

BIKE TOUR #2
EXIT #157-Devil Dog S&E
1922 and 1932 Route 66
4.6 mile *7.4 km* loop

This is a special treat for mountain bikers, as the Forest Service has marked portions of the 1922 and 1932 alignments of Route 66 as the Devil Dog Bike Tour. Take Exit #157-Devil Dog. As you come off the interchange the paving ends at a cattle guard. Turn your odometer to **Zero** here. You are now on FR 108. Just across the cattle guard (R) is the parking area at the trailhead, with a sign and map. Ride FR 108 0.4 miles *0.6 km* to a crossroad. Turn left, still on FR 108 (which is the 1932 version of 66) and go to the 0.7 mile *1.1 km* point, where you will see the 1932 road going uphill. Turn right and ride to the 0.9 mile *1.4 km* point, where you turn left on FR 45 (which is the 1922 version of 66). Ride it to the 2.0 mile *3.2 km* point, where you will find the 1922 route going uphill and FR 45 turning right. Bike up the 1922 road to the point where it meets the 1932 road at 2.5 miles *4.0 km*, then turn left and come downhill. When you reach the bottom of the hill at 3.9 miles *6.3 km*, follow FR 108 back the way you rode in to return to your car.

Bill Williams Mountain

At MP 159 you are getting close to the base of Bill Williams Mountain, the highest mountain in this area.

Exit #161—Williams

Gas, Food, Lodging

Take Exit #161-Williams-Grand Canyon to go into the town of Williams. Turn right at the Stop Sign. (Detour #2 begins at this point).

DETOUR #2
EXIT #161-Williams
Old Route 66
1.2 mi. *1.9 km* one-way
Time 10 minutes

Take Exit #161-Williams. At the stop sign, **Zero**, turn right, and then turn right again, following the sign that reads, "Williams District Ranger." You are now on Route 66 headed west. You will come to the Williams District Ranger turnoff (L). Pass by this. Next you will come to Ragtime Morgans (L). This bit of 66 ends here. Don't take the dirt road that seems to extend beyond the end of the paving. Turn around and drive back to the stop sign. Turn right and drive into town

Entering Williams

Soon after you take Exit #161 you will enter the Williams City Limits. As you drive closer to the town center you will find the Route 66 commercial district, with old

Route 66 in Williams today

motels, service stations and cafes lining the sides of the road. Route 66 was divided in Williams in 1955, so you pass into town on a one-way street system. Eastbound traffic is carried on a street that was named Bill Williams Avenue until 1995 when its name was changed to Route 66. Until the highway was divided in Williams, all of it was funneled along Bill Williams Avenue, so most of the commercial buildup is there rather than along the westbound route, which was located on Railroad Avenue.

End of Tour

This tour ends at the Visitor Center, our **Zero** point at 19.0 miles *30.4 km*. To get there watch the street signs for the corner of 2nd St. and Route 66. Turn left (N) at this corner and drive one block to the Williams Visitor Center. Here you will find parking, toilets and information.

About Williams

Although Williams is a small town, it has a rich heritage of Route 66 history and there is much to do there. Since the 1890s Williams and Flagstaff have each claimed the title "Gateway to the Grand Canyon". The honor was clinched for Williams when the Grand Canyon Railroad began taking passengers from Williams to the South Rim on September 17, 1901.

The Grand Canyon Railway has been resurrected and now thousands of visitors take the train to the Grand Canyon every year. So important to the economy of Williams has the railroad become that most would consider it the mainstay. Every visitor to northern Arizona should see the Grand Canyon, and taking the railroad is one of the best ways to make the trip. For information, dial their website, http://www.thetrain.com.

Williams has the distinction of being the last town in the United States where Route 66 was bypassed by Interstate-40, the date being October 13, 1984.

You will find many stores filled with Route 66 souvenirs. Our favorites are the Route 66 Publishing Company at 401 W. Railroad Ave. and Twister's at 417 E. Route 66.

Where To Eat

Rod's Steak House, 301 E. Route 66, 635-2671. A Route 66 classic, it has been turning out prime steaks and other good food for decades. Moderate-exp.

Pine Country Restaurant, 107 N. Grand Canyon Blvd., 635-9718. Huge selection of pies. Home cookin'. Inexpensive.

Rosa's Cantina, 411 N. Grand Canyon Blvd., 635-0708. Mexican food. Inexpensive.

Twister's, 417 E. Route 66, 635-0266. Fun, with a Route 66 theme, big curio shop. Burgers and milk shakes. Inexpensive.

Where To Sleep

Red Garter, 137 W. Railroad, 635-1484. Ideally located in a historic building that once housed a busy brothel. Moderate.

What to See and Do In Williams

Take the train to the Grand Canyon. The depot is on Grand Canyon Blvd. just north of the Visitor Center.

Enjoy outdoor activities: fishing, hunting, camping, hiking, mountain biking, rock climbing, skiing. Ask at the Visitor Center for information. Williams is in the heart of the great Kaibab Forest, with miles and miles of public land available for you to use and enjoy.

Play a round of golf at their excellent 18-hole grass course, Elephant Rocks. Drive west on Railroad Ave. for 1.3 miles from the Visitor Center, turn right on Golf Course Road and follow the signs. 635-4935.

Take the Williams Historic Walk, see page 33.

Visit the historic Railroad Depot & Museum. These are located at the office of the Grand Canyon Railway.

Shop in the Williams historic district. This is a compact area that is easily walked. Fine for a stroll on a summer evening.

The Grand Canyon

Williams is the home of the Grand Canyon Railway, and if you plan to travel to the scenic wonder by train, then you will want to use Williams for your base.

Many users of this guide will drive to the Grand Canyon. There are three good highways to the Grand Canyon from Route 66, one from Williams and two from Flagstaff.

1. Highway 64 (from Williams)
Distance: 60.0 mi. **Driving Time**: 1 hour

Drive east from Williams for 2.4 miles *3.8 km* and follow the signs for Highway 64. This is the easiest of the roads and is a good paved highway, kept open all year. The distance is 60.0 miles *96.0 km* and it is an easy drive, but is the least scenic. There are few roadside businesses along the way, but the Planes of Fame Air Museum and Bedrock City Theme Park are both located at Valle, at the 28.0 mile *44.8 km* point. As you enter the boundaries of Grand Canyon National Park you will come to a ticket office where you must pay an admission fee. The ranger will give you a Grand Canyon Guide. Follow signs into the Park.

2. Highway 180 (from Flagstaff)
Distance: 80.0 mi. **Driving Time**: 1.5 hours

From Flagstaff City Hall drive north on Humphreys Street, then follow signs. The distance is 80.0 miles *128.0 km*. The first 40.0 miles *64.0 km* take you through beautiful forests, including aspen groves, along the base of the San Francisco Peaks. This road reaches higher elevations than the other roads, so snow is more of a problem. It joins Highway 64 at Valle and follows it into the Park.

3. Highway 89 (from Flagstaff)
Distance: 107 mi. **Driving Time**: 2 hours

From Flagstaff City Hall, drive east on Route 66, following the signs. Where Historic Route 66 goes off to the right, stay on Highway 89. In addition to being a route to the Grand Canyon, Highway 89 provides access to Sunset Crater National Monument and Wupatki National Monument, as well as being a road to the Grand Canyon, and you will pass the entrances to these great natural attractions along the way. You will travel through a pine forest for 15.0 miles *24.0 km* until you reach a high point near the entrance to Sunset Crater. From this high point you will begin a long descent down into piñon-juniper country, all the while seeing the Painted Desert in the distance. You will enter the Navajo Reservation and travel to the junction with Highway 64, which is about 1.0 mile *1.6 km* before Cameron. You turn to the left onto Highway 64 here to get to the Grand Canyon. Actually, we recommend that you continue to the Cameron Trading Post, about one mile *1.6 km* north of the turnoff, as it is worth a trip.

We have driven to the Grand Canyon from Williams and Flagstaff dozens of times. Our favorite way to make the trip is to take Highway 180 from Flagstaff to the Canyon and to return to Flagstaff via Highway 89. This is the most scenic and interesting route, but it takes the most time. The Williams route via highway 64 is the shortest and fastest, but if you have time, try it our way, we think you'll like it.

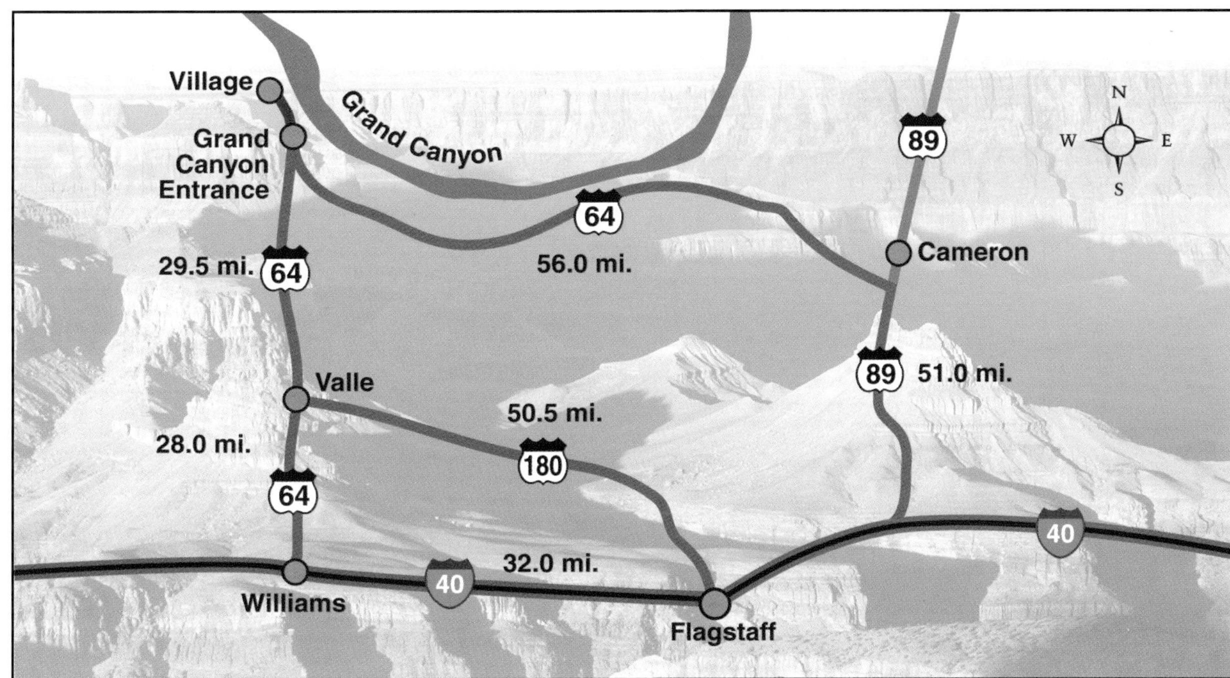

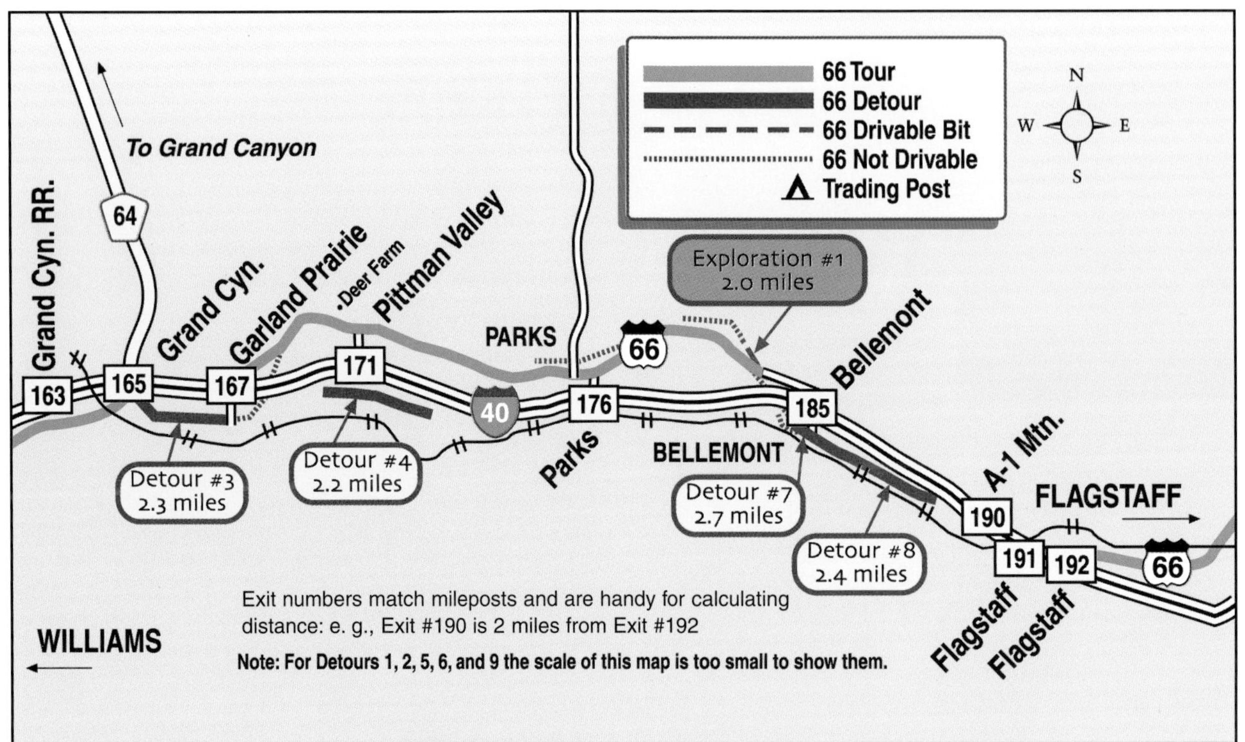

Tour 7-W Flagstaff to Williams pp. 28-33

Tour 7-E Williams to Flagstaff

Distance: 34.0 miles *54.4 km*

Highlights: Good long bits of Route 66, Deer Farm, Parks Store, Arboretum

Driving Time: 1 hour

Wagon Wheel Lodge

Tour 7-E takes you from Williams to Flagstaff staying in the pine forests. The tour is able to use a long segment of Route 66 that has been posted and signed as an Auto Tour by the Forest Service office in Williams. This makes for an enjoyable trip. Along the way you will visit the historic Parks Store, have a chance to pet the animals at the Deer Farm and enjoy some good photo opportunities.

Visitor Center in Williams

START

0.0 miles *0.0 km* Visitor Center, our **Zero** point. Drive south one block on Grand Canyon Blvd. and then turn left, which places you eastbound on Route 66. There is an interesting alternative way to leave Williams eastbound, which is to follow the stair-step course of the original Route 66 alignment. We think it is fun, and describe it in Detour #1.

DETOUR #1
Original Rt. 66 from Williams
1.6 mi. *2.6 km* one-way
Time 10 minutes

As you drive this original alignment you will wonder why on earth the roadbuilders ever chose this erratic path full of speed-killing right angle turns. From the Visitor Center driveway, **Zero** and exit onto Grand Canyon Boulevard (2d St.), turn left and drive north to the first stop sign, at Edison Avenue. Turn right on Edison. Drive four blocks on Edison and then turn left on Airport Road. Drive Airport Road for one block and then turn right on Rodeo Road. Drive Rodeo Road to its end, at a stop sign, where it meets the newer Route 66 heading east out of Williams near the overpass. Turn left and follow this road, which will lead you to Exit #165-Williams on I-40.

(Detours for roadies: As you are leaving town you can sample short segments of the 1921 alignment of Route 66 by following the directions for Detours #2 and #3 on the next page. Both of these detours require driving on unpaved roads.)

DETOUR #2
1921 Old Trails-Route 66
0.3 mi. *0.5 km* one-way
Time 10 minutes

Zero at the Visitor Center and drive east on Route 66. (From the end of Detour #1, it's 0.2 miles *0.3 km*). As you leave town look for a bunch of buildings and vehicles to your right at 1.5 miles *2.4 km* and turn right there, onto Echo Canyon. Then turn immediately left, going over a cattle guard. **Zero** at the cattle guard. You'll be on the never-paved 1921 road. The road curves right at 0.1 miles *0.16 km* where a two-lane track goes straight. The track is the 1921 road. High-clearance vehicles can drive it to the 0.3 miles *0.5 km* point ending at a massive 1960 railroad embankment.

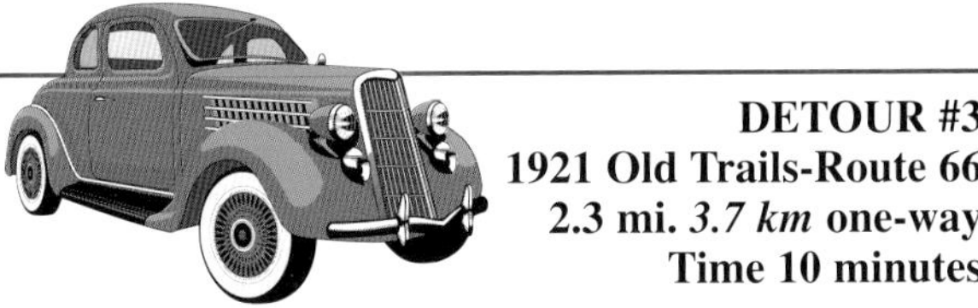

DETOUR #3
1921 Old Trails-Route 66
2.3 mi. *3.7 km* one-way
Time 10 minutes

Zero at the railroad overpass. At 0.2 miles *0.3 km* turn right onto a paved road, then turn left, still on paving—old 66. Drive to the barrier at 0.6 miles *1.0 km,* then turn right onto a gravel road. Ignore the Primitive Road sign, the road is OK. At 0.7 miles *1.1 km,* where the road curves left, you will see a track running to your right—1921 66. Don't take it; turn left and head east. At 1.5 miles *2.4 km* you reach the Old Depot Rd. junction. Go straight on Mountain Man Tr. At 2.3 miles *3.7 km* is another road junction. Old 66 goes straight here, but private property inhibits access to it. Turn left. **Zero** as you enter the bridge and drive over I-40 at Exit #167. Start the Auto Tour on the other side.

Exit #165—Williams/Grand Canyon

For the regular tour get onto I-40 eastbound (toward Flagstaff) at Exit #165-Williams.

Exit #167—Garland Prairie Rd./Circle Pines Rd.

Take Exit #167-Garland Prairie Rd./Circle Pines Rd. At the stop sign **Zero** and turn left, going over I-40 and then circling right on the paved road. At 0.8 miles *1.3 km* the 1931-1964 alignment of Route 66 begins. At 0.9 miles *1.4 km* paving ends temporarily and the road changes to a wide and well-maintained gravel road. The Forest Service has prepared an Auto Tour for us, which we will follow. There are three interpretive signs at parking areas on the Forest Service tour. At 1.8 miles *2.9 km* you have an unfolding view of the San Francisco Peaks in the distance.

Davenport Lake

2.6 miles *4.2 km* The road curves to skirt Davenport Lake to your right. You will motor along the northern margin of the lake and may wonder why it is called a lake, since it is usually dry. In wet weather, though, it can be full of water. I-40 (to your right) goes across the middle of the lake on a built-up roadbed. The paving resumes at 3.5 miles *5.6 km.*

Deer Farm

At 4.1 miles *6.6 km* you will see the Deer Farm to your left. It's a must-stop for animal lovers and kiddies.

SIGHTSEEING #1
Deer Farm
Time 1.0 hours

The Deer Farm is to your left in a big barn-like structure. They have restrooms, snacks, a gift shop and a petting zoo. Although they specialize in deer, having several varieties, they have other animals as well. Many of these are so tame that they will eat food from your hand, and you can buy feed for them. A paved trail winds around through the animal enclosures. Children love this place and if you are an animal lover, you will find it a treat. The owners are very nice, and on a recent visit presented us with a baby wallaby to pet. This is an old 66 business that seems to be surviving very well.

Auto Tour Stop #1

At 4.6 miles *7.4 km* you come to a stop sign. Turn right and you will see the first of the three Auto Tour signs to your immediate left. Don't turn onto I-40 here.

Pittman Valley

4.7 miles *7.5 km* At this point you are beginning to enter an open area called Pittman Valley. It is an attractive mountain meadow. At 5.1 miles *8.2 km* you will pass by the old Wagon Wheel Lodge (to your left), which was a

DETOUR #4
Old Route 66
2.2 mi. *3.5 km* one-way
Time 20 minutes

At 5.8 miles *9.3 km* **Zero** and turn right (S) on Sherwood Forest Road. Drive over I-40. On the other side turn right (W) on the nameless paved road. This is old 66. If you look in the opposite direction you can see the unpaved raised bed of the road, running through a ranch property, so it's inaccessible. Drive west on the paved road and at 1.7 miles *2.7 km* at the interchange for Exit #171-Pittman Valley, turn left on Mountain Ranch Rd. Notice the raised unpaved roadbed running to your left at the interchange. The road takes you in front of a big resort, presently called the Quality Inn. At 2.1 miles *3.4 km,* where the access road turns left into the resort, keep going straight, onto a very brief stretch of old 66 asphalt-topped concrete, ending at a barrier at 2.2 mi. *3.5 km.* You can see how I-40 came right over the top of 66 here. You can return to I-40 at Exit #171-Pittman Valley.

favorite inn. It is rumored that in the World War Two era it was a brothel. It is now private property, so do not trespass. You will drive across the valley and then climb uphill on some great 1939 concrete.

DETOUR #5
Old Route 66
0.2 mi. *0.3 km* one-way
Time 10 minutes

At 7.4 miles *11.8 km* turn right onto an unmarked gravel road. You will immediately go over a cattle guard. Drive in for 0.2 miles *0.3 km* and park by the corral. The entry road intersects another road at this point. Walk the road to your right, noticing the bits of thin old macadam paving, a sure clue that this is old 66. It ends at I-40 at 0.25 miles *0.4 km*. Old 66 went south of I-40 here and turned west, visible on Detour #4. Return to the parking place and walk the other arm of the road. We did not find any paving on this longer arm, but it is elevated and has concrete culverts, things found only on a major road. It runs 0.75 miles *1.2 km* to I-40, which has buried it. This old road forms a big curve, and near the place where you parked, in the fold of the curve, was the campground Rittenhouse described, "A tree-shaded camping spot here...maintained free by the U. S. Government."

Garland Prairie Vista Picnic Area

8.0 miles *12.8 km* Garland Prairie Vista (to your right) This is a picnic area created many years ago, a favorite stopping place for travelers. Today it has a few picnic tables and a toilet. There's a great photo-op of 66 looking to the Peaks. The picnic ground is at a high point, and formerly provided wonderful views over the country to the southeast, where there is a very large open park called Garland Prairie. Today the trees, which were seedlings then, have grown so high that the views are blocked. It is hard to see much but you can at least get a feel for how things used to be by stopping here.

As you drive east of the picnic area the concrete roadway continues for a while, full of cracks that have been sealed with asphalt. This is one of those places where you can really imagine yourself on the old road. At 9.6 miles *15.4 km* there are some houses, the older ones dating back to the 1930s and the newer ones having been built since I-40 was opened. At 9.8 miles *15.7 km* is the abandoned Three Bears Trading Post (R). At 10.1 miles *16.2 km* you can see the raised bed of the 1931 road in the trees to your left, not far from your car. The old paving is clearly visible on portions of this road. It leads up to the Parks Store, passes it, disappears for a bit, and then reappears, going all the way to the Auto Tour Stop #2.

Parks In the Pines Store

10.5 miles *16.8 km* Parks Store (to your left). By 1921 the Old Trails Highway had been constructed and Williams and Flagstaff competed to have a road to the Grand Canyon from the highway. Both towns are in Coconino County so the Board of Supervisors, not wanting to show favoritism, decided to run the road from Parks (then called Maine), which was about equidistant between the two cities. The Maine-Grand Canyon road was built in 1921 and this store was built in November the same year at the corner where the two roads intersected. After Old Trails became Route 66 in 1926, this corner was still the Grand Canyon junction until Highway 64, which is closer to Williams, was built in 1928, after which the Maine-Grand Canyon road was not maintained except to serve local ranchers and farmers. Stop in and buy something in order to see the store and to help the owner survive.

1941 Alignment

As you drive east of the store the road climbs. Look for a cattle guard sign at 11.5 miles *18.4 km* where you will see a wide red gravel road overgrown with weeds angling off to your right. This is the 1941 alignment of Route 66. You can hike it. See the Hike box below.

Auto Tour Stop #2

11.6 miles *18.6 km* Auto Tour Second Interpretive Site (L) As with the first site, there is a pullout with a map and sign. The map shows the 1921, 1931, and 1941 versions of Route 66. There is something special here: the Forest Service has made the 1931 version of the road into a hiking trail. The trail is 0.75 mile *1.2 km* long. If you have the time for it, this is a refreshing walk. The path goes downhill, an elevation change of about 50 feet *15 meters* and you walk right on top of the 1931 highway. It was paved

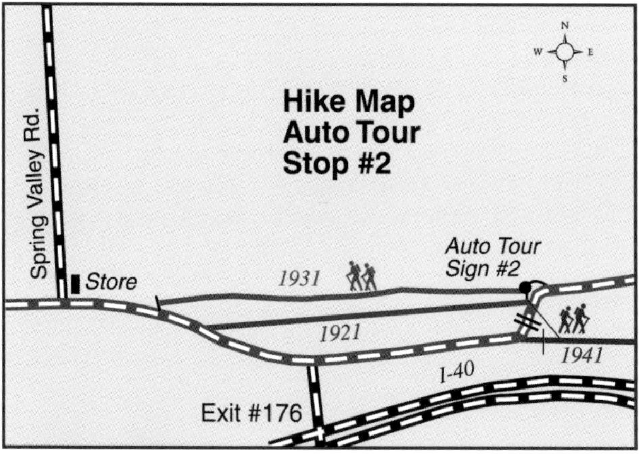

HIKE
1941 version of Route 66
0.4 mi. *0.6 km* one-way
Time 20 minutes

(Red line on above map). From the second Auto Tour sign walk south across the paved road and follow FR 097 to the point where it intersects a wide red gravel road. Turn left and walk the red gravel road to its end. You will find some pieces of paving and a culvert along it. This is the Route 66 alignment used from 1941-1964 and was built to avoid the high point at 49 Hill. This bit of historical 66 ends where it bumps up against I-40.

but the paving is crumbling, so that there is almost none of it left. There was a Forest Service campground about midway, where you will see a little stone building to your left, which was a springhouse supplying water for campers. The hike ends where the 1931 and 1941 alignments merge. As you stand at the interpretive site, if you look to your left (S) you can see the raised grade of the 1921-1931 alignment. It is possible to walk 30 paces to it and hike it almost to the bottom, where it ends against a fence. The 1921 roadway was never paved. This hike is a wonderful way to stretch your legs if you have been driving for a while. Highly recommended. (Map, page 74).

From Auto Tour Stop #2 drive back onto the paved road, turn left and drive on to the east. The paving ends at 12.1 miles *19.4 km* but will resume.

Fortynine Hill

13.6 miles *21.8 km* Fortynine Hill. This was the high point on Route 66 at 7,410 feet *2,245 meters* until 66 was rerouted in 1941. One wonders why the road was located here, as it goes through a narrow mountain pass that is shaded in the winter so that the sun cannot melt snow. Route 66 was relocated in 1941 to avoid this hill. If you look off to your left into the trees, you will see an even older grade running along beside you, playing tag until the road starts downhill, when it veers off to your left. If you keep watching it until you are down on the flat, you can see it running along the center of the meadow.

Brannigan Park

14.1 miles *22.6 km* Brannigan Park (to your left) This is a beautiful spring-fed open meadow in a bowl surrounded by hills and mountains. There are still a few old homes in Brannigan Park, and you will see that some have fallen down. Some newer homes have been built. The paving resumes at a cattle guard as you leave the park. **Zero** out here. Notice the home to the left at the cattle guard: it has a fence made of skis.

DETOUR #6: If you turn left onto the paved road at the cattle guard and drive for 0.6 miles *1.0 km* you will see a white gate to your left. This is where the 1921 road comes across. Look right and you can see it, though not as plainly, to the east. Turn around and go back to the cattle guard, **Zero** out, and turn left (E).

Auto Tour Stop #3

1.3 miles *2.1 km* Auto Tour Third Interpretive Site (to your left). You will see a gravel-surfaced pullout with a pine-log fence. There is an informative sign here, illustrated with a map showing the old alignments that went through this area. There is also text giving information about the road.

At 1.7 miles *2.7 km* you are entering a curve to your left. Look across I-40 and you can see the 1931 lane cut through the trees on the other side. 0.25 mi. *0.4 km* farther you see the lane for the 1921 road. The 1931 alignment joined the 1941 version of the road at the spot where your car is sitting. The road from here to Exit #185-Bellemont is pure frontage road, and never was 66.

At 1.8 miles *2.9 km* Exploration #1 is available on Forest Road 9229K, which turns sharply to the left. This is for high-clearance cars and only when the road is dry.

EXPLORATION #1
Old Trails Highway
2.0 mi. *3.2 km* one-way
Time 25 minutes

Turn left on unpaved road 9229K, which runs along a power line. This is the original 1921 Old Trails Highway, which became Highway 66 in 1926. It was never paved. You must have a high-clearance vehicle and a dry road to do this. Drive along the old road for 2.0 miles *3.2 km* to a point where it starts down a grade on a raised bed. It is blocked beyond here and you must retrace your path. Few people know about this forgotten version of the Mother Road. It was replaced in 1931. This is the road you saw if you took the little Detour #6 at the eastern edge of Brannigan Park.

Exit #185—Bellemont

3.8 miles *6.1 km* Stop sign at Exit #185. **Zero** here. You are now at the I-40 interchange. Get onto the eastbound lanes to go to Flagstaff. Roadies will be interested in Detours #7 and #8 available on the other side of I-40.

DETOUR #7
EXIT #185-Bellemont S&W
Old Route 66
2.7 mi. *4.3 km* one-way
Time 15 minutes

Where the frontage road meets the I-40 overpass **Zero** out and drive over I-40. On the other side, turn right on Bellemont Camp Road. As you begin to drive west look down to your left, and you will see a raised roadbed, the original Old Trails Highway through here. The paved road you are driving replaced it in 1941. At 0.6 miles *1.0 km* is Bellemont (left). There's not much left today but a tavern and some dilapidated buildings. You can turn left on the next road and drive 0.1 miles *0.16 km* to a water tank (L) and photograph the collapsing building that fronted the 1921 road. West of this are some new industrial buildings. At 1.8 miles *2.9 km* the 1921 version of the road comes in from your left and crosses your road, running about 0.2 miles *0.3 km* to your right. [For a good walk, stop here and hike along the old raised roadbed (L), which runs 0.5 miles *0.8 km* to a fence]. The paving disappears briefly west of here, so drive carefully. The paving resumes but soon ends at a wire fence. A gravel road continues west for a short distance, but it is not worth taking. Turn around and go back to Exit #185.

Eastbound>

DETOUR #8
EXIT #185-Bellemont S&E
Old Route 66
2.4 mi. *3.8 km* one-way
Time 15 minutes

If finishing Detour #7 go straight ahead at the stop sign and **Zero** there. If starting near the truck stop on the north side of I-40, **Zero**, drive over I-40 and on the south side, turn left on East Bellemont Rd. This is old 66. It runs right in front of the Harley-Davidson dealership and cafe and if you are a Hog fan you will want to stop in. The road runs along parallel to the railroad. At 1.3 miles *2.1 km* you will see the crumbling remains of a Whiting Brothers motel (left). At 1.6 miles *2.6 km* you will see the old Pine Breeze Inn and gas station (left). Rough old concrete surfacing begins here. The old highway ends at a barricade at about the 2.4 mile *3.8 km* point. Return to Exit #185-Bellemont.

Bellemont

0.5 miles *0.8 km* Bellemont. Bellemont Flat, a large prairie is out of sight to your right. In the early days it was used for grazing, but in World War Two it took on a different role, when the U. S. government located a major ammunition depot there. In 1942, the 5,000 residents of Flagstaff were startled to find that 12,000 construction workers had come to town to build the depot, spending over $100 million dollars (in today's values) on the project. Once the construction horde moved out, the base employed 2,000 workers, including many Navajo Indians. First called Navajo Ordnance Depot, the facility was later renamed Navajo Army Depot. It was at its peak during WWII, and then had a resurgence during the Korean and Vietnam wars. After that its activities dwindled down to the point where the federal government turned it over to the State of Arizona, which now uses it as a National Guard camp, and has changed its name to Camp Navajo.

Arizona Divide

5.1 miles *8.2 km* The Arizona Divide. As you drive toward Flagstaff, you will reach the top of a hill where you will see a sign for the Arizona Divide (R). All water falling on the north side of this divide drains into the Little Colorado River Basin, while all that falling on the south side drains into the Verde River Basin. The point is 7,335 feet *2,222 meters* high, making it—after 1941 when 66 was rerouted around 49 Hill—the highest point on Route 66 (the Continental Divide in New Mexico was 7,263 feet *2200 m).* East of the divide you pass over the railroad on the Riordan Overpass, a major railroad crossing on Route 66.

Exit #191—Flagstaff

6.3 miles *10.1 km* Exit #191-Flagstaff. Take Exit #191. Curve around underneath I-40 and follow the signs toward Flagstaff. Once you leave I-40, you are back on a nice segment of Route 66, one that has stood the test of time, as it was used for the entire life of the Mother Road, from 1926-1968. (I-40 bypassed 66 in Flagstaff in 1968). For the first couple of miles you pass through a stretch of still largely unspoiled forest, although a few homes are being built there now.

The Arboretum at Flagstaff

8.8 miles *14.1 km* The road to the Arboretum at Flagstaff is to your right.

SIGHTSEEING #2
Arboretum at Flagstaff
Time 1.0 hour

At the 8.8 mile *14.1 km* point you will see a sign for the Arboretum (right). This is a horticultural study facility that is open to the public. If you love plants then you will want to see this place. It is 4.0 miles *6.4 km* off of Route 66, and the last 3.0 miles *4.8 km* of the road is a good gravel road.

Pine Springs

8.8 miles *14.1 km* Pine Springs (L).You can see that this was once a service station. There was also a restaurant here and a few tourist cabins in back. Pine Springs has been closed for many years, but was once popular with truckers, who wanted to take their big rigs out of town so that they could find a parking lot large enough for their trucks. Pine Springs used to be way out in the country, but since 1990, there has been much development in this area, so that it now feels like part of urban Flagstaff.

Outskirts of Flagstaff

10.1 miles *16.2 km* The first traffic light. East of here you will enter what used to be the outskirts of town, where the tourist facilities began. There were many motels, restaurants and service stations from here into the heart of Flagstaff. There are still a few motels and restaurants (including the recommended Galaxy Diner) along this strip now, but most of the service stations have closed, though you can still tell what they were by their shape.

Modern Flagstaff roadside eatery with a Route 66 theme

Highway Junction

10.8 miles *17.3 km* Junction of Highways 66 and 89A. You will see road signs for Route 66 here. Follow the signs and turn to the left, onto Milton Road, getting into the curb lane, because you will need to make a right turn into the Visitor Center soon. This junction is in the neighborhood of the Northern Arizona University campus.

Northern Arizona University

10.9 miles *17.4 km* Northern Arizona University campus (R). Starting in 1899 as Northern Arizona Normal School, with an enrollment of twenty-three students, this institution grew slowly over the years, changing its name and its focus several times. It reached university status in 1964, after which it grew dramatically, and now has an enrollment of almost 20,000, making it one of the mainstays of Flagstaff's economy and adding many amenities to the quality of life in the city. As you continue driving into the heart of Flagstaff, you can see the distinctive remains of its Mother Road tourist-oriented businesses.

DETOUR #9: (Map below) Old 66 into Flagstaff. At 10.9 miles *17.4 km*, turn right on Mike's Pike and follow it for three blocks, then turn right on Phoenix Avenue. Notice the old motels along Phoenix. Drive Phoenix three blocks to San Francisco Street. Turn left on San Francisco and drive just over the railroad tracks, then turn left into the Visitor Center (V.C. on the map)

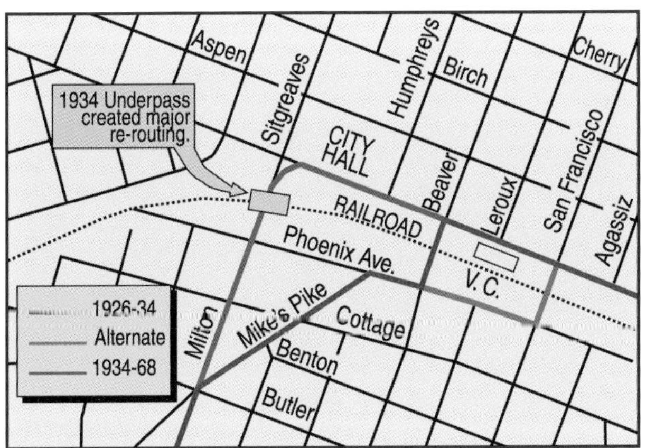

Railroad Overpass

11.3 miles *18.1 km* Railroad Overpass. You will drive under a railroad overpass built in 1934 (Route 66 was then realigned to go under it) and follow the curve of the road to the east into downtown. Since the railroad is on your right (S) beyond the underpass, all businesses along Flagstaff's main street were built on the left (N) side of 66. When Route 66 was king, almost every one of the businesses along the highway was tourist-related, including the block now covered by City Hall.

Flagstaff Visitor Center—End of Tour

11.5 miles *18.4 km* Intersection of Route 66 and Beaver Street. Turn right (S) onto Beaver and then make an immediate left (E) into the parking lot for the Visitor Center. At the center you can get information about Flagstaff, find a toilet, and buy snacks and souvenirs. You can call the Visitor Center for information: 1-800-842-7293, or locally at 774-9541.

Flagstaff Coffee Houses

Because Flagstaff is a college town, it supports a wide variety of coffee houses. If you are like us, you've just gotta have that caffeine fix.

Macy's European Coffeehouse, 14 S. Beaver

Late for the Train
107 N. San Francisco St. (Downtown)
1800 N. Ft. Valley Road (Northside)

Campus Coffee Bean, 1800 S. Milton (University)

Latte Shack, 1566 S. Riordan Ranch Rd. (University)

Jitters, 3504 E. Route 66 (Eastside)

And for those who prefer tea, there is

Tea & Sympathy, 409 N. Humphreys

Route 66 in Flagstaff today

Eastbound>

Sedona and Jerome

Sedona—Northern Arizona's redrock vacation Mecca

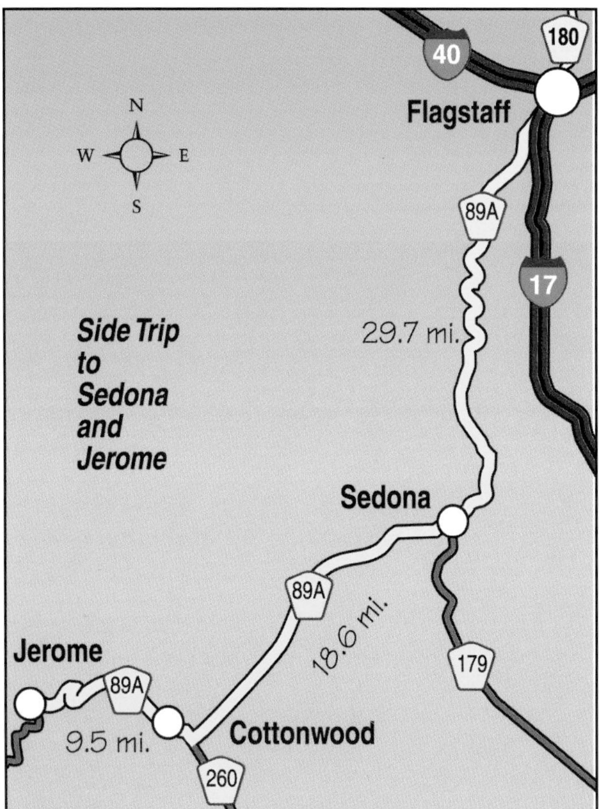

Sedona

Many travelers through northern Arizona want to see Sedona, the Redrock Mecca. Flagstaff, with its many fine places to eat and stay, is the base for a side trip to Sedona.

From Flagstaff City Hall, drive west, then curve south on Route 66, going through the underpass. Continue south on Milton Road, following signs for Highway 89A. You will drive 13.9 miles *22.2 km* through the pine forest to the rim of Oak Creek Canyon, and then drive a narrow curving road through the gorgeous canyon for an additional 15.8 miles *25.3 km* to Sedona, a total of 29.7 miles *47.5 km*. We love the drive to Sedona, never tiring of it, though we have taken it hundreds of times.

Most Sedona visitors will want to stop first in Uptown Sedona, the first part of town that one comes to. There are many interesting shops in this area, and it is a fine place for walking, gawking, having a meal or a snack, buying anything from souvenirs to fine art, and enjoying the majestic red cliffs in the background. From uptown, go south and turn left on Highway 179 at the junction, to go to Tlaquepaque, another wonderful place to stroll and enjoy yourself. There is additional fine shopping at the Hillside, about 0.5 miles *0.8 km* farther down Highway 179.

There are many fine restaurants and places to stay in Sedona. We do not have space here to list them.

Jerome

Jerome is another of our favorite places. It is located 28.1 miles *45.0 km* south of Sedona on Highway 89A. You will drive to Cottonwood where you will reach a road junction at the second stoplight, at 19.0 miles *30.4 km*. You can either turn left here on Highway 89A or go straight ahead on Historic Highway 89A, which takes you to Jerome through Old Town Cottonwood and Clarkdale. The two roads join beyond Clarkdale and become one winding road up Mingus Mountain to enter Jerome.

Jerome is now a semi-ghost town, a fascinating relic of its glory days as the home of one of Arizona's biggest copper mines, and now a sanctuary for artists and craftsmen. It is very picturesque and reminds many travelers of an Italian hill town.

Sightseeing in Jerome is confined to the compact old downtown historic district, where there are many interesting shops and some satisfying restaurants. For history buffs, just wandering through the town is a rich experience. There is a mine museum downtown, which is well worth a visit.

If you visit both Sedona and Jerome and take the time to enjoy them, you will spend an entire day, so allow plenty of time. Your visit will be a memorable experience.

Jerome, former queen of the copper camps

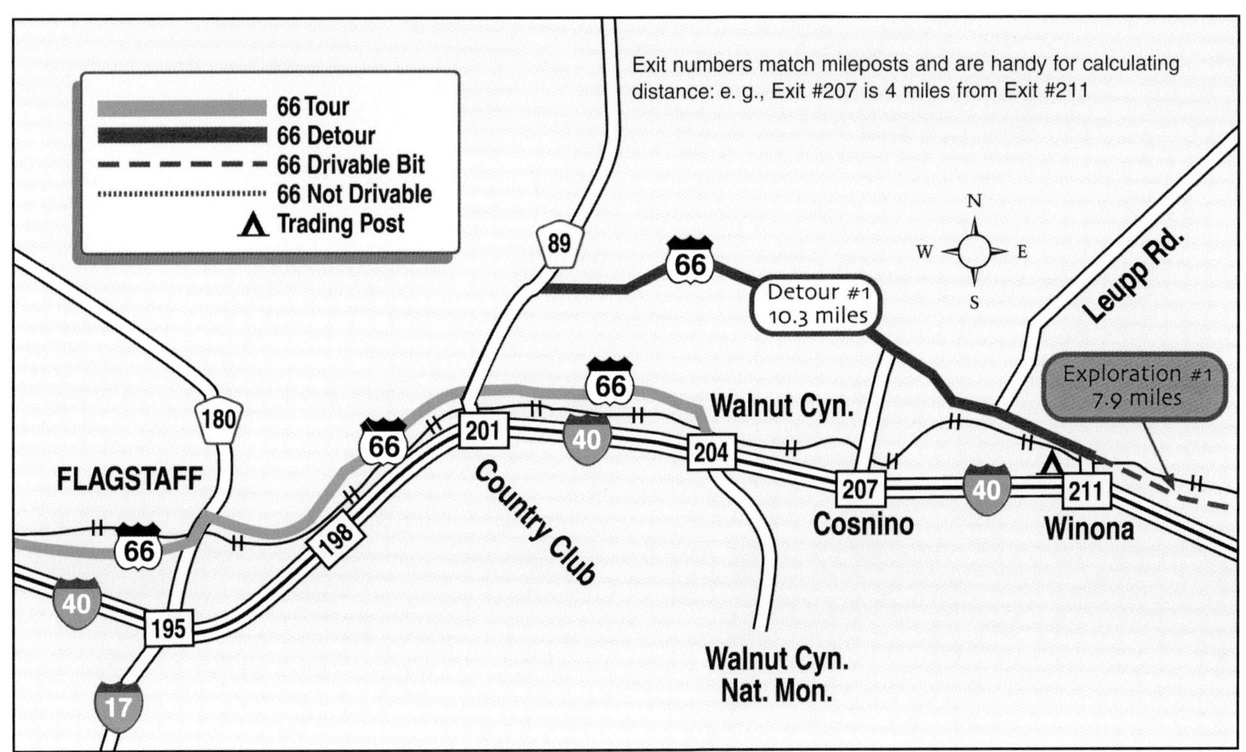

Tour 6-W Winona to Flagstaff pp. 24-27

Tour 8-E Flagstaff to Winona

Distance: 14.7 miles *23.5 km*
Highlights: Museum Club, Walnut Canyon, Winona
Driving Time: 30 minutes

Route 66 icon in Flagstaff. It disappeared in 1980—OP

Tour 8-E takes you from the heart of downtown Flagstaff to the east along motel row. You will follow the 1947 alignment of Route 66 out into the country (the 1921-1947 alignment is available as a detour). Along the way you will see some interesting old roadside businesses, including the justifiably famous Museum Club, to end your tour at the place made famous in a song, Winona.

START

Start at the Visitor Center in downtown Flagstaff.

Flagstaff Visitor Center

0.0 miles *0.0 km* Drive out the east side of the parking lot onto San Francisco Street and get into the curb lane so that you can make a right turn. Turn right (E) at the stoplight. You are now on Route 66.

Flagstaff's Old Motel Row

0.3 miles *0.5 km* Motel Row. In the glory days of Route 66 it seemed that almost every one of the businesses along the highway was devoted to tourism, furnishing some kind of service to the motorist. Today many of these businesses have been converted into something else. All are on the left side due to the presence of the railroad on the right. The first of the old motels you will see is the Snowbowl. Others as you drive along are the Whispering Winds, Red Rose, King's House, Western Hills, Frontier, Wonderland, Twilite, 66, Flagstaff, Paradise, Pinecrest, and El Pueblo. The El Pueblo was built in 1936 by Philip Johnston, who won fame in World War Two when he invented the Navajo Code Talker program. There is a recommended restaurant, Miz Zip's, at 2924 E. Route 66. The late Bobby Leonard, who created the restaurant, built his business by developing a better hamburger. He bought choice beef and ground it fresh daily on the premises, a tradition his family still carries on. You can taste the difference and you will enjoy the old-time ambiance. The 1921 and 1947 versions of the road followed the same path to the turnoff, next page.

Museum Club

3.3 miles *5.3 km* The Museum Club (L). This grand old building with its inverted tree trunk doorway has been an eye-catcher since it was first built in 1931 by Dean Eldredge. He was a collector of curios who hoped to prosper on this good site, with frontage on Highway 66, by constructing a museum-curio store on the edge of town, where he would be the first business that westbound tourists would see. Since Eldredge's death in 1936, the place has been a nightclub. Present owner Martin Zanzucchi is a Route 66 buff, a director of the Route 66 Association of Arizona and the man who was responsible for having Flagstaff's Santa Fe Avenue renamed Route 66 in Flagstaff in 1992. The place contains Route 66 memorabilia and is also a great place to see real Arizona cowboys at their leisure. Be sure to pay it a visit.

Route 66—Highway 89 Junction

3.6 miles *5.8 km* 1947 Historic Route 66 Turnoff. Watch carefully as you approach this point and get into the curb lane. You will first see a road sign for Fanning Drive. The turn you are to take is just beyond Fanning Drive where there is a big overhead sign reading, "Historic US 66" and another reading, "Local Traffic Only." As you begin to drive this historic road you will see that most of it consists of a concrete surface. It its heyday, these concrete sections of Route 66 were asphalt-covered. Much of the asphalt has worn away, leaving patches. The highway construction specifications for this road called for concrete a foot thick *0.3 meters*, heavily reinforced. No wonder it is still in good condition. You will see that Route 66 runs parallel to the railroad, which is very close to it on your right.

Flagstaff Truck Center

4.2 miles *6.7 km* Flagstaff Truck Center (L). What is left of one of the well-known service station-motel combinations is seen here. This operation started as a service station with a small motel attached, called The Tourtel. (The Tourtel's sign now hangs from the ceiling of Main Street Catering in downtown Flagstaff). Later, when I-40 was being built, the owner turned the service station into a business specializing in servicing big trucks and it was called the Flagstaff Truck Center. After that the guests in the motel were almost exclusively truck drivers. After hanging on for a few years, the motel was abandoned.

New Industrial Area

4.6 miles *7.4 km* Ralston Purina Tower, right. Today this part of East Flagstaff has become an industrial area, but that is a recent development. In the days of Route 66, this area was rural, with only a few homes. Drivers would likely have seen cattle grazing along here. The tall tower with the checkerboard painted at the top is part of the Ralston Purina plant, where pet food is made and shipped all over the region.

Cinder Mine

5.8 miles *9.3 km* Big cinder operation (L). The operators of this cinder mine have cut away the volcanic cinder mountain to its core, giving motorists an idea of the composition of these mountains and hills which dot the landscape. Beyond this mine, the area becomes rural, looking like it did in the old days.

Cosnino Overpass

7.7 miles *12.3 km* Cosnino Overpass. A writer who described Route 66 in 1955 noted that in its entire length across Arizona, the highway crossed the railroad seven times, all of them at under or overpasses. This is one of them, called the Cosnino Overpass. Traffic is so light here that it is a safe place to park off the road and then stand on the bridge to see and photograph oncoming trains.

Route 66 Segment Ends

8.4 miles *13.4 km* Stop Sign. This is the end of this segment of Route 66. While short, it provides a worthwhile traveling experience. We find that it is almost as fast to travel east of Flagstaff on this route as it is on I-40, and it is much more interesting. From the stop sign follow the road signs to return to I-40 eastbound to get to Winona.

Walnut Canyon National Monument

If you want to visit Walnut Canyon (recommended) you can drive straight ahead. Coming out on old Route 66 is our favorite way to go to Walnut Canyon, the one we usually take.

SIGHTSEEING #1
EXIT #204
Walnut Canyon NM
Time 1.5 hours

Drive across I-40, then follow the signs on the other side, which lead you to the National Monument, 3.0 miles *4.8 km* from I-40. There is a Visitor Center with toilets, a gift shop, and museum. The highlight of the attraction, however, is the Island Trail, which takes you down to a butte around the rim of which are numerous cliff dwellings at trail level. The trail is not long, only a loop of 0.8 miles *1.3 km,* but there is a steep flight of 240 stairs—easy to climb down but hell coming up. An easier path, the Rim Trail, is 0.4 miles *0.6 km* one-way, running along the edge of the scenic canyon. You can see some cliff dwellings from this trail but they are across the canyon.

This photograph shows the cliff dwellings at Walnut Canyon, as seen from the Island Trail, which allows visitors who are willing to climb the 240 steps to have the unforgettable experience of walking along beside these ancient ruins in a beautiful picturesque canyon setting. Highly recommended.

Exit #204—Walnut Canyon

As you travel east of Exit #204-Walnut Canyon on I-40 you will notice that the Ponderosa pines begin to thin out and smaller trees take their place. These smaller trees are piñon pines and junipers.

Exit #211—Winona

__Gas, Food__

As you approach Winona, at Exit #211-Winona you may be looking for a town. Winona was never a town, even though the lyrics in Bobby Troup's famous song, *Get Your Kicks on Route 66* make it seem that it's a town. Winona started as a little railroad section house. When the Old Trails Highway was built in 1921, the road crossed the railroad tracks at Winona. This made it an important point, and a local rancher named Billy Adams, who also ran a barber shop in Flagstaff, decided that it might be a good place for a gas station and tourist camp. He located his operation a little to the north and east of the present gas station but there are no longer any tourist cabins on the site. You can stop in at the gas station and refuel or go into the store. They have snacks, a deli, and some Route 66 souvenirs. The owners still call their business the Winona Trading Post.

The trading post is the end of this tour.

The 1925 Walnut Creek Bridge, seen on Detour #1

DETOUR #1
EXIT #211-Winona
1921-1947 Route 66
10.3 mi. *16.5 km* one-way
Time 20 minutes

At Exit #211-Winona, take the exit. **Zero** at the stop sign, turn left and go over I-40. On the other side follow the main road heading north. This is the first alignment of Route 66 into Flagstaff, going back to the earliest days of motor travel. It was used until 1947, when the version of Route 66 on Tour 8-E was opened. Just follow the red line on the map on page 79. Along the way you will see (and photograph) the great old steel truss bridge over Walnut Creek. On both sides of the road, but mainly the right, you will see old farming fields. How the real Dust Bowl refugees characterized by Tom Joad and his family from *Grapes of Wrath* must have been heartened to see cultivated land after so much desert. At the end of this piece of 66 you will join Highway 89 at a stop light. You can turn right here and drive to the Grand Canyon (details on page 71). Turn left to come into Flagstaff. Elden Pueblo, a small Indian ruin, is on your right. It's free and interesting.

EXPLORATION #1
EXIT #211-Winona
Route 66 and 1914 bridge
7.9 mi. *12.6 km* one-way
Time 1 hour

Take Exit #211-Winona and turn left at the stop sign and then right on the first drivable road. Go downhill on old paving—Route 66. At the bottom **Zero** at the 0 milepost sign (R). The paving lasts for 1.0 miles *1.6 km* then becomes patchy, turning into a good wide gravel road at 2.0 miles *3.2 km*. At 6.0 miles *9.6 km* you will find paving again, but it's rough. At 6.6 miles *10.6 km* the road meets a wire fence. Take either dirt road to the left. At 6.8 miles *10.9 km* there is more paving to the 7.3 mi. *11.7 km*, point from where you can see how the road ran in a straight line to today's I-40. Park here if you are not in a high-clearance vehicle. Otherwise, keep driving the dirt road. At 7.7 miles *12.3 km* you are at the edge of Canyon Padre, with the I-40 bridge to your right. If you get out of your car and walk over toward the bridge, you can see the piers of the 1937 bridge under the I-40 bridge. Drive the old road down into the canyon until you reach the 1914 bridge at 7.9 miles *12.6 km*. It is very scenic for photos. Look for the faint letters "66" on the posts at the far end of the bridge. You can drive over the bridge, but the road ends at 8.8 miles *14.1 km* at a gate. Instead, hike around the old alignments. The oldest 1914 alignment went over the bridge and then made a hairpin turn, hugging the canyon wall. You will see the rock walls that supported it and it makes a good walk. A later alignment—perhaps in 1926 when Route 66 was created—blasted the side of the butte away and followed the side canyon making a wide sweeping arc to the east. On the canyon floor you will see huge chunks of paving, probably put there when I-40 replaced Route 66 in the area in the 1960s. It's a great place to explore.

In 1937 the state built a new bridge to replace the old 1914 concrete model, stating, "The mile of roadway, including the bridge, has six curves, all of them far sharper than our present standard permits". The route was so dangerous that there were several wrecked cars lying on the bottom of the canyon (none are visible today). The 1937 bridge was replaced in 1952, and again in the 1960s by the I-40 bridge.

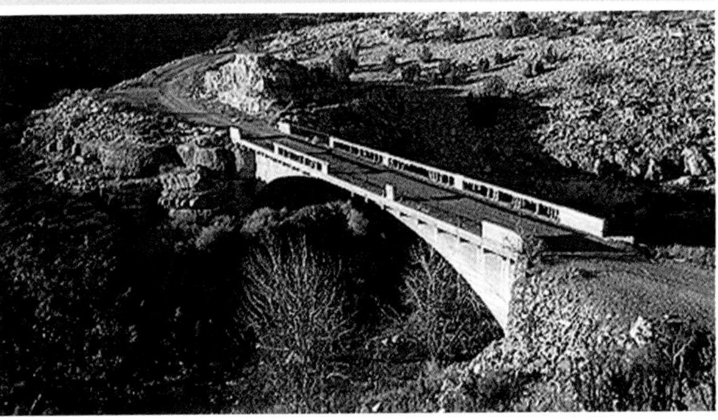

The 1914 bridge over Canyon Padre

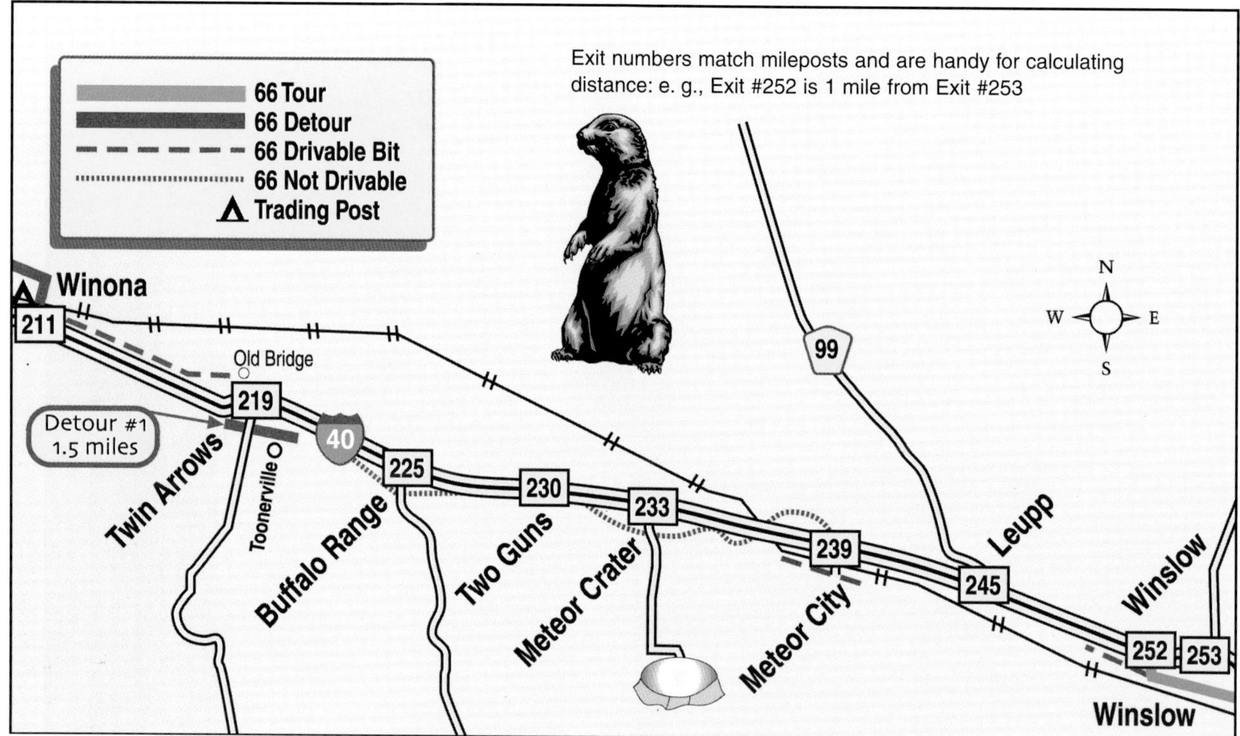

Tour 5-W Winslow to Winona pp. 20-23

Tour 9-E Winona to Winslow

Distance: 42.8 miles *68.5 km*
Highlights: Winona, Twin Arrows, Meteor Crater
Driving Time: 1 hour

Twin Arrows

Tour 9-E takes you from the wooded highlands of the Flagstaff area onto the open plains of Winslow. On the way you will see sites of Twin Arrows, Two Guns, and Meteor City, all of them now closed, reflecting a significant change in travel that has occurred since the freeway replaced the Mother Road. You will have the chance to visit Meteor Crater, one of the world's great natural wonders.

START

Winona

Exit #211- Winona. As you drive to the east from the Winona Interchange, you will see a gravel road running along parallel to I-40 on your right (S). We believe that this is not a portion of Route 66, but is simply a frontage road.

Exit #219—Twin Arrows

No gas, No food, No lodging, Photos

Take the exit and follow the sign for Twin Arrows, which you will see as you come to the end of the off-ramp. Twin Arrows is one of the prime photo opportunities on Route 66. The service station, trading post and café are closed but the famous arrows are still there to photograph. When you are finished at the arrows continue east on the

DETOUR #1
EXIT #219-Twin Arrows S&E
Toonerville Trading Post
1.5 mi. *2.4 km* one-way
Time 10 minutes

After you visit the arrows, drive east on the frontage road. At the stop sign, **Zero**, turn right and then make an immediate left onto the old gray paving, which is Route 66. At 0.5 miles *0.8 km* (R) is the former Toonerville Trading Post, which opened in the 1920s, catering to both the Navajos who lived to the north and to the motoring public. It is older than Twin Arrows. In 1972 the owner, Slick McAlister, was murdered there by robbers. Today there are no signs or any other icons to show that this place was once the Toonerville Trading Post. It got its name from a comic strip popular in the 1920s. You can continue to drive old 66 to the 1.5 miles *2.4 km* point, where it curves to the right (S). We believe that the highway actually went straight ahead here and did not curve. In any event, the paving ends at this point today. Return the way you came and get onto I-40 eastbound at Exit #219.

Meteor Crater from the observation deck

frontage road. At the stop sign turn left and take I-40 eastbound, toward Winslow. As you drive east you will see a line of poles and stones about 0.25 mile *0.4 km* to your right (S), running along parallel to the freeway. This is not Route 66, only a pipeline. The junipers disappear east of Twin Arrows and you enter into a wide-open bare desert. The first travelers through this area reported that the ground was covered with knee-high grass, but the country was overgrazed and the grass cover is now very thin

Exit #225—Buffalo Range Road

No gas, No food, No lodging

The buffalo range was created many years ago when it seemed that the American Bison was on the verge of extinction. Concerned individuals created this buffalo preserve to insure the survival of the species. The Arizona Fish and Game Department operates the Raymond Buffalo Range, maintaining a small herd here. Even though it is open to the public, it is rather difficult to visit the place. You drive in several miles on a dirt road until you come to the caretaker's living quarters, an old ranch house. In order to see the buffalo, you have to be lucky enough to find the caretaker at home and willing to take you out on the land where the animals are grazing. Call 928-774-5045 for information. As you approach Exit #225 you can see the raised bed of old 66—just dirt—to the right of I-40, but you can't drive it. The paving was ripped up and sagebrush has grown up on the grade so that even a jeep could not drive it. Our advice is to pass by Exit #225 and keep going. At this point on I-40 you can see in the distance to the left an area of colored sand with mystical black hills and promontories rising above it. The colored sand is part of the Painted Desert and the black hills are the volcanic formations of the Hopi Buttes.

Exit #230—Two Guns

No gas, No food, No lodging

Two Guns is a major disappointment these days, as it is locked up, and closed to visitors, with No Trespassing signs displayed in an unfriendly fashion. You might pull off to take a photo from a distance, but otherwise, you can only pass by. It is too bad that Two Guns is closed, for it was one of the most interesting trading posts along the road, with a long and colorful history. East of Exit #230 you can see an unpaved older version of Route 66 running along the right side for about a mile.

Exit #233—Meteor Crater

Gas, Food, No lodging, Natural Wonder

From a distance you can see a white dome south of this exit. The dome is a modern service station, not an old Route 66 business. If you take the exit and drive up the Meteor Crater Road, at the far side of the service station you will see old 66 running east-west on both sides of the paved road, where there is a *faux* cattle guard. No Trespassing signs have been erected on both ends of old 66 here, so that it is no longer possible to drive the Mother Road on this old alignment. We really regret that one can no longer drive east to the old Meteor Museum. You can still see the ruins of the building with its tower in the distance, but you can't drive to it.

Meteor Crater itself is a genuine natural phenomenon—no trumped up publicity was necessary to make it seem important. For years it baffled scientists, who argued

SIGHTSEEING #1
EXIT #233
Meteor Crater
Time 1.5 hours

Take Exit #233-Meteor Crater and follow the signs into the place, a 6.0 mile *9.6 km* drive on paved roads. You will pass a gas station. At the far edge of the gas station Route 66 runs east-west across the Meteor Crater road, but it is blocked by No Trespassing signs, so drive on. The road takes you up to the parking lot. You buy a ticket at the entrance and then walk up steps to a courtyard where there is an interesting display about astronauts. From there you enter the main building where you will find restrooms, a snack bar, book shop and gift shop including some Route 66 things, and some Indian jewelry. There is a well-designed museum that tells the history of Meteor Crater, and also a theater in which programs about the crater are presented.

The main attraction is outdoors. You walk out onto the rim of the crater and are enthralled by the sight. Three observation stations have been set up, at a low, medium and high level, with lensless telescopes trained on points of interest. Signs guide you. It is not possible to walk around the entire rim unless you are escorted by a guide. Guided tours are available and are excellent.

Meteor Crater is privately owned, but the owners have done a good job developing and caring for it.

When you are finished, drive back out to Exit #233 and return to I-40 heading east.

about how it was created, but the modern view is that it is an impact crater where a meteor struck the earth. It is such a rare phenomenon that NASA used it for training astronauts during the Apollo Program. For several decades Winslow advertised itself as Meteor City in order to capitalize on the fame of this great crater. No Route 66 or I-40 traveler should miss it. See Sightseeing #1 for details.

Site of Rimmy Jim's

The famous old Rimmy Jim's Trading Post was located directly north of the road to Meteor Crater and was a natural stopping place for motorists who wanted to see the crater. In addition to the usual gas station, Rimmy built a collection of tourist cabins shaped like Indian hogans.

Rest Area

From Meteor Crater as you drive toward Winslow, at 1.0 mile *1.6 km* east of Exit #233 is a Rest Area, with toilets, picnic tables and informational maps and signs. East of MP 236 you can see an old concrete bridge (R) where Route 66 went over Cow Canyon.

Exit #239—Meteor City

No gas, No food, No lodging

Many people confuse Meteor City and Meteor Crater; however, the only thing they share is the word "meteor." The confusion was compounded years ago when Winslow was known as The Meteor City. The Meteor City Trading Post was housed in a dome with a rainbow haircut. It first started as a typical Route 66 trading post, in a flat rectangular building which was replaced with the original dome. That dome burned in 1990, and today's dome was built to replace it. This was the last of the Route 66 trading posts between Winona and Winslow, a stretch of road that used to support six of them. Starting at Winona, they were Twin Arrows, Toonerville, Two Guns, Rimmy Jim's, Meteor City, and Hopi House. I-40 killed them all. The last operators of Meteor City hung on for seven years, finally giving up the business on July 31, 2000. On the north side of Exit #239 is the Red Gap Ranch Road, a 1931 version of Route 66. This is now completely closed to the public, with barriers, signs and a locked gate.

Exit #252—Winslow

Gas, Food, Lodging

There are other exits for Winslow, but be sure to take Exit #252. **Zero** at the stop sign. Turn right, then left at the next stop sign to drive into town.

Winslow Historic District

You drive into town on Route 66, which is lined with holdover businesses from the glory days—lots of motels, service stations and cafes. In 1951 Winslow became the first city in Arizona to create one-way traffic for Route 66, with the eastbound motorists going into town on Second Street and the westbound drivers using Third Street.

Drive to the 1.8 mile *2.9 km* point, where you reach the intersection of Second Street and Kinsley. Turn left on Kinsley and park your car along the street. You will see the famous (although quite new, having been opened in 1998) **Standin' on the Corner** park here. Give it a look and take some photographs. Across the street are the Old Trails Museum and Roadworks, both of which are recommended. This is the end of this tour. See page 19 for our recommendations about where to eat and sleep in Winslow.

Old Trails Museum in Winslow

Winslow Historic District Map

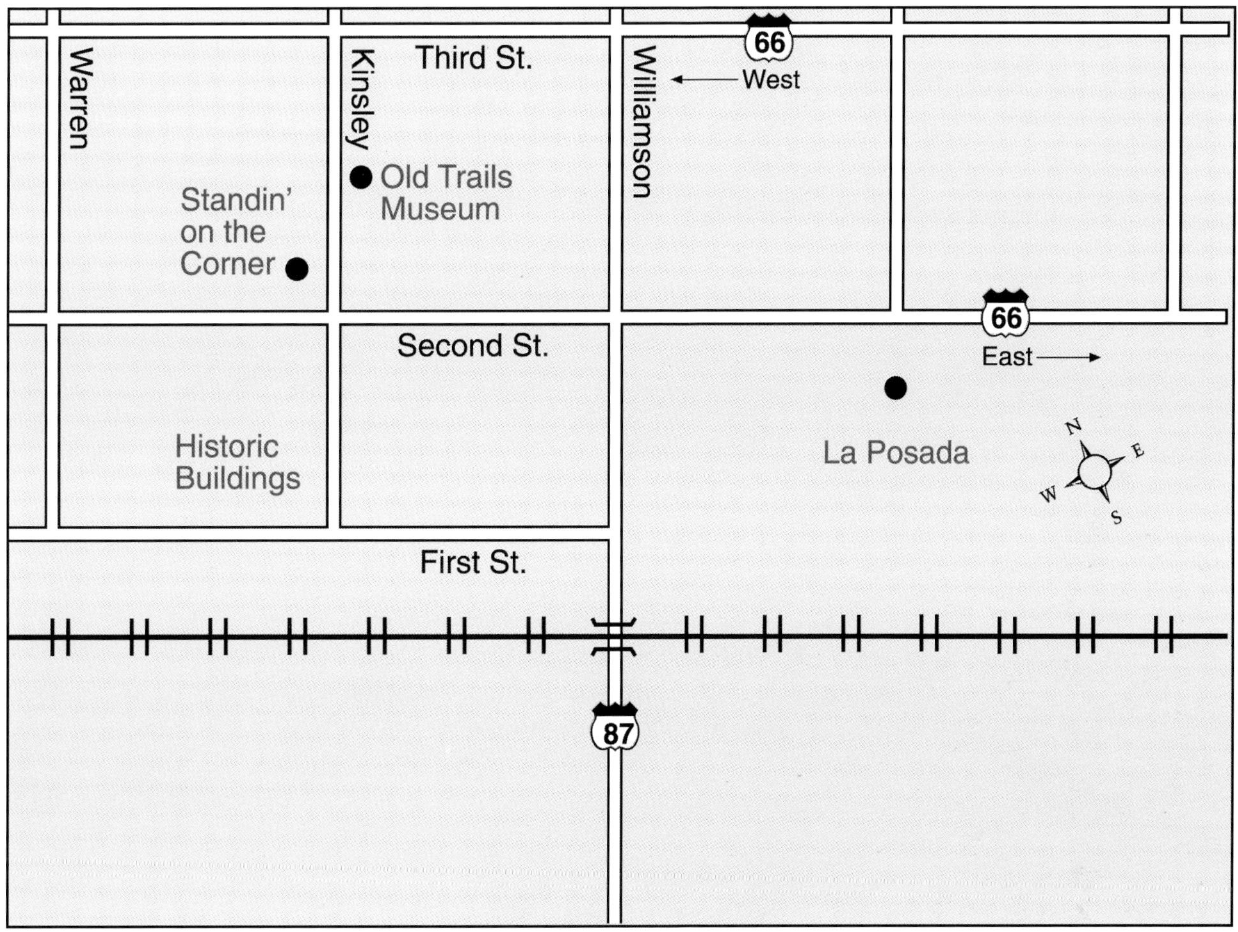

Points of Interest to Explore

The **Winslow Visitor Center**, available by taking I-40 Exit #253 is well designed and has a wealth of brochures and information for travelers. We are impressed also by the large mural on the inside walls depicting points of interest and Winslow history.

The **Old Trails Museum** is one of our favorite stopping places on the road, as we always drop in to see what Janice is doing. Janice Griffith, the curator, is full of local information and "talks 66." There are interesting displays and occasional programs.

Standin' On A Corner Park is endearing. It doesn't sound like much. There is just a statue and a wonderful mural, but somehow it transcends these and takes on an engaging personality. Wander around, look at the names on the bricks that pave the park and "take it e-e-easy."

La Posada is the last of the great Harvey Houses. Built in 1930, it is an historic and architectural treasure, designed by the talented Mary Colter. Self-guided tours inside.

We enjoy historic walks and were delighted to discover that Winslow has a hidden treasure along First Street. Although it is hard to picture it now, First Street, adjacent to the railroad tracks, was the primary commercial street of Winslow, lined with business houses. This worked fine in the days of the horse and buggy, but broke down when the transcontinental automobile highway was run through town. There was not enough room between First Street and the tracks for a wide two-way street with curbs and gutters. So, the highway was located one block to the north, along Second Street, where it is today. For a while the old businesses on First Street held out, but soon an exodus to Second Street began. The owners left behind a row of the largest commercial buildings in Winslow, many of which were torn down or have burned down. A few remain. Take a stroll and see for yourself. Interesting.

Our research led us to the discovery that much the same thing happened in Holbrook on North and South Commercial, in Seligman on Railroad Avenue and in Kingman on Topeka Avenue.

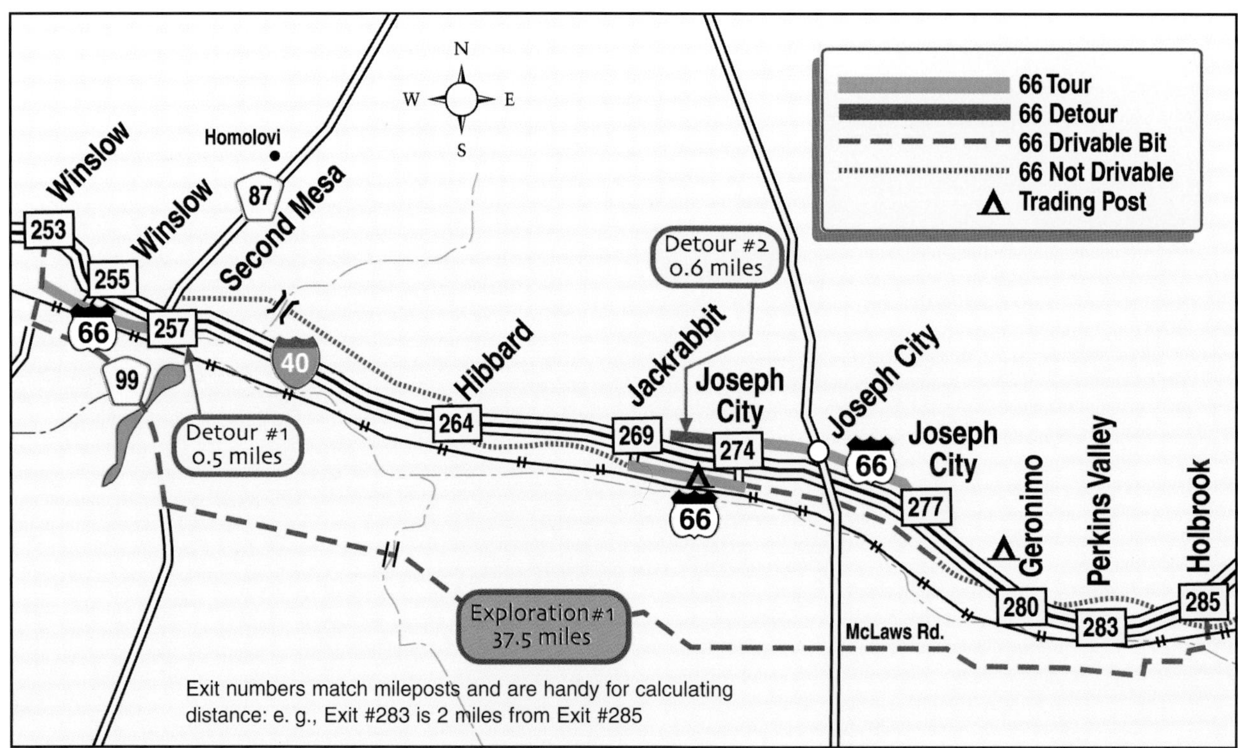

Tour 4-W Holbrook to Winslow pp. 18-19

Tour 10-E Winslow to Holbrook

Distance: 33.0 miles *53.0 km*
Highlights: Jack Rabbit Trading Post, Joseph City
Driving Time: 45 minutes

La Posada 1930—OP

Tour 10-E takes you from Winslow to Holbrook across the grasslands that characterize so much of northern Arizona. The design of our tour is to take you to the famous Jack Rabbit TP, and then through nearby Joseph City, an historic Mormon town founded in 1876. There is an optional stop at the Geronimo Trading Post to see the "World's Largest Petrified Log!"

Standin' on the Corner Park

START

0.0 miles *0.0 km* Second Street and Kinsley **Zero** point. (Standin' on the Corner Park). Drive east on Second Street, which is old 66.

La Posada

At 0.1 miles *0.16 km* you pass the famous La Posada (Right). This grand old building, designed by architect Mary Elizabeth Jane Colter, was finished in 1930, the showpiece of the Santa Fe Railroad's Harvey House system. Closed for years, it was reopened in 1995 and is in the process of restoration. It is worth a visit, and is a wonderful place to stay.

0.8 miles *1.3 km* There is a closed Whiting Bros. Service Station, in classic shape and colors (L). Photo stop?

1.3 miles *2.1 km* You are now leaving town. Don't take the I-40 entry. Continue east on old 66. It is a divided highway at first, and then merges down to a single road.

The famous Wigwam Motel is located in Holbrook

Little Colorado River Bridge

2.7 miles *4.3 km* You drive over the Little Colorado River (usually dry) on a bridge. The river parallels the road's path all the way to Holbrook but is mostly out of sight.

Exit #257—Second Mesa

3.4 miles *5.4 km* I-40 turnoff to Exit #257-Second Mesa.There is a short segment of Route 66 that can be driven east of here, see Detour #1. Exit #257 is also the access to Homolovi Ruins State Park. Until the fall of 2000 you could drive north and east of Exit #257 on old 66 to the west side of the Cottonwood Wash Bridge, but this is no longer possible as the Arizona State Highway Department has blocked the road. If you don't take either Detour #1 or Homolovi, get onto I-40 here headed east.

DETOUR #1
EXIT #257-Winslow S&E
Minnetonka Trading Post
0.5 mi. ***0.8 km*** **one-way**
Time 10 minutes

Zero where you meet the onramp onto I-40 at Exit #257. You will see a Dead End sign to the east. Go east anyway. At 0.2 miles *0.3 km* you will see the Minnetonka Trading Post (L). This was a classic Route 66 tourist operation, but it has changed in recent years and is now a bar and feed store. You might want to take a photo of the petrified wood facing on the front wall. Beyond Minnetonka, at 0.5 miles *0.8 km* old 66 paving ends at a Road Closed sign. It continues as a dirt road beyond the sign, but we rate it as not worth driving. Return to Exit #257-Second Mesa.

SIGHTSEEING #1
EXIT #257
Homolovi Ruins Park
Time 1 hour

At Exit #257-Second Mesa, **Zero** at the stop sign, drive over I-40 and continue driving straight (N) on Highway 87. At 1.6 miles *2.6 km* you will reach the entrance to Homolovi where you turn left to enter the park. Follow the signs to the Visitor Center. Homolovi is a State Park and you must pay an entrance fee. At the Visitor Center is a restroom, book store, and information. You can drive through the park and see various ruins which have been restored in this large deserted city of the ancients.

On I-40 east of Exit #257-Second Mesa you can see old undrivable 66 following a line of power poles to your left.

Exit #264—Hibbard Road

The north road, which used to go west to Cottonwood Wash bridge is now blocked by a locked gate. By taking Exit #264 and driving south and east, one can find two old alignments of 66, the earlier one—apparently never paved—running along close to the railroad track, and the newer one, which was paved, to the north. Both are just rough raised beds of interest only to diehard roadies, so we merely mention them without showing them as a Detour. East of Exit #264 old 66 crossed under I-40 and can be seen running along to the south. Beyond Exit #264 you can see culverts on old 66 to your right (S).

Exit #269—Jackrabbit Road

Trading Post, Gas

Coming up is a classic example of successful advertising gimmickry. The Jack Rabbit Trading Post was made famous by its large rabbit statue, which you can ride (How could you possibly pass up the chance?) and the "Here It Is!" signs. Take Exit #269. At the stop sign, **Zero** and turn right (S), then left (E). You will see the big "Here It Is!" signs. Follow them to the trading post, which is on your left. By all means stop and check it out and get your picture taken astride the rabbit.

Buckaroo Sherry tames the savage beast

After your visit to the Jack Rabbit TP, drive east on old 66, which runs very close to the railroad, on your right. Drive old 66 until you come to an on-ramp for I-40 at Exit #274-Joseph City at 4.7 miles *7.5 km*. Turn left (N) and drive over I-40. Follow the "Historic US 66" signs.

Joseph City

After you drive over I-40 at Exit #274-Joseph City, turn right (E) at the stop sign and follow the "Historic US 66" signs, through the center of town on Main Street. Only a couple of roadside businesses remain, but you can see the skeletons of the enterprises that were able to thrive here. As you leave town you will see the Old Fort Monument (L), worth a brief stop. East of here, you are forced back onto I-40. Be sure to follow the signs to take I-40 east.

All over the Joseph City area you can see the Cholla Power Plant, with its huge smokestacks. Joseph City residents sold their water rights to the electric company in 1960. The plant created sorely needed jobs for the residents, but it also sucked up underground water, dropping the water table so low that farming was abandoned.

Joseph City was the home of Western poet San Diego Rawson, a real Route 66 character. Rawson moved to Joseph City in the 1920s and built the trading post that later came to be known as Ella's Frontier. He sold trinkets to tourists and continued to write verse until he died, at which time ownership passed to Ella.

Bushman home in Joseph City

Exit #283—Perkins Valley Road (Golf Course)

Here old 66 shifts to the north side of I-40. There is a sign for "Holbrook City Limits" at this exit, but pass by this exit and take the next exit.

Exit #285-Holbrook/Show Low

Follow the "Historic US 66" signs into town. Old Route 66 (not drivable) goes off to the right, next to the railroad. You reach a stop sign where you turn right and drive into the main part of town, passing the classic Wigwam Motel (R). There is a stoplight at the junction of Navajo and Hopi. This was the heart of downtown in the days of the Mother Road and is the end of this tour.

DETOUR #2
EXIT #274-Joseph City
Route 66 Trading Posts
0.6 mi. *1.0 km* one-way
Time 10 minutes

Go into Joseph City following the Historic US 66 signs as above. When you reach the stop sign north of the overpass at Exit #274, **Zero** and turn left. You are now driving old 66. Drive about 0.5 miles *0.8 km* and you will see the site of Howdy Hank's Trading Post to your right, identified by its plywood tepee. Just past it on your left is the log cabin structure of Ella's Frontier. Ella used to advertise that hers was the oldest post on Route 66, but we think that it was not. Stop here, even though the paving continues, as it is uninteresting. Turn around and drive east through Joseph City.

Exit #280—Hunt Road/Geronimo Road (optional)

If you want to visit Geronimo TP, take Exit #280. You come to a stop sign. There is a piece of 66 to the right, on Hunt Road, but it is blocked within 0.25 miles *0.4 km* by Private Property. Not worth taking. Instead, turn left and visit Geronimo Trading Post by driving Geronimo Road. As you approach, you will see a white tepee on top of a red stone butte. You drive around to the other side of this butte and enter the trading post parking lot. There are some things worth seeing at Geronimo, particularly the very large pieces of petrified wood, one of them an upright 80-ton tree trunk, "The World's Largest Petrified Tree!" The main feature of this trading post is its collection of stones. They have everything from local petrified wood to rare specimens from distant places. The inside of the trading post has the usual tourist fare including rubber tomahawks, but they also have some genuine Indian crafts and lots and lots of stones. Geronimo is a dead end eastbound. When you leave, you must go back the way you came in and get back onto I-40 eastbound, taking the turn marked "Albuquerque." As you drive east, you will see bits of 66 to your right (S).

EXPLORATION #1
McLaws Road
37.5 mi. *60.0 km* one-way
Time 1 hour

This was the National Old Trails Road from 1913 until 1922, when it was rerouted to the north to the alignment that became Route 66. **Start**: 2nd St. and Kinsley in Winslow. Drive east one block, then turn right and drive under railroad. You are on Hwy. 87. At 1.2 mi. *1.9 km* turn left (E) on AZ 99, paved. At 7.5 mi. *12.0 km* turn left (E) on Territorial Road, unpaved. At 14.2 mi. *22.7 km* you reach the interesting 1913 Chevelon Creek Bridge, very scenic over a deep watery gorge. Get out and explore. At 26.6 mi. *42.5 km* you come to a stop sign at Obed Road. Go straight ahead onto the paving—it's all paved from here. At 29.5 mi. *47.2 km* you enter an area of ranch houses, where the highway is called McLaws Road. At 36.5 mi. *58.4 km* is a stop sign; turn right on Apache. At 36.7 mi. *58.7 km* is another stop sign; turn left on Hwy. 77 and cross the bridge over the Little Colorado into Holbrook. At 37.5 mi. *60.0 km* you are at the junction of Hopi and Navajo in downtown Holbrook, the end point, which is also the end point of Tour 10-E.

Holbrook Recommendations

Things to See:

The Museum in the Old Courthouse.

Places to Eat:

Mesa Italiana, 2318 E. Navajo, 524-6696. Good Italian food. Moderate.

Ms. Viv's Coffee Queen, 265 Navajo Blvd., 524-2757. Coffee bar, but also light lunches. Inexpensive.

Romo's Cafe, 121 W. Hopi, 524-2153. Mexican food.

Places to Stay:

Arizonian Best Western 2508 E. Navajo, 524-2611.

The Wigwam, 811 W. Hopi, 524-3048.

Holbrook Historic Walk

1. START Old Navajo County Courthouse—1898
Replaced in 1976, the old building is now home to the Navajo County Museum. The old jail is a must-see. In January 1900 a gallows was built, probably in front of the building, and George Smiley was "swung into eternity" before the gaze of Holbrook citizens. (See #9 for details).

2. Masonic Lodge—1916 (200 N. Navajo)
Still used by Holbrook's Chalcedony Lodge No. 6, chartered in 1887, the first Masonic Lodge in Arizona.

3. Campbell's Coffee House—1928 (110 N. Navajo)
Built by Chester B. Campbell, this building was a coffee house and then also the Greyhound Bus Station from 1947 until 1983. Campbell's menu specialty was the original Son-of-a-Bitch Stew.

4. J & J Trading Post—1910 (100 N. Navajo)
Not long ago a thriving trading post. A movie theater was operated during the 1920s at the east end of the building.

5. Blevins' House—ca. 1887 (216 Joy Nevin Ave.)
This was the site of the famous bloody shootout between Sheriff Commodore Perry Owens and the Blevins gang in 1887. The basic structure of the original cottage is still the same, although additions have been made to the back.

6. Historic Roads Monument. (216 Joy Nevin Ave.)
In front of the Blevins house you will find a small monument with a bronze plaque telling the story of the historic roads and trails which came through the area.

7. Santa Fe Depot—1882
Sitting quiet and abandoned, it is hard to realize that this depot was the railroad's major shipping point west of Albuquerque in its heyday.

8. Bucket of Blood Saloon—1888 (Bucket of Blood St.)
The saloon was one of the first rock structures built in Holbrook. It replaced a wood building destroyed by the fire of 1888, which wiped out the entire town. The notorious saloon was named for the violent brawls and the shootings that stained its floors as well as its reputation.

9. Wattron Drug Store—1888 (Bucket of Blood St.)
Located next to the Bucket of Blood, this drug store was owned and operated by Frank Wattron, one of the most interesting pioneers of Holbrook. While he was Sheriff he issued a flippant invitation to a hanging that scandalized the nation: "You are hereby cordially invited to attend the hanging of one George Smiley, Murderer. His soul will be swung into eternity on December 8, 1899, at 2 o'clock p. m., sharp. The latest improved methods in the art of scientific strangulation will be employed and everything possible will be done to make the surroundings cheerful and the execution a success."

10. ACMI Store—1888 (Bucket of Blood St.)
Located only two doors west of the Bucket of Blood, this store was founded by devout Mormon settlers in 1881 at the original Holbrook, then moved to Woodruff in 1882, and moved again to this site after the big fire of 1888. The counterpart of the famous ZCMI in Salt Lake City, the ACMI was a cooperative store that served both Mormons and non-Mormons in the area.

11. A&B Schuster Store—ca. 1890 (Bucket of Blood St.)
The Schusters were twin brothers who came to the West from Germany and made a name for themselves with their Holbrook store.

This row of buildings, from the Bucket of Blood to Schuster's, was the heart of old Holbrook. Look to the west from here and you can visualize the row of buildings that once flanked this busy and prosperous area. In 1929 the roads in town were altered to accommodate Route 66, which was located one block north of the tracks. When the road construction was finished, the commercial district shifted to the new highway and the old commercial corridor became a forgotten corner.

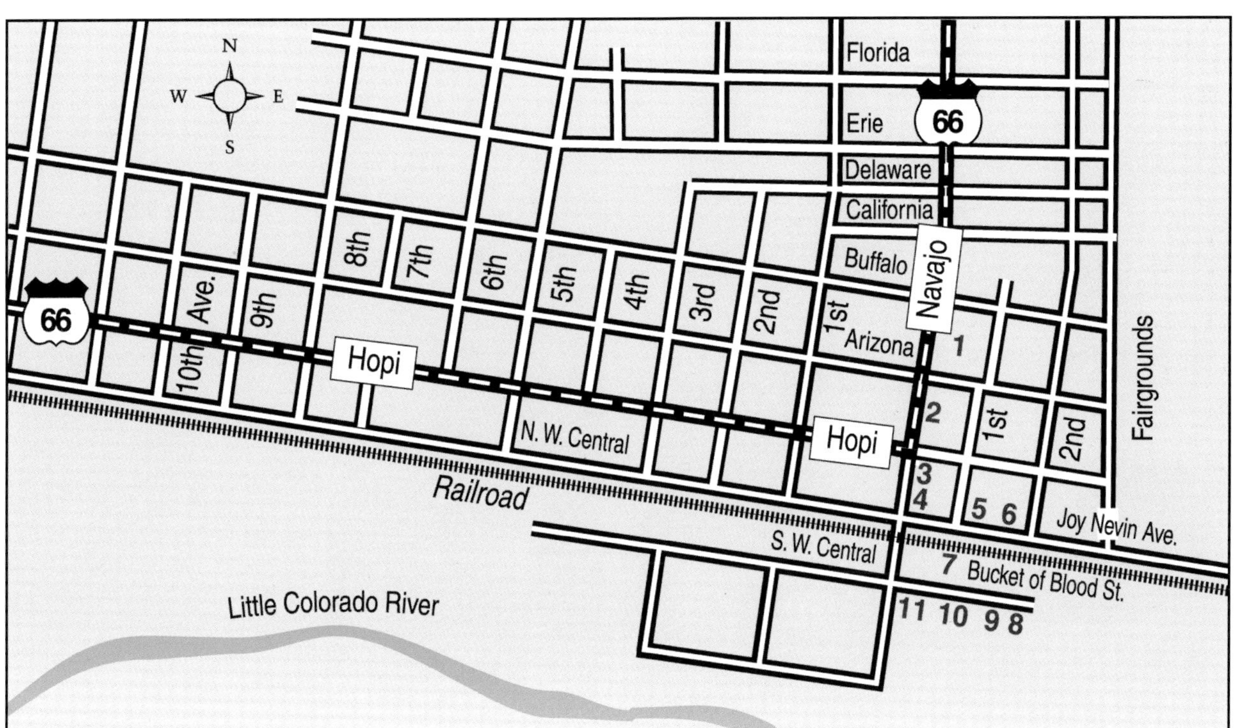

Eastbound>

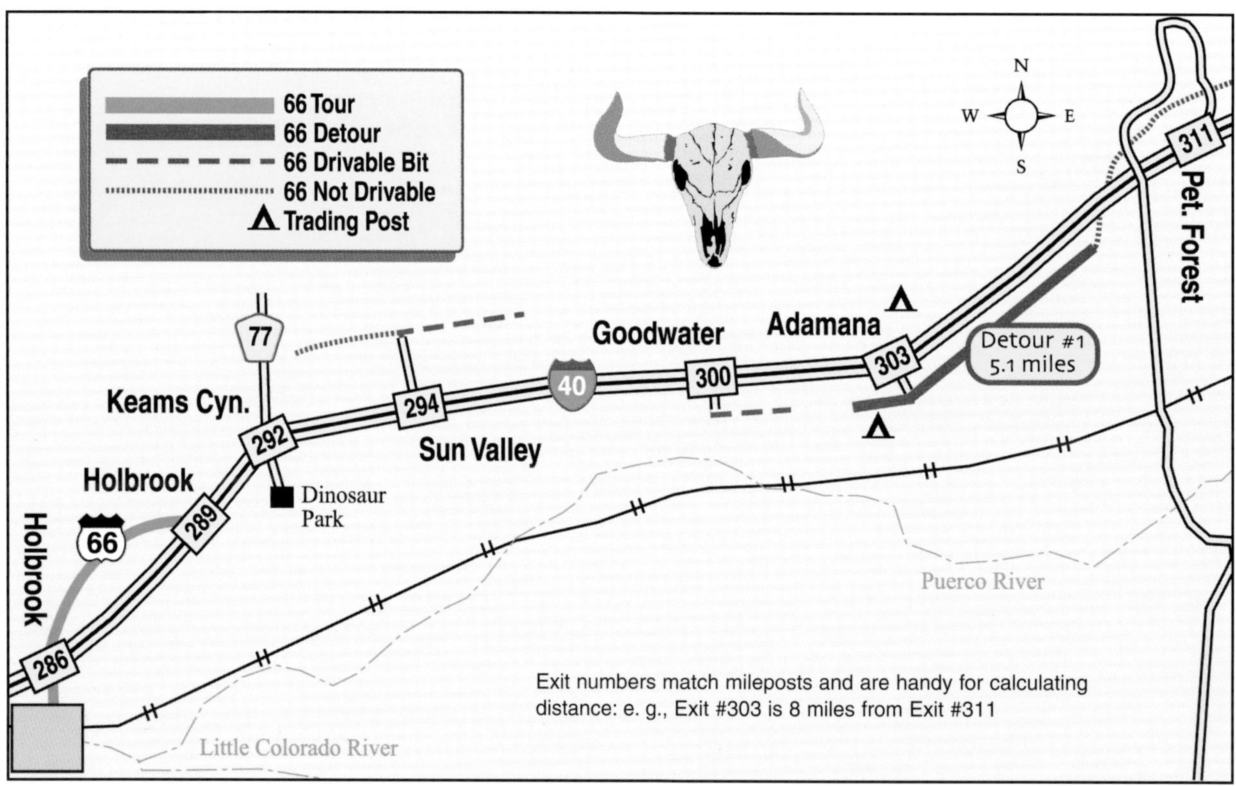

Tour 3-W Petrified Forest to Holbrook pp. 16-17

Tour 11-E Holbrook to Petrified Forest

Distance: 25.0 miles *40.0 km* (via I-40), 18.3 miles *29.3 km* (via Highway 180)
Highlights: Dinosaur Park, Petrified Forest National Park
Driving Time: 40 minutes

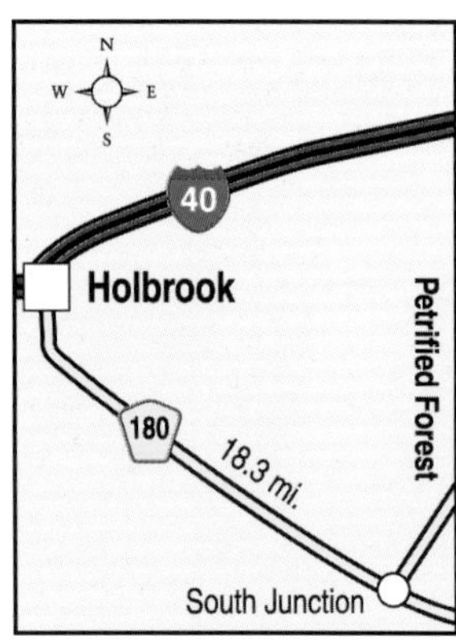

Tour 11-E is highlighted by the Petrified Forest. If you want to see it, the smart way is to take the southern route on Highway 180 instead I-40. Turn south on Navajo Blvd. and follow it for 0.7 miles *1.1 km* to Hwy. 180. Turn left and on 180 drive to the 18.3 mile *29.3 km* point, the south junction of the road into the Petrified Forest. *If you drive I-40 then see below.*

Navajo & Hopi Streets (start: if driving I-40)

START

0.0 miles *0.0 km* Intersection of Navajo and Hopi Streets, the **Zero** point. Turn left (N) on Navajo and drive out of town.

0.7 miles *1.1 km* Don't take the I-40 entrance to Exit #286 found here. Keep going up the hill, straight. You will see Historic US 66 signs along here. You climb up onto a hilltop known as "The Mesa". In the days of 66 this was out of town, with almost no development on top.

3.2 miles *5.1 km* You reach the I-40 approach to Exit #289. Take it, following the signs to Albuquerque, emerging onto the freeway on a high tableland. Overall the landscape is of scanty grasslands. You will see many petrified trees along the righthand side of the road. These are not natural, but were placed there as a tourist attraction by the operators of Dinosaur Park, coming up at Exit #292. Note the colored soils you will see down to your right, the purples and blues of the Painted Desert at MP 291.7.

Exit #292—Keams Canyon/Highway 77

This is where you exit to see the business that advertises itself three ways: (1) International Petrified Forest, (2) Dinosaur Park, and (3) Museum of the Americas. If one of these doesn't appeal to you, then another one will. This is a very modern attraction, opened in 1999, but is the kind of experience 66 travelers would have been glad to enjoy. We sampled it and are happy to report that it is something really worth seeing. The collection of ancient Indian pottery in the museum is outstanding.

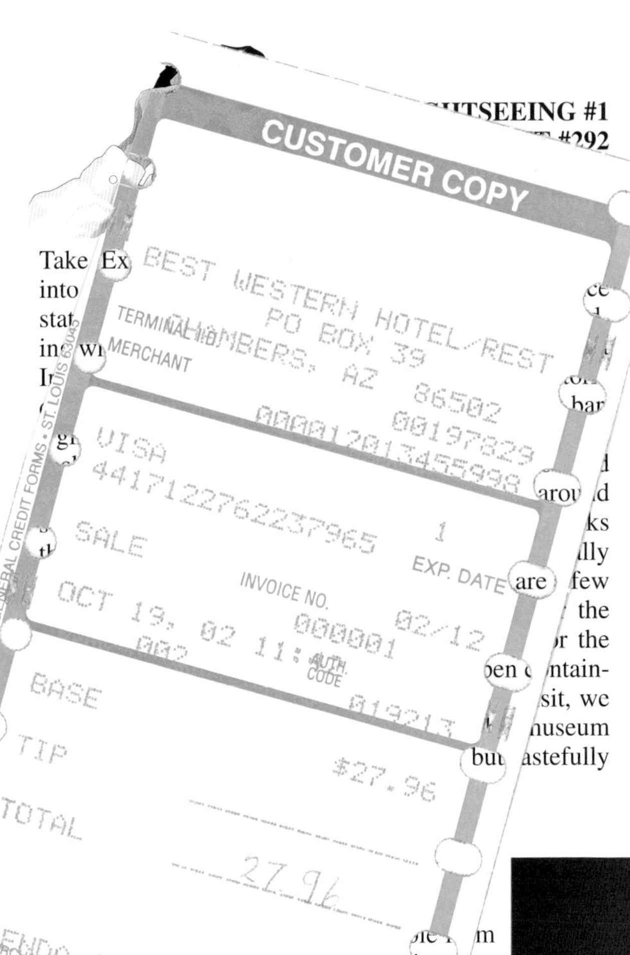
CUSTOMER COPY

BEST WESTERN HOTEL/REST
PO BOX 39
CHAMBERS, AZ 86502

TERMINAL ID 00197829
MERCHANT 000012013455998

VISA
4417122762237965
SALE 1
EXP. DATE 02/12
INVOICE NO. 000001
OCT 19, 02 11:
002
AUTH. CODE 019213

BASE $27.96
TIP
TOTAL 27.96

BRENDA J POWELL
X PURCHASER SIGN HERE B J Powell

Cardholder acknowledges receipt of goods and/or service in the amount of the Total shown hereon and agrees to perform the obligations set forth in the Cardholder's agreement with the issuer.

GENERAL CREDIT FORMS • ST. LOUIS
3 PART RECEIPT
5.5531CF

DETOUR #1
EXIT #303-Adamana
S&E
Route 66
5.1 mi. *8.2 km* one-way
Time 20 minutes

At Exit #303-Adamana, from the stop sign, **Zero** and turn right, and then left on the frontage road, which is Route 66. It runs along uneventfully for 5.1 miles *8.2 km* parallel to I-40 to a point where the paving ends. Here a gravel road turns sharply to the south, going to Adamana (access is blocked, don't try it). Rocky's Old Stage Station, a Route 66 roadside business, looking like a junkyard, is straight ahead. Back track to I-40 and head east.

EXIT #303—Adamana
Trading Post, Rock Shop, Old Bridge

To get to the Painted Desert Indian Center, a trading post, take Exit #303-Adamana and turn right at the stop sign, then turn right (W) again. The post is 0.1 miles *0.16 km* down the road and has some good merchandise, including dead pawn. 0.2 miles *0.3 km* farther west you will see (but can't drive) the old 66 bridge across Big Lithodendron Wash. Return to Exit #303. On the north side of the exit is Stewart's Petrified Wood. It's like one of the old-time 66 attractions. You drive up a winding road to reach it. The owners have tried every advertising gimmick, including plastic dinosaurs, old cars, mannequins, signs—even the old ploy of parking junk cars in front to make you think that it has visitors. We like the inside of the store, which is funky and very personal, a far cry from the formula places east on I-40. They sell petrified wood in all shapes and sizes if you are interested in having a souvenir. Return to Exit #303 and go east on I-40 or take Detour #1.

Eastbound>

Exit #311—Petrified Forest

Savvy eastbound travelers take Highway 180 from Holbrook and enter the Park from the south, then drive north through the Park. If you enter from Exit #311 for the park tour, you have to drive back through the park for 26.3 miles *42.1 km* to return to I-40. See our map on the next page for the south-north drive.

The old Navajo County Courthouse in Holbrook, now home of a museum

The Petrified Forest National Park—South to North

For the North to South tour, see pp. 14-15

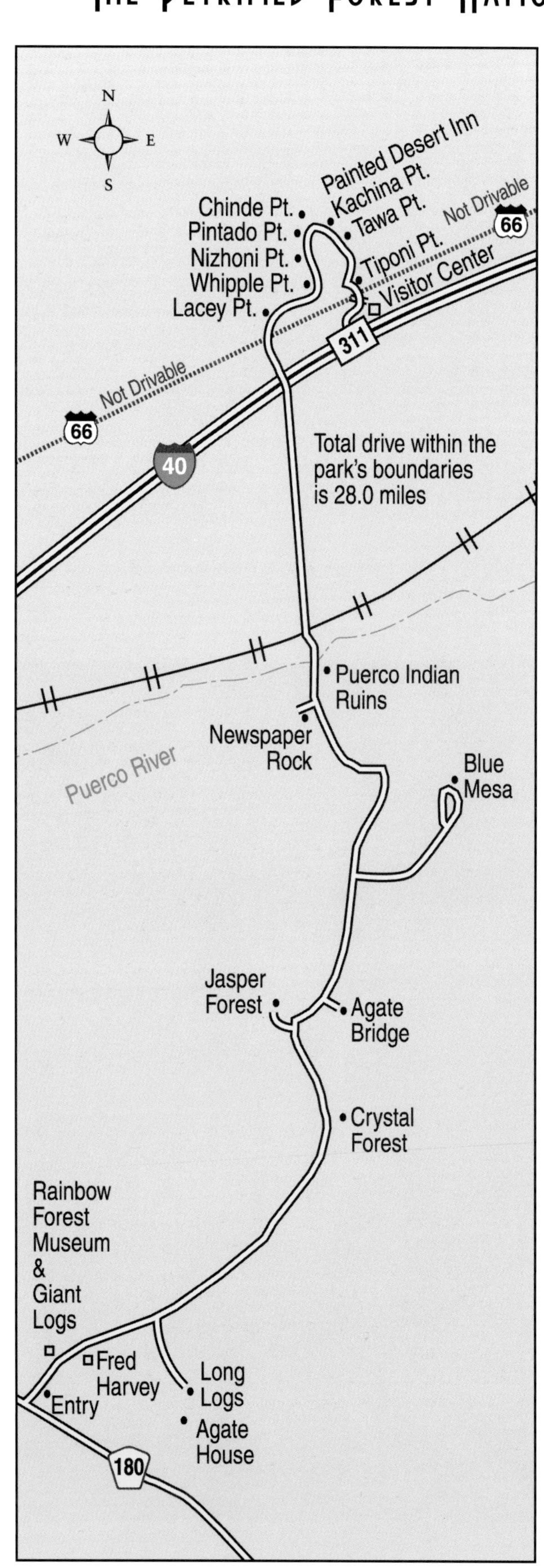

Distance: 28.0 miles *44.8 km.* (This is the distance within the park boundaries, and is used by the Park Service).

Time: Half a day

The Petrified Forest is not to be missed. Be sure to allow enough time to see and enjoy it. How much time do you need? We think half a day. We like to get out of our car and hike at places in the park but some travelers will be content to settle for what they can see from the windows of their vehicles. Hours are 7am-7pm Summer, and 8 am-5 pm Winter MST. See www.nps.gov/pefo/

If you follow our directions, you will enter the park from the south, into the Rainbow Forest. In the early years of automobiling this was the only auto entrance. **Zero** at the turn from Highway 180. Just off Highway 180 you will find two privately owned businesses. Turn left and drive north 0.7 miles *1.1 km* to the entrance station, where you will have to pay a fee. Then you will begin the drive northward through the park.

0.0 mi. *0.0 km* **Entrance Station—Zero again**

1.6 mi *2.6 km* **Rainbow Forest Museum** & **Giant Logs**. The museum is run by the Park Service and is worth a stop. In addition to the museum it contains a book shop and restrooms. You can get information from the rangers. Behind the museum is the 0.4 mi *0.6 km* long Giant Logs hiking trail, which is fun. Recommended.

Just north of the museum on the right is the **Fred Harvey Curio Shop and Cafe**.

1.8 mi *2.9 km* **Long Logs** and **Agate House** to the right. 0.25 mi *0.4 km* to parking lot. There is a good paved 0.5 mi. *0.8 km* hiking trail through Long Logs with a 0.75 mi *1.2 km* branch going to Agate House. Recommended.

7.5 mi *12.0 km* **Crystal Forest** to your right. A foot trail of 0.75 mi *1.2 km* winds around this beautiful forest. Lots of color. Lots of wood. Easy walk. Recommended.

9.3 mi *14.9 km* **Jasper Forest**, left. Access road is 0.5 mi *0.8 km*. You look off a cliff edge onto a wood-covered valley. This was once one of the most famous sights in the park but theft has damaged it severely. Skip this if your time is limited.

10.0 mi *16.0 km* **Agate Bridge**, right, a favorite. A paved road takes you to a high point where you will find the bridge after a short walk. There is a toilet at the site.

12.1 mi *19.4 km* **Blue Mesa**, right. If you are pressed for time, bypass this. A 3.5 mi *5.6 km* access road takes you to the top of a mesa to see blue and white haystacks and some petrified wood. There is a 1.0 mi *1.6 km* hiking trail.

15.9 mi *25.4 km* **Newspaper Rock**, left. Drive 0.25 mi *0.5 km* to parking area and make a short walk. Formerly one could hike down a trail to see and touch this rock but so much damage was done that park officials closed the

Agate Bridge

trail. Now you are limited to looking at it through a telescope.

16.7 mi *26.7 km* **Puerco Pueblo Indian Ruins**, right. The paved trail through the ruins is 0.3 mi *0.5 km* long. There are about 100 rooms, many unexcavated. It was inhabited from 1250-1380. There are some petroglyph panels on the site. For the comfort of visitors there is also a toilet here.

21.8 mi *34.9 km* You drive over the **I-40 Overpass**.

You have now left the Petrified Forest area and have entered the **Painted Desert** portion of the park.

22.1 mi *35.4 km* You will see the old alignment of **Route 66** to your left and right here, lined by power poles. No asphalt remains. You can stand here and look in both directions and see where the road ran across the park.

23.1 mi *37.0 km* **Lacey Point**, left. The first Painted Desert viewpoint. No walking necessary.

23.4 mi *37.4 km* **Whipple Point**, left. No walk needed.

23.6 mi *37.8 km* **Nizhoni** ("beautiful" in Navajo) **Point**, left. No walking needed.

24.8 mi *39.7 km* **Pintado Point**, left. Requires a short walk from the parking area. Broad panoramic views, varied colors.

25.5 mi *40.8 km* **Chinde** ("ghost" in Navajo) **Point**, left. You must drive 0.4 mi *0.6 km* to the viewpoint, where there are picnic tables and a toilet. The view is over the Black Forest.

25.6 mi *41.0 km* **Painted Desert Inn**, left. The inn was built by H. P. Lore in 1924, as Stone Tree House, a tourist attraction. The United States Government bought the property in 1935 and remodeled it using CCC labor from 1937-1941. The government turned the operation of the inn over to a concessionaire. The inn was closed 1942-1947 due to the war. In 1947 the Fred Harvey Company took over the concession and brought its famous architect, Mary Colter, out of retirement to decorate the place, which was finished in 1948. Ms. Colter did her usual superb job. The inn was operated as a hotel until closed in 1963. Though scheduled for demolition in 1975, supporters saved it. Made a National Historic Landmark in 1987, it is now a fine place to visit, to admire the architecture, the history and the views from Kachina Point, where it is situated. There is a hiking trail going down onto the floor of the Painted Desert from the inn. As you walk out to the Kachina Viewpoint, you will find a Wilderness sign pointing to the trailhead. The trail goes to the bottom of the valley. This is not a "tame" trail like the ones you have found so far. It requires planning and preparedness.

26.1 mi *41.8 km* **Tawa Point** (L). Another good Painted Desert lookout point. It does not require walking. The views are wonderful.

26.8 mi *42.9 km* **Tiponi Point** (L). The last of the Painted Desert lookout points.

27.1 mi *43.4 km* You will see an unpaved road, left, which is barred to traffic. This is **Route 66**, which followed this alignment from the 1920s until 1961.

27.5 mi *44.0 km* **Visitor Center**, left. Here are two buildings. In the first one you will meet there is a Fred Harvey gas station and convenience market. On the back side of the building is a cafeteria and gift shop. In the second building there is an information desk, gift shop, bookstore, museum and toilets. The selection of food here is much broader and better than the Fred Harvey Rainbow Forest facility at the south end of the park.

From the Visitor Center, you will drive 0.5 miles *0.8 km* south to **Exit #311-Petrified Forest** and follow the signs on the interchange to get onto I-40.

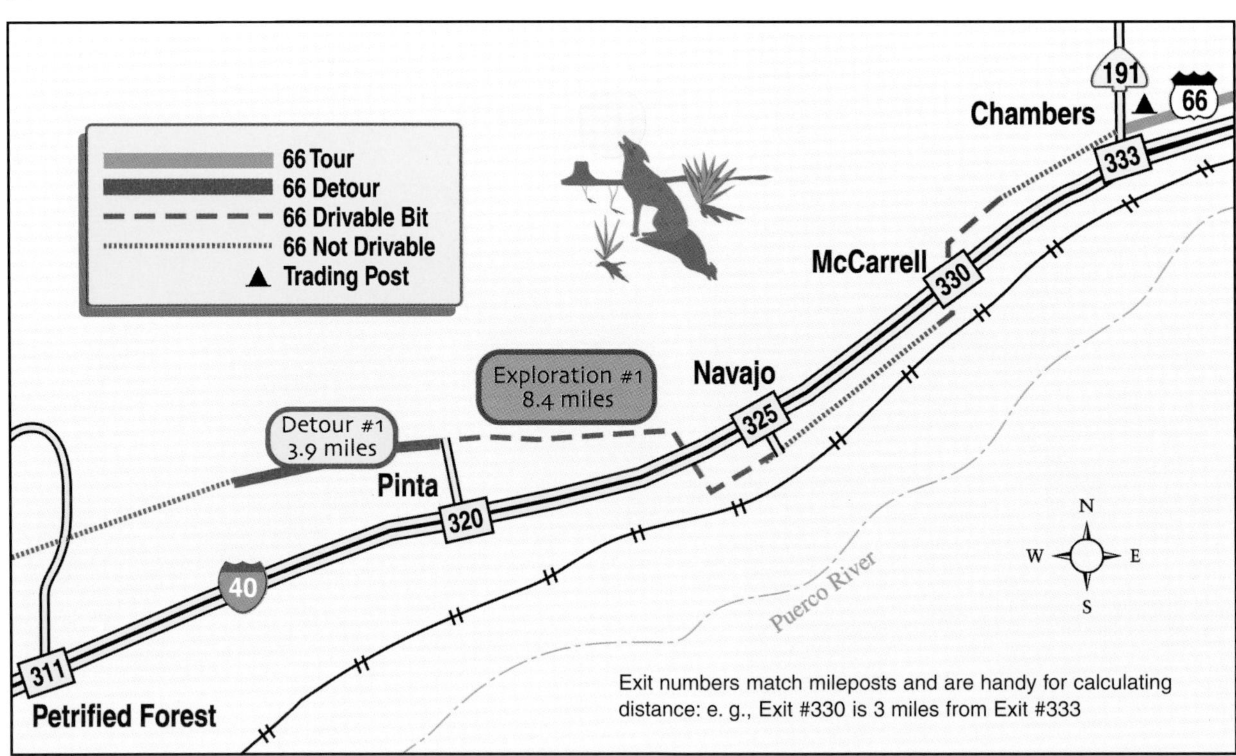

Tour 2-W Chambers to Petrified Forest pp. 12-13

Tour 12-E Petrified Forest to Chambers

Distance: 22.0 miles *35.2 km*

Highlights: Rangelands, Navajo Indian country

Driving Time: 45 minutes

Tom of Ganado—OP

Tour 12-E begins at the Petrified Forest National Park. You will drive easterly from here through a broad flat landscape of thin grasses where cattle roam. In the distance are mysterious mesas, colorful cliffs and forbidding canyons, the ancestral homes of the Hopi and Navajo tribes. Except for the scenery there isn't much of interest on this particular drive.

START

Petrified Forest

If you made the Petrified Forest, tour from north to south, you end it in the south part of the park, some 26.3 miles *42.1 km* from I-40. There is no southern road for eastbound travelers to take, and you will have no choice but to travel north back to Exit #311-Petrified Forest, to get onto I-40 eastbound. If you followed our recommended route, taking Highway 180 from Holbrook and entering the Petrified Forest at the south end and then traveled north through the Park, you will end the Petrified Forest tour at the north end of the Park where you get onto I-40.

EXIT #320—Pinta

No gas, No Food, No Lodging

Detour #1 is located here, for any car. Exploration #1 is also available, but is only for high-clearance vehicles.

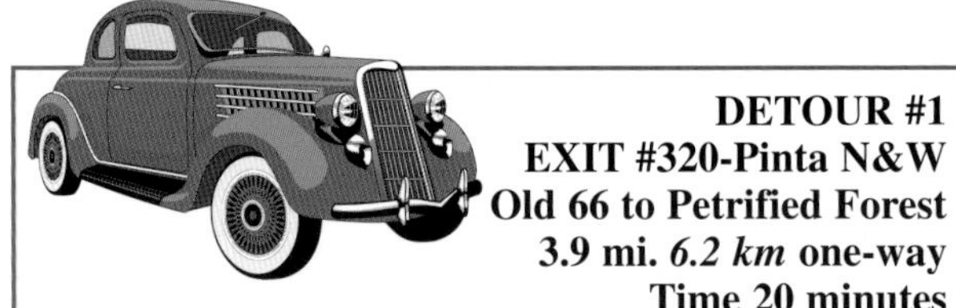

DETOUR #1
EXIT #320-Pinta N&W
Old 66 to Petrified Forest
3.9 mi. *6.2 km* one-way
Time 20 minutes

Take Exit #320-Pinta. **Zero** at the stop sign, turn left, go over I-40 and take the offramp downhill to your right. Ignore the Dead End sign. Where the paving ends don't take the straight dirt road to the left just beyond, stay on the main dirt road, going uphill. At 1.3 miles *2.1 km* you intersect old 66. Turn left and drive on the old paving. At about 3.9 miles *6.2 km* you will find the remains of the Painted Desert Trading Post (R) overlooking the valley of the Dead River. Very scenic for photos. Just west of this is an old but still drivable bridge, a good place to stop. You can drive over the bridge and go another 2.4 miles *3.8 km* west of the bridge, but the road is bad and is blocked at the boundary fence for the Petrified Forest. Return the way you came in. At a point 2.6 miles *4.2 km* from the ruins, high-clearance vehicles can begin Exploration #1.

EXPLORATION #1
EXIT #320-Pinta N&E
Old Route 66
8.4 mi. ***13.4 km*** **one-way**
Time 25 minutes

Take Exit #320-Pinta. **Zero** at the stop sign, turn left, go over I-40 and take the offramp that curves downhill (R). Ignore the Dead End sign. Follow the curving road west. The paving ends. Don't take the straight dirt road to the left, but stay on the main dirt road. At 1.3 miles *2.1 km* you will intersect old 66. Turn right. You are on old paving, worn but OK. We drove at 40 mph. At 2.6 miles *4.2 km* is a cattle guard at a wire fence signed "Wild Life Sanctuary." Go through the gate, which is usually open. The road is not so good east of the gate, so one must drive more slowly. At 3.7 miles *5.9 km* the road curves to the right and starts downhill toward I-40. At 4.2 miles *6.7 km* is a gate at a barbed wire fence where you leave the sanctuary. At 4.8 miles *7.7 km* is a washout leaving just enough roadway for a car to pass over it. There is an old box culvert here but it is obviously inadequate to deal with the flash floods which hit the area periodically. The road is bad here with scary crumbling banks. At 5.2 miles *8.3 km* is another repaired washout. At 5.6 miles *9.0 km* the paving disappears and the road becomes sandy. You can see that 66 went toward I-40 at an angle, which you can't drive. At 5.9 miles *9.4 km* you drive through a tunnel under I-40. On the other side turn left on the gravel road heading east, a good road, marked Apache County 7385. It is old 66. The Puerco River and railroad are to your right (S). At 8.0 miles *12.8 km* is a crossroads. Turn left (N) on the paved road. There are several homes in this area. At 8.4 miles *13.4 km* is a stop sign. Turn right (E) to get onto I-40 at Exit #325-Navajo. There is an historic marker telling the story of the 1863 governmental party which formally created the Arizona territory to your right at the base of the on-ramp.

EXIT #325—Navajo
Gas, Food

There isn't much to see at Navajo except for a gas station and a few homes. Rittenhouse described it having a population of 52, with Marty's Trading Post, a cafe and five tourist cabins. Navajo is an historic site, for at nearby Navajo Springs a key event in Arizona history took place. In 1863 during the depths of the Civil War, New Mexico was one giant territory. President Lincoln thought it wise to split it and create Arizona. He picked a governor and territorial officials and sent them to Arizona to establish a new government. On December 29, 1863 the party, including the Governor, John Goodwin, camped at Navajo Springs, a place that was definitely in Arizona, so they proceeded to organize the government and move on to Prescott, the capital. Maps show that there is a marker at the springs, some 3.5 miles *5.6 km* SE of Exit #325. In May 2000 we tried to drive to the site and found the gate to the road locked so that it cannot be visited.

Abandoned car on the bank of the Dead River

EXIT #330—McCarrell
No gas, No food, No lodging

There are two drivable bits of Route 66 from this exit but they are very short and uninteresting, for die-hard roadies only.

EXIT #333—Chambers
Food, Gas, Trading Posts

Chambers is a little community with its own post office, but is not a town. There is a motel and cafe, The Chieftan Inn, on the south side of I-40. We stayed there and the room was good. The food in the cafe was OK. At a point 0.6 miles *1.0 km* north from I-40 on the right (E) side of Highway 191, there is a trading post, with a separate gallery. This is also a gas station and convenience market.

This is the end of this tour.

Decoy Cars

Many of the trading post operators used a ploy: they parked a couple of their own cars in front of their establishments and left them there permanently, the idea being that travelers would be more likely to patronize a place where they thought there were already other customers present, a sort of Join the Bandwagon effect. As time went by, some of these decoys developed flat tires, cracked windows, etc. and looked pretty ugly, more likely to repel customers than to attract them.

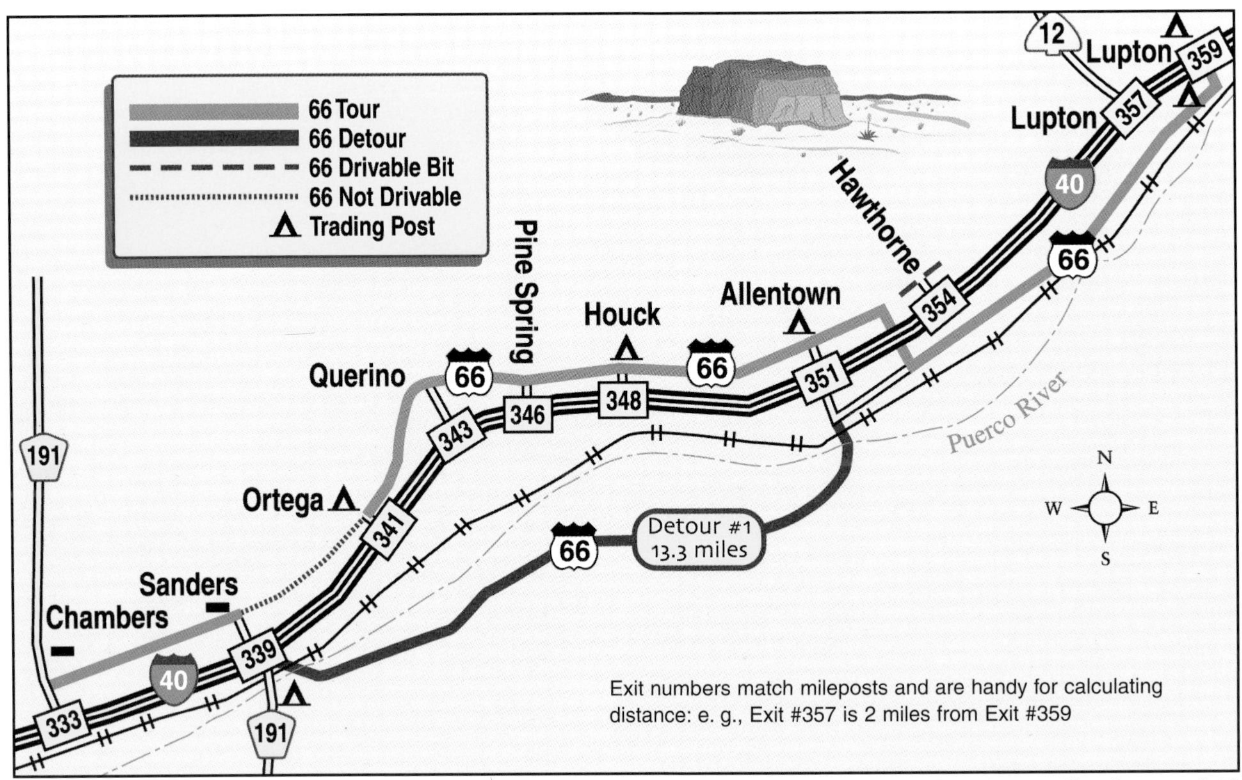

Tour 1-W New Mexico State Line to Chambers pp. 8-11

Tour 13-E Chambers to New Mexico State Line

Distance: 26.7 miles *42.7 km*
Highlights: Sanders Diner, Outstanding Trading Post, Arizona State Line
Driving Time: 1 hour

Old Roadside Sign

Tour 13-E takes you into Navajo Indian homeland. The main body of the immensely large Navajo Reservation lies to the north of the highway, although pockets of it are sprinkled around to the south. East of Sanders you will actually travel through the reservation. For over a hundred years trading posts have been an important fact of Navajo life and you will find several of them along the road.

START

EXIT #333—Chambers

Zero at Exit #333-Chambers.

0.0 miles *0.0 km* Exit #333. Take the exit, **Zero** at the stop sign, turn left and drive over I-40. At 0.5 miles *0.8 km* turn right and drive on paved Apache County 7060, which is Route 66. You will now enjoy a nice 6.2 mile *9.9 km* stretch of Mother Road. This fine old segment of Route 66 runs alongside old garages and a few homes, ending at a stop sign at the community of Sanders. Most drivers will want to re-enter I-40 here, but an alternative is to visit Sanders.

Old-Style trading post at Chambers, over sixty years ago—OP

EXIT #339—Sanders

Gas, Food (Classic Diner), Outstanding Trading Post

Sanders is one of those little northern Arizona communities that started as a trading post. Today it is an educational center for the Navajo Nation for children living on this part of the reservation. The largest part of the reservation lies to the north of I-40 but from Sanders east to the state line, the road goes through the reservation. There are three large schools here. For the Route 66 traveler, there is a great old Valentine diner, an appealing trading post and Detour #1.

66 Diner. You will enter Sanders on the north side of I-40 facing one of the schools. Turn right at the stop sign and drive over I-40. You will then drive over two bridges. When you come to the end of the last bridge, take the first paved street to the left and drive east one block, turning right on the paved street past the post office. The 66 Diner is on your left in the next block. As you enter the diner you will see what appear to be a mail slot and a mail box on the inside wall. These were part of the Valentine system and were actually strongboxes into which the day's receipts were deposited. The food here is good and the portions very large. We were astonished by the wide-ranging variety of items on the menus.

Burnham TP. From the diner drive south one block to a stop sign. Turn right and drive another block, where you will intersect Highway 191, which runs to St. Johns and other points. There are several businesses on the sides of Highway 191. Turn left and drive about 100 yards (*30 m*) to the R. B. Burnham & Co. Trading Post, on your left. The Burnham family is now in its fourth generation of traders. When you enter the store it seems that it is only a convenience market for the local Navajos. You will find some interesting goods in stock, including the largest selection of wool skeins we have seen anywhere. They also have weaving tools. But the real treasure is in the back room, which you must have permission to enter. Inside you will find real Navajo arts and crafts, authentic beautiful goods. This is the place to buy something that is really good with confidence that you are getting high quality merchandise.

DETOUR #1
EXIT #339-Sanders S&E
Pre-1930 Route 66
13.3 mi. *21.3 km* one-way
Time 25 minutes

This detour takes you along the road that was the alignment of 66 until December 1930 when the road over Querino Canyon was opened, made possible by the construction of the Querino Canyon bridge, which you will see if you take the blue-line tour. **Zero** at the stop sign. Turn right and drive over the I-40 bridge at Exit #339. Next, drive over the railroad bridge. Then turn left at the south end of the railroad bridge and drive over the Rio Puerco on the old iron bridge with yellow rails. As you exit the old bridge you come to a V fork. Turn left on the major road, heading east. It is wide and graded but unsurfaced. There are quite a few homes to the south, along the right hand side of the road. They seem rather new, since the 1980s. At 2.0 miles *3.2 km* there is a V fork. Turn left on Apache County #7240, a maintained dirt road. There are few homes from now on. At 12.5 miles *20.0 km* you reach a T junction. Turn left and drive over the new bridge. The 1923 bridge is just a few yards away, to your right and is literally falling apart. It is scenic, so haul out the camera. At 12.8 miles *20.5 km,* on the other side of the bridge, you drive over the railroad tracks and the roadway becomes paved. At 13.3 miles *21.3 km* you reach I-40 at Exit #351-Allentown. Turn right onto I-40 eastbound.

Eastbound>

When you drive out of Burnham's, turn right and head back to I-40 on Highway 191. Across the highway and closer to I-40 there is a gas station, inside of which is a Taco Bell Express, which serves pretty good food. When you reach the freeway, get onto it heading east.

EXIT #341—Ortega

We include what we call our **Blue-line Tour** here, named for the blue line on the map on page 96. If you like driving backroads and experiencing the oldest parts of Route 66 in this area, you will enjoy this trip, which takes you all the way to Lupton. From Exit #341, at the stop sign, turn left and go across I-40, **Zero**, then turn right on the frontage road. This is paved for a short distance, and then becomes unpaved where it turns uphill. Don't worry about the condition of the road unless it is muddy. When dry, it is fine. You drive up on top of a mesa where the road levels out and at 2.7 miles *4.3 km* reach the scenic Querino Canyon Bridge. Stop for photos if you wish. Continue east on this 1930 road. Just across the bridge (L) are the ruins of the old Querino Trading Post. Beyond that, where a sideroad comes in from your left, at 3.2 miles *5.1 km* is the new Querino Trading Post, which caters to Navajos rather than tourists, and is an interesting visit. You will come down hill past a church (L) and pick up paving again at 5.1 miles *8.2 km* at Exit #346-Pine Springs, where there is only an access road.

EXIT #346—Pine Springs

Pass by this Exit.

Blue-line Tour. Stay on the frontage road at Pine Springs and drive it to Houck at 6.9 miles *11.0 km*, where the Fort Courage Trading Post is located.

EXIT #348—Houck

Food, Trading Post

Houck (pronounced "Howk" not "Hoke") is a historic spot. James Houck established a trading post here in 1877 making it one of the oldest on Route 66. Today it is the site of Fort Courage, a big modern trading post, the main feature of which is a replica of the fort seen in the old TV series *F-Troop*. The series was not filmed here. We rate the goods in the trading post as typical tourist fare. There is also a convenience market and a post office. In a separate building are a restaurant and gas station. Guests used to be able to climb the tower, but it is now closed. **Blue-**

1923 Allentown Bridge ruins—Detour #1

Old style Navajo family—OP

line Tour: From Houck continue to drive the northside frontage road, which is Route 66, to the east, to reach Allentown at 10.0 miles *16.0 km*.

EXIT #351—Allentown Rd.

Food, Trading Post

Allentown is not a town, just a trading post site. You will find two trading posts here, the largest one on I-40 in Arizona called Indian City and a small one called Chee's. Indian City is two-stories high and very modern. Inside is a Taco Bell Express and a fountain, with an eating area. The ground floor contains typical tourist goods, and there is an upstairs gallery, but we found its merchandise to be typical tourist fare too. Chee's little place has three parts, a curio store with typical tourist stock, a rock shop and a book store.

Blue-line Tour: East of Allentown, keep driving the frontage road, a part that we really enjoy, as it winds and dips over hills and into washes. East of Allentown the road goes to a double tunnel at 12.4 miles *19.8 km*. Turn right and drive through one of the tunnels under I-40. Turn left on the other side and drive the frontage road you will find there. This is a 1950s edition of Route 66, wider and smoother, and it will take you all the way to the Lupton underpass at 18.0 miles *28.8 km*.

I-40 Drivers: From Allentown you are only about 8.0 miles *12.8 km* from the New Mexico State Line. You have two choices for heading east. The easier choice but less interesting one is to get onto I-40 eastbound. The choice we recommend and have designed for Tour 13-E is at Exit #351-Allentown; turn right at the stop sign, then turn left (E) and drive the frontage road. This way you will drive into the border area on Route 66. There is another of those little settlements that look like a town on a map but aren't, called Lupton, at the border.

EXIT #359—Lupton—End of Tour

Food, Gas, Trading Posts

If you are approaching Exit #359 on I-40 then take the exit and turn left from the stop sign. If you have followed the tour and are approaching it from the frontage road, then you will come to an underpass at Exit #359. To your left here is a trading post, Ortega's Indian Market, a dome with a sign on top. It sells typical tourist fare. Beyond this trading post you can turn left and drive under I-40 to get to the group of trading posts on the other side, against the red cliffs. At the turn you will see an example of true roadside kitsch, the life-sized plastic animals perched on the cliffs above the first trading post. You will turn right to cruise along the row of trading posts. The one with the plastic animals is John Yellowhorse's group of buildings, next is Chaparral, third is Tepee Trading Post and finally there is Fort Yellowhorse, slightly over the line in New Mexico, in front of a cave. The Arizona-New Mexico state line runs through the Ft. Yellowhorse store and is painted on the floor. All of these trading posts sell typical tourist fare. Speedy's Truck Stop has gasoline and the only food at Lupton as the Tepee Trading Post has closed its cafe.

You have now reached the end of Route 66 in Arizona.

The Arizona-New Mexico Border in the 1950s—OP

The Las Vegas Connection

Many visitors come into Arizona from Las Vegas, so we have field-tested this trip. It is about 105 miles *168 km* from Las Vegas to Kingman, with a possible stop at Hoover Dam.

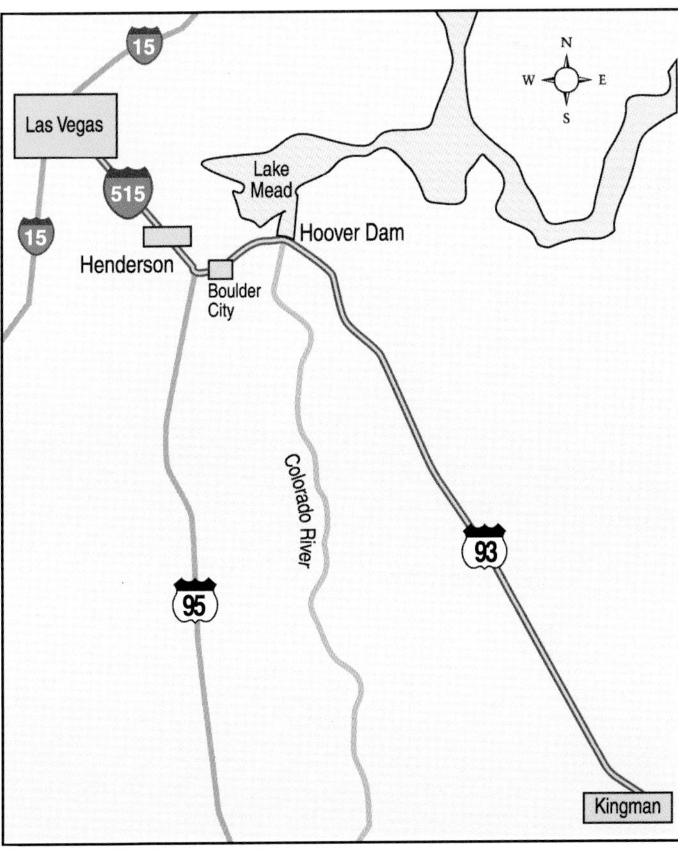

Leaving Las Vegas:
Starting from The Strip, take either Flamingo or Tropicana east for about 5.0 miles *8.0 km* to reach the freeway. Turn right, headed south, to Henderson.

At 7.7 miles *12.3 km* you will reach the first of four exits for Henderson, which has grown so large that it now seems to be part of Las Vegas. Stay on the freeway, which skirts Henderson. The freeway ends at 19.0 miles *30.4 km*, but the roadway continues to be divided.

At 20.6 miles *33.0 km* you will reach the city limits of Boulder City. This town was created from bare desert in 1931 for the workers on the nearby dam project, which was then called Boulder Dam, which is how the town got its name. Later the name of the dam was changed to Hoover Dam but the town did not change its name.

You reach a stoplight where you have a choice of taking the 93 Truck Route to the left or going straight ahead, into the old downtown area. We recommend that you go through the town. It may take ten minutes extra but it is worth seeing, a pleasant and prosperous place with many parks. The business district looks like it was frozen in time in 1955. In fact, we think it looks more like a classic 1950s Route 66 town than the present Route 66 towns in Arizona do.

At 32.6 miles *52.2 km* you will reach Hoover Dam, coming down a long, twisting approach road. Hoover Dam is a very interesting place, one that photographers love, situated dramatically in a steep desert canyon with the Colorado River surging below. However, all traffic narrows down to one small channel as the roadway passes over the top of the dam. Visitation is heavy and you should expect dense crowds, especially if you are there at peak season. Parking is extremely scarce. A multi-story parking garage has been built to relieve the problem, so if you intend to stop at the dam, keep a careful lookout for the parking garage, which is to your left. You pay an entrance fee and then drive up the ramps to the upper stories, looking for a space. If the place is busy you can circle up and down for a long time. There are a few public parking areas, much smaller, on the Arizona side, but don't count on finding a space there. Two tours of the dam are offered. Although the basic tour is 35 minutes long, by the time you park, buy your ticket, look around, etc., you can easily spend an hour and a half.

Hoover Dam spans the Colorado River, which is the boundary between Nevada and Arizona; so as soon as you drive over the dam, you enter Arizona on the other side. From the dam you will go through a lonely desert for 73.0 miles *116.8 km* more to reach Kingman. This is true desolate desert Arizona desert with no services.

At the 105.6 mile *169.0 km* point you will enter Kingman where Highway 93 meets I-40. Drive under I-40 following the Beale Street sign. Turn right at the next intersection, then left, and you'll be on Route 66 (Andy Devine). Travel east for two blocks, looking for the Powerhouse on your right. It is a huge building, well marked, and is the **Zero** point for our tours east and west of Kingman.

What you do from here depends on how much time you have and what your plans are. Many travelers want to mix a trip to the Grand Canyon with a Route 66 experience. Die-hard Route 66 fans want to travel every inch of it. We suggest that for many visitors, the following is a good itinerary: Combine Tours 3-E, 4-E, 5-E, and 6-E, which will take you along many miles of original old 66 pavement, passing through Hackberry, Peach Springs, Seligman, Ash Fork and ending at Williams. The distance is 130 miles *208 km* and the driving time, allowing for stops, is 4 hours. There are good places to stay and to eat in Williams. The next day you can make an easy drive of about 60.0 miles *96.0 km* to the Grand Canyon and have time to enjoy it. If you plan an overnight at the Grand Canyon you must have advance reservations. Otherwise exit the Grand Canyon via Cameron and drive to Flagstaff. An alternative to staying in Williams is to drive an additional 34.0 miles *54.4 km* to Flagstaff. See page 71 for Grand Canyon details.

A Brief History of Route 66 in Arizona

[Note: this is a distillation of our forthcoming book, *The History of Route 66 in Arizona*. We found so much interesting material that it went way beyond the bounds of the amount of history needed for this Guide. Therefore we are working on a separate volume containing only the history, which will be detailed, footnoted and indexed].

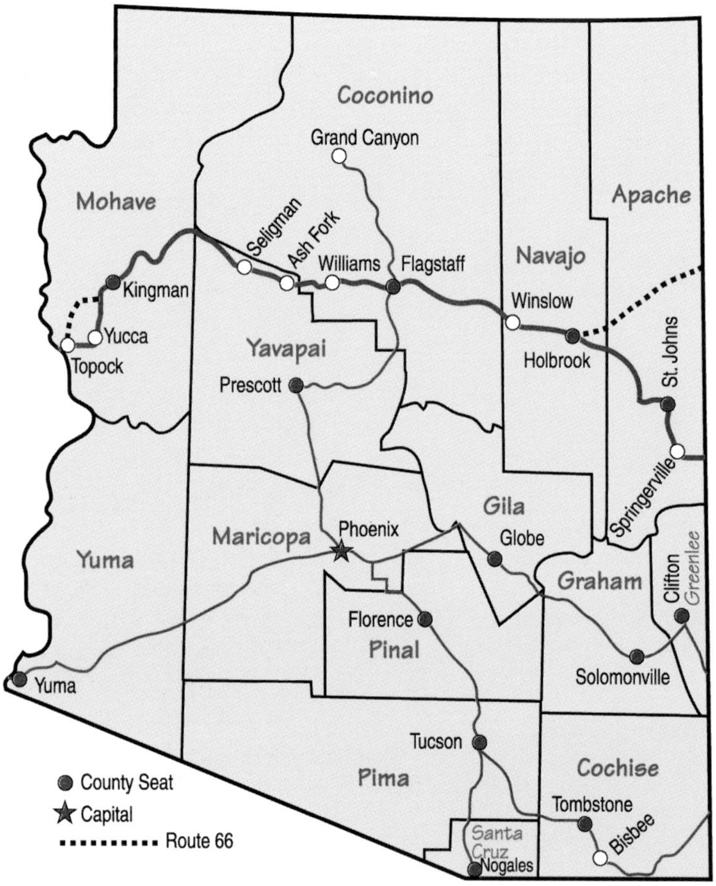

Horse and Buggy Days

The first true vehicle road across northern Arizona was blazed in 1857 along the 35th Parallel by Lt. Edward Beale, who led a camel caravan from Ft. Wingate to the Colorado River. Railroad engineers later followed The Beale Road, and the rail line that was built from 1880 to 1883 tracked it closely.

Early Auto Roads

Arizona began planning for automobile roads in 1909, while it was still a territory. The post of Territorial Engineer was created and handed to J. B. Girand, who devised a system of four primary roads that touched each of Arizona's fourteen county seats. Girand's east-west road running across northern Arizona—the forerunner of Route 66—followed the railroad from the Colorado River to Holbrook but from there it dipped to the south to connect to St. Johns, the seat of Apache County, as can be seen on the map. The railroad went northeast, to Lupton.

In addition to the roads that were to be built within its borders to serve Arizona citizens, it became apparent by 1910 that the legislature was going to have to look beyond Arizona's boundaries and think in broader terms: there was talk about building transcontinental highways.

Arizona was favorably situated for a transcontinental highway because it is so far south. No one wanted to build a road north of Colorado because of the heavy winters in the northern tier of states. At the level of Colorado, drivers heading west had to get over the Rocky Mountains and then faced the difficult basin and range landscape all the way to the Pacific Coast. By going south as far as Santa Fe, road planners could do an end run around the Rockies and deal with much less difficult mountains on the way west. This fact of geography caused roadbuilders to look at both northern and southern Arizona. The north avoided the worst of the desert sands but had a high-elevation section between Flagstaff and Williams that was subject to snow. The south, through Phoenix and Yuma, had the opposite problem, heat and sand.

There was fierce competition between northern and southern Arizona for the prized highway.

In those early days the roads were given names rather than numbers, and Arizonans began to hear alluring tales about the Ocean-to-Ocean Highway, the Lincoln Highway, the National Old Trails Highway and many others.

The associations planning transcontinental routes inspected Arizona and landed in the middle of a factional dispute between northern and southern Arizona. Arizona became a state on Valentine's Day, February 14, 1912, while competition for the National Old Trails Road, the Ocean-to-Ocean Highway and the Borderland Road was intense.

Because more than 80% of Arizona's population was concentrated south of Prescott, southern-route boosters were confident that they would get all the good roads. However, in 1913, northerners pulled a coup by convincing the National Old Trails Road Association to choose the northern route with two modifications to the Girand Plan. The first was to follow the railroad east of Holbrook, following it along the valley of the Rio Puerco into New Mexico via Lupton. The second was to depart from the Girand Plan at Kingman by going over the Black

Mountains via Oatman. In 1915 Springerville citizens convinced the National Old Trails Road Association that there was no decent road from Holbrook to Lupton and that a road from Holbrook to Springerville should be added as a branch of the Old Trails Highway.

From 1913 to 1916 Arizona worked on parts of the Old Trails, financed mostly by county bond monies, supplemented by state appropriations, but a chronic shortage of funds made progress painfully slow.

The hazards of driving early Arizona roads—OTM

The Federal Aid Era Begins

Arizona's roadbuilding effort was given a major boost in 1916 when the Federal Road Aid Act was passed. Under this bill Congress agreed to give the states $25 million according to a formula based on population, land size, and extent of roads used to carry mail. The program was interrupted by America's entry into World War One, and it was not until after the war that Arizona was able to use federal money. Crews built major pieces of the Old Trails, using the aid money and a large amount of war surplus equipment.

In 1921 there was a fundamental change in the Federal Aid program, when the 7% System was enacted. This new law was designed to knock a hole in the Pork Barrel and force states to put federal aid money into major roadways that could be linked together into a nationwide system. The law required each state to make an inventory of its entire road system and then designate 7% of the total for federal aid, subject to federal approval. The National Old Trails Road in Arizona was included as part of the state's 7%. Construction was performed under individual contracts for small portions of the road at a time, as the money would allow, being further divided by fiscal years. By 1926 Arizona had 420.1 miles of the National Old Trails Road, only about 25 miles of which, from Flagstaff to Canyon Padre, was paved.

National Standards Are Adopted

By 1924 road groups and the government were seeking a way out of the bewildering maze of state roads, unofficial interstate highways and random signage. The American Association of Highway Officials worked with the Bureau of Public Roads to devise a plan for a uniform highway system. In March 1925 an AASHO committee led by Cyrus Avery suggested a road design and numbering system to the Bureau of Public Roads. This was approved and signed into law by President Coolidge. Several interstate road systems were approved, to be identified by numbers rather than names. The east-west roads would have even numbers, while the north-south roads would have odd ones. The decimal numbers, 10, 20, 30, etc. were coveted. Avery, who was from Oklahoma, noted that none of the existing east-west highways went through his state, so he seized the opportunity and plotted out a brand-new highway running from Chicago to Los Angeles. This was a departure from the existing conventions because it ran southwest from Chicago to St. Louis before turning west. Nevertheless, Avery had what it took to get his highway approved. He also wanted to obtain one of the prize zero-numbers, U. S. Highway 60, for his road, and almost landed it. However, the backers of a true transcontinental road from Newport News to California complained so bitterly that Avery yielded and took the number 66 as a consolation prize. U. S. Highway 66 came into existence on November 11, 1926.

U. S. Highway Number 66

In Arizona the result of the national road plan was that the path of Route 66 was fixed, running from Lupton via Holbrook, Winslow, Flagstaff, Williams, Ash Fork, Seligman, Kingman, and Oatman to Topock. Planners refused to have any branches, so the Holbrook to Springerville highway was split off to become U. S. 70,

Construction on the new Highway 66 proceeded as before, under the 7% System. The major difference before and after the creation of U. S. Highway 66 as far as Arizona was concerned, was in the promotion of the road.

Immediately after 66 was created, Avery and others organized the U. S. Highway 66 Association, which had two main goals: (1) to entice travelers to take 66 instead of some other road, (2) to get all of it paved. It was found that Arizona had the least amount of paving of the eight states on 66, so much attention was focused on it.

In 1928 the publicists for the U. S. Highway 66 Association dreamed up a real attention-getter, the transcontinental footrace, better known as the Bunion Derby. This event was heavily publicized and all of the press and radio services followed it. Starting in Los Angeles, 275 contestants began running toward New York on March 4. They came into Arizona on March 12, while

Bunion Derby, Peach Springs, Maxwell House pot—MMHA

the race was still fresh and getting lots of attention from the media, and spent 11 nights in the state, leaving it on March 22, when the contestants ran from Lupton to Gallup. While the race was a financial failure for the promoter, it did bring the attention of all America to the new road and made Highway 66 a household name.

The Thirties

Triggered by the Wall Street Crash of 1929, the Thirties were the time of the Great Depression. While the Depression was very bad news for most Americans, it had its benefits for Highway 66. In the first place, the federal government appropriated millions of extra dollars for roadbuilding projects as a way of providing employment. This spurt of new road money allowed Arizona to improve

Dust Bowl Refugees—NA

Highway 66 and to get it completely paved. The final bit of pavement was done on a 3.9-mile strip through Crozier Canyon in July 1937. This meant that the entire Route 66 from Chicago to Los Angeles was paved. It was a first, being two years ahead of the next competitor, the Lincoln Highway, and gave 66 bragging rights and solidified its reputation as the best road to take.

The second event that had an impact on Highway 66 during the Thirties was the migration of Dust Bowl refugees. Low farm prices and bad weather culminating in huge dust storms drove thousands of farmers from their smallholdings in Oklahoma, Texas, Kansas and other states, forcing them to seek new opportunities elsewhere. Many chose to go to California, and a migration of perhaps half a million people headed west. Thousands of these migrants chose to travel on Highway 66. Their travails were highlighted in John Steinbeck's famous novel *Grapes of Wrath*, which appeared in 1939. The book and the movie made from it the following year tied the migration and Highway 66 together in the imagination of the public. It made Highway 66 a symbol of hope, a way to get that last chance, and fed into the idea of going west for a fresh start that had been part of the American psyche for decades.

World War Two

America entered World War Two in 1941. By then Highway 66 had its own identity. It was well known, the road of choice for most westbound travelers, and its route was fixed. All of it was paved. From this time onward, there would be improvements on the road, a few curves taken out here, widening there, and so on, but no major change of route (until 1952 when the Yucca Cutoff bypassing Oatman was opened). By then the borders of the highway were lined with roadside businesses, mostly small operations, eight-room motels operated by Mom and Pop, built on a shoestring.

During the war there was very little construction on the highway because manpower and materials were concentrated on the war effort. But there was traffic. Lots of it, including huge military convoys that transported thousands of servicemen to West Coast camps and ports. Many of these servicemen had a glimpse of Arizona for the first time and liked what they saw, resolving to return to Arizona when the war was over.

Little noticed at the time was the passage of the Federal Highway Act of 1944. This law assumed that most of the nation's highways were unsafe and outmoded and needed replacement by a 40,000-mile system of modern superhighways. The proposed highway system was presented as being necessary to the national defense system, vitally needed to transport troops and equipment. Some planning took place but little else was done. Nevertheless, a little seed had been planted that would wait until it was time to sprout. From this point forward Highway 66 would be maintained but would not evolve.

Postwar and The Fifties

The war ended in August 1945. During the war no new cars were built, gasoline and tires were rationed and pleasure travel was nearly nonexistent. Many defense workers had earned big money and their pockets were bulging with unspent savings. The result was a postwar explosion of consumerism and travel. Once Detroit made the shift back to civilian production, eager buyers snapped up everything it could offer and took to the highways. The

Postwar Route 66 in Flagstaff—OP

favorite highway of all was U. S. Highway 66. Drivers shattered all visitation records at the Grand Canyon and other sites. Highway 66 saw a new kind of motorist, the pleasure driver, with money to spend, unhurried and willing to stop off to see Wonderful Roadside Zoos and Arizona's Oldest Trading Post. Service stations, cafes and every other tourist-oriented business zoomed to undreamed of heights.

It was during this heady era that Bobby Troup traveled the fabled highway to California and wrote a song about it, *Get Your Kicks on Route 66*. This hit song became the anthem for the highway and people began to refer to the road as Route 66 instead of Highway 66.

The Fifties family takes to the road

As the nation sprinted into the 1950s, the newly formed families of the Baby Boom took to the road as never before, and Disneyland was added to the list of reasons to go to California. Traffic on Route 66 became so heavy that it was hard to walk across the street in places like Flagstaff and Kingman in peak season.

This heavy traffic, however, exposed the weakness of Route 66, a road that had evolved from wagon tracks into the National Old Trails Highway and from there had been built to 1920s standards, and in some places upgraded to 1930s standards. By the 1950s Route 66 was a dangerous road and fully earned the nickname given it at the time, Bloody 66.

The Interstate Freeway System

Congress had been studying the nation's roadway needs, and spurred by President Eisenhower, who had been impressed with the efficiency of Germany's autobahns, passed the Interstate Highway Bill in 1956. The seed planted in 1944 had sprouted. The Act authorized a 41,000-mile road system, quite different from the Route 66-style highway. Where 66 had deliberately made a point of going through the heart of cities and towns, the new freeways would go around them. Where 66 allowed travelers to get off the highway anywhere they chose, the freeways would have strictly controlled access, so that one could leave the highway only at a few selected exits. These were controversial features. The aspect that everyone agreed upon was that the freeways would be divided so that there would be no more of the dreadful head-on crashes that were such devastating killers on 66 and other roads of the time.

Bypass

Work on the freeway system took place little by little in Arizona but it wasn't long before the impact of the new system could be foreseen. Bypass meant death to towns. Controlled access meant death to many roadside businesses. Local groups tried to fight off the freeways, but to no avail. The decisions had been made at the highest levels and it was only a matter of time before the freeways would be built and many places bypassed. The best anyone could do was to forestall the inevitable. So the late 1950s and early 1960s saw the dwindling of Route 66. During the 1960s there was a renewed spate of interest in the road even as it was disappearing, when the *Route 66* TV show became popular.

Flagstaff was the earliest Arizona 66 town to be bypassed, in 1968. Williams somehow hung on, fighting and stalling, until it became the last 66 town in the nation to be bypassed. A sad little ceremony observing the event was held in Williams on October 13, 1984. Bobby Troup appeared and sang *Get Your Kicks*. Then the ribbon was cut and the last 66 downtown died.

Highway 66 was officially declared dead in 1985 when AASHO approved its decertification. The signs came down, and the name was erased from maps.

Later that year Angel Delgadillo, a lifetime resident of Seligman, who ran a barber shop there, decided that 66 should not be allowed to die. He called a meeting of selected business owners along Route 66 in Arizona at the Copper Cart restaurant in Seligman. Only 15 people attended. Nonetheless, Angel kept fighting. In February 1987 he succeeded in creating the Historic Route 66 Association in Arizona. Later that year he convinced the Arizona legislature to adopt "Historic Route 66" and post it with signs. At first only the road from Seligman to Kingman was included, but now most of the Arizona Mother Road is so designated.

Angel Delgadillo in his Seligman barber shop, 2000

PLACES

Even today northern Arizona is sparsely settled. There was virtually no population along the path that became Route 66 until the arrival of the railroad, which began in 1880 as the Atlantic & Pacific constructed the final leg of its line, running west from Albuquerque to California. The path it followed was that of the 1857 Beale Road, which its surveyors determined to be the best course. Construction of the line across Arizona lasted until 1883, and gave rise to several towns: Holbrook, Winslow, Flagstaff, Williams, Ash Fork, Seligman, and Kingman. The trains of the era were driven by steam engines and needed to stop every 20 miles for water; so a large number of stations were created, many of them simply a water tank and a house, where a caretaker lived. These stops were given names. As the only habitations for miles around, these stops appeared on maps. As the trains switched away from steam, many of these points were abandoned, but their names remained on maps. Many have been dismayed to find that what looked like a town on a map of Arizona turned out to be nothing more than a shack or the place where a shack used to be.

Adamana. For two generations of railroad travelers Adamana was known as the portal to the Petrified Forest. Pioneer Adam Hannah started a ranch in the area in 1884. About that time the railroad began to advertise the natural wonders along its line. The Petrified Forest was one of the best, so the A&P created a stop at Adam Hannah's ranch and called it Adamana, a contraction of his name. Visitors were met at the train station by Hannah and taken by horse-drawn wagon to the forest. Al Stevenson bought the land and built the Forest Hotel with rooms for thirty-five tourists in 1908. In 1925 Adamana had a hotel, a post office, a railway station and a store. Route 66 travelers could drive south through Adamana and reach the Petrified Forest, but this meant fording the Rio Puerco. The river was bridged in 1932 when Arizona Highway 63 was built, about two miles east of Adamana. This diverted auto traffic away from Adamana. By the end of the 1930s trains no longer stopped at Adamana. The opening of I-40 isolated the place. The hotel burned down in the 1960s, marking the end of Adamana.

Allentown. This is also spelled Allantown. Why anyone ever called it a town is a mystery. It was a railroad section point. Later a trading post adopted the name, and by the time the highway came through the area the name of the trading post was put on the maps as if it were a town. A typical Route 66 roadside business was run here, with gas station, curio shop and a grocery store.

Ash Fork. The vast prairies surrounding this little town were like nature's invitation to pioneer families of stockmen who moved in and established ranches on the grasslands on a fork of Ash Creek. At first these were sheepmen. Then the railroad came, reaching the area in October 1882 and bringing with it the boon of easy transportation

Adamana in the early days—NCM

of livestock. The railroad decided to build a station at the place and make it a division point. The little town qualified for a post office on April 21, 1883, picking the name Ash Fork (not Ashfork). The economy was based on ranching, railroading and sandstone quarrying. In April 1893 a new railroad opened, the Santa Fe, Prescott & Phoenix, connecting with the Santa Fe at Ash Fork. The Santa Fe built a grand Harvey House called El Escalante in Ash Fork in 1907. The arrival of Route 66 through the heart of Ash Fork converted it from a railroad town to a highway town, and added tourism to its list of industries. Ash Fork's peak population was 1,000, reached in the 1950s, the residents depending on a four-legged economy: railroading, livestock, quarrying and tourism. In the late 1950s the Santa Fe rerouted its main line north of the town, knocking out one of the legs. Then the I-40 bypass knocked out another leg in 1979. Since the mid-1960s Ash Fork has lost population, El Escalante has been torn down and the town is trying to re-define itself.

Bellemont. In 1876 sheep rancher Walter Hill began the settlement of this area, though he had no neighbors until the railroad ran through the place in 1882, when it acquired a name in honor of Belle Smith, daughter of a railroad official. A sawmill was set up nearby and a section house was located at Bellemont, giving it enough vitality to support saloons and a store (1886), a post office (1887) and a school (1893). It became a major stock-shipping point on the railroad. In 1897 a tie-pickling plant and a big cinder mine were established by the railroad employing four hundred men. In 1908 the railroad closed its station at Bellemont. The National Old Trails Highway came through Bellemont in 1921 giving it new life from tourism and the distinction of being the highest town on the road at 7,130 feet. By that time the pickling plant and cinder mine were closed and Bellemont was a sleepy little spot in the road, though it still had a post office, school, store, garage, and service station. It had a population of 35 in 1940. Then, in 1942, in the early days of America's involvement in WWII, the government announced plans to build a major munitions base there and 12,000 construction workers descended on the little burg to construct a $100,000,000 (inflation adjusted dollars) base. Finished later that year, the Navajo Ordnance Depot employed over 2,000 people. Because of the wartime labor shortage, the government hired many Navajo Indians, building a village for them complete with trading post. It was the largest Indian town in Arizona. Employment was cut after the war, to surge again during the Korean War and again during Vietnam. Afterwards it became military surplus and was transferred to the state of Arizona, which uses it as a National Guard facility named Camp Navajo. The post office was closed in 1957. Some of the buildings on the base have been removed, but a good many of them remain, giving today's traveler an idea of the gargantuan size of the facility. Today Bellemont is only a spot on the map, its only old business being a tavern, though a new industrial park is being built around the old community.

Chambers. Like many of the places in Indian country, it started as a trading post. Charles Chambers opened his post some years before the railroad arrived on the scene, so the railroad section house was named for him. While never a large place, it was able to keep going as a point on Route 66 and a crossroad for an important road going north into the heart of Navajo country. In the mid-1920s a large deposit of halloysite was discovered about four miles away and a mine for the rare earth was opened. The name was changed in 1926 from Chambers to Halloysite, then changed back to Chambers in 1930. Senator Carl Hayden of Arizona, explained the change in a letter to the *Holbrook Tribune* in 1927: "The main reason presented in support of the proposed change in the name of Chambers post office was on account of its similarity to the Chandler office, it being represented that a certain sheep grower in Chambers lost $300 through delay in receiving a bid for his wool due to the latter being made to Chandler and not having been remailed to him until five days later."

Earliest photo of Flagstaff, 1882—MNA

Flagstaff (Pop. 52,894). The first settlement of this mountain city began in 1876 when a handful of sheep ranchers who had come through the area on the Beale Road years earlier, decided to leave drought-stricken California and take their chances on the green country in northern Arizona that they had seen while getting to the Golden State. Later that year a group of young men in a Boston-organized colonizing party celebrated the 4th of July at a spring, where they raised a pine tree, hung Old Glory from its tip and had a Centennial ceremony. When they moved on, they took their flag with them, but left the flag staff, which became a landmark. In April 1880 the Atlantic & Pacific RR began its long-delayed push to finish the railroad from Albuquerque to California. A group of surveyors led by Lewis Kingman set up a construction camp between a spring and the right-of-way in April 1880, a camp whose population waxed and waned as different groups of workers: graders, tie-choppers, etc. came and went. Merchants moved in to supply the needs of these workers and by 1881 residents of the camp decided the place was a permanent settlement and should have a post office. At a citizens' meeting the name Flagstaff was chosen. The rails arrived in Flagstaff on August 1, 1882, and opened the little town to the world, enabling industry to begin. For years the mainstays of Flagstaff's economy were the "Ls" lumber and livestock. It became the county seat of newly created Coconino County in 1891 and was the shopping hub for the region. In 1892 Flagstaff got into the tourism business when a stagecoach to the Grand Canyon began running. In 1899 the town leaders created a little teachers' college. The National Old Trails Highway came through the center of town in 1914, the same path followed by Route 66 a decade later. Flagstaff was a natural stopping point for Mother Road travelers, being a good day's drive from Los Angeles or Albuquerque. Its high 7,000 foot elevation meant that it was cool in the summer, giving a respite from the grueling heat experienced on either side of the town. By the end of the Roaring Twenties, Route 66 tourism was firmly established as one of the mainstays of Flagstaff's economy. The Thirties saw many a migrant family trying to get through Flagstaff to California. Some of them stayed. During the Forties, the construction of the giant Navajo Ordnance Depot at Flagstaff's back door (see Bellemont) injected a huge amount of cash into the town, much needed, as tourism was reduced to minimum levels for the duration. At the end of World War Two, Flagstaff saw an explosion of tourism, and it enjoyed its double-barreled position of being both a major stop on Route 66 and the Gateway to the Grand Canyon, and the owners of roadside businesses built motels, cafes and gas stations on every available piece of highway frontage. The I-40 bypass hit Flagstaff in 1968, and there was an immediate slump, as town leaders had guessed wrong about the habits of freeway travelers. They believed that the best plan was to have only two freeway exits, one on each end of town, forcing motorists to exit, come into town and travel the length of it. They did not foresee that drivers often buzz right by the first exit so that they can get a better look at a place before they get off the freeway. For years Flagstaff played catch-up for this mistake, but finally has five exits. Today tourism is still the major industry for Flagstaff, but it is based on travel to the Grand Canyon, rather than the Mother Road. The town has become a city and is by far the largest in northern Arizona.

Goldroad. The name is variously seen as Gold Road, Goldroad, and Goldroads, but the authoritative book, *Arizona Place Names*, shows it as Goldroad, so we will stick with that. There was a little gold mining in the area as early as the 1860s, but large-scale operations had to wait until a major discovery was made in 1902 when prospector Jose Jerez found a rich outcrop of gold-bearing quartz while searching for his burro. He was grubstaked by Henry Lovin, a Kingman merchant. Assays showed that Jerez had located high-grade ore and a stampede started to the district. There was one major mine, working Jerez's claim, which was sold to bigger and bigger fish until a corporation financed by French capitalists had the money to develop the property. By February 1903 150 men worked at the mine. By the end of 1907 the mine had yielded over $2 million but the easy-to-work vein played out. Eventually a subsidiary of the giant U. S. Smelting, Refining and Mining Co. bought the claim and successfully worked it into the 1930s, by which time the total yield was over $7 million. Falling gold prices in the 30s caused closure. Decades later, when gold price controls were removed and the free market shot the price up the mine was reopened, only to close again in 1998. Since 1998, tours have been given in the old mine. Old Goldroad was quite a town, with many buildings, including large and imposing structures in a truly picturesque setting, best appreciated driving west over Sitgreaves Pass. In 1949, the greedy Arizona legislature passed a law taxing idle mining properties at the same rate as active ones. This caused the owner to tear down almost all the buildings so that today there is no town to visit.

Grand Canyon Caverns. It was discovered in 1927 when a heavy rain widened the funnel-shaped entrance. A wood cutter for the Santa Fe found the entrance one evening while on his way to a poker game with the boys at the nearby Yampai section house. The railroad workers and ranch hands then explored the find, calling the place Yampai Caverns. When it was learned that the caverns were big enough to attract visitors, they were purchased and developed. At first, visitors were lowered into the cavern by ropes and a hand-operated winch. By the 1930s the caverns were leased by Stan Wakefield, who installed stairs and landings. Wakefield operated a service station at Deer Lodge on 66 and used it as tourist headquarters for cave visitors. Later Hyde Park was built even closer to the entry road to the caverns and became another gateway. It was not until the 1960s that an elevator was installed. In the meantime the name of the attraction changed to Dinosaur Caverns and then to its present name, Grand Canyon Caverns, and the present facilities were built.

Hackberry. In the 1870s a group of prospectors found a outcropping of gold ore near a spring where a hackberry tree grew, so they named their find the Hackberry Mine. Soon there was a little town of 100 people. When the Atlantic & Pacific Railroad came through the area in 1882, Hackberry became a cattle shipping point, the third most active in Arizona. The mines began to play out about the time that The National Old Trails Highway came through the town, which by then had a school, stores, post office and all the other amenities of a small town. After the mines closed only a few families remained, making their living from ranching and Route 66.

Holbrook (4,917). Settlement began in 1878 at the strategic point where the Rio Puerco meets the Little Colorado River, then called Horsehead Crossing. In 1881 after construction of the Atlantic & Pacific Railroad began, the population shifted a bit to the west, where a railroad camp was named Holbrook in honor of an A&P official. An investor in the railroad, Edward Kinsley, visited the area in 1884 during a wet cycle and found the plains flowing with beautiful grasses and all the ponds full of water. Brimming with enthusiasm, he went to New York and convinced several investors, including the Seligman brothers, to incorporate a giant cattle outfit called the Aztec Land & Cattle Company, better-known as the Hashknife Outfit because its brand looked like a cutting tool used by camp cooks. With ample funds from well-heeled backers, the outfit bought one million acres of land from the railroad at fifty cents an acre and shipped in

Holbrook after 1888 fire—NCM

40,000 head of cattle from Texas. There were already some Mormon ranchers on the range, so in addition to hiring competent cowboys, the Aztec did not ask too many questions when a very rough outlaw element appeared, ready to do the dirty work of shouldering the Mormons off the range. The shift was dramatic: one year there were lush ranges lightly grazed by cattle under the care of a few sedate family men; the next year the plains were loaded with cattle and badmen under the aegis of the second largest cattle company in the West. Violence ensued. Once the Mormons had been pushed back into their stronghold of Joseph City, a range war broke out with sheep ranchers in the Pleasant Valley, and America's worst feud was underway, the Grahams vs. the Tewksburys. Many Western towns today—in an effort to claim a Wild West heritage—make exaggerated claims about their past. Holbrook has no need to inflate or invent. It was as wild as they come. In time the badmen turned on their employers and the Hash Knife suffered tremendous losses from rustling. Theft, bad weather, the Panic of '93 and overgrazing doomed the company, which sold out in 1902. Holbrook settled down. Ranching was still important, but trade and shipping also rose to the fore, as it became an important crossroads. In addition to the railroad, there were roads going south to St. Johns and other points and north into Indian country. All of these brought in trade. Both the northern and southern routes of the Old Trails Highway converged on Holbrook and it enjoyed status as a highway town, soon blossoming into the gateway to the Petrified Forest. Navajo County was created in 1895 and Holbrook became its seat. In the heyday of the Mother Road, Holbrook was definitely a highway town, with tourism taking the top rung on the ladder of industries. When the town was bypassed in 1981 forty-five businesses closed within a year. Today it is a good place to visit, with a historic walk, good restaurants and places to stay.

Hashknife cowboys, a tough bunch, 1880s—OTM

Houck. Houck is named after James Houck, who entered the area in 1874 as a mail carrier on the old road between Fort Wingate, New Mexico and Fort Whipple, Arizona. He set up a trading post at Houck in 1877 because of its access to the military road and the Navajo reservation. When the railroad came through in 1881, a section house was built near the trading post and given his name. Houck learned the sheep business from the Navajo and in 1885 gave up trading for sheep ranching. He was involved in the Pleasant Valley War and while working as a deputy sheriff in 1887 killed one of the Grahams. Eventually he moved to the area north of Phoenix and prospered in the sheep business for years. When business turned bad, Houck committed suicide in 1921. Houck is probably the longest-lived trading post on Route 66/I-40 today.

Jack Rabbit. Is it Jackrabbit or Jack Rabbit? We have seen the name both ways. This is one of the best-known roadside businesses in Arizona, perhaps on the entire Main Street of America. James and Nora Taylor bought the property in February 1949 and changed the name to Jack Rabbit, using an existing building. It was just another business until they conceived the brilliant marketing idea of plastering the roadsides with advertising signs, and "Here It Is!" became a 66 icon. The business survived the I-40 bypass and is one of the last remaining gimmick-driven roadside businesses along Route 66 in Arizona. Go there. Ride the rabbit.

Joseph City. Unlike most Route 66 towns, Joseph City's birth had nothing to do with the railroad or ranching, but came about as a result of the Mormon church's decision to extend its reach into Arizona. In 1876 a hardy group of the faithful under the command of William Allen set up a community they called Allen's Camp. Later the name was changed to St. Joseph. In 1923 the post office department asked that the name be changed as it was being confused with St. Joseph, Missouri, and the name was then changed to Joseph City. The town has always been small, with a population of perhaps two hundred. When Route 66 came through the middle of the little place, roadside businesses sprang up everywhere, and Joseph City became a Mother Road town. Today there is little left of the farming that once characterized it. The I-40 bypass wiped out all the roadside businesses.

Kingman (20,069). Kingman is a bustling place today, enjoying a renaissance born of people seeking the Sunbelt as a retirement haven, but minerals and the railroad made the town. The mountains around Kingman are rich in minerals, some of which were worked as early as 1858. When the railroad arrived in 1883 Kingman became the shipping point for the mines and ranches. It became the seat of Mohave County in 1887. The location of Highway 66 west of Kingman was the subject of hot controversy, as two competing groups argued their cases. The Oatman group wanted to run the highway over the Black Mountains through their town. The Yucca group wanted the road to make an end run around the mountains, as the railroad had done. The decision was made at the time that Oatman was approaching the zenith of its power, and the road was sent over the mountains, not around them. This was changed in late 1952 when the Yucca bypass was opened. Kingman had a huge military facility in World War Two, the Kingman Army Air Field, which brought hundreds of GIs and civilian workers to the desert city. After the war Kingman continued to enjoy a lively health, boosted by the emergence of Las Vegas as the new American playground, because Kingman is the major Arizona Route 66 road junction for travelers to Nevada.

Kingman, first known photo, ca. 1883—MMHA

Lupton. This is another of those places that looks like a town on the map but isn't—never was. For many years there has been some kind of commercial activity here because it is the first community of any kind for travelers coming into Arizona from New Mexico along Route 66.

Meteor City. A trading post that capitalized on its proximity to Meteor Crater. Meteor City now has a new fame—alas!—as the last trading post between Winslow and Winona to close, shutting its doors on July 31, 2000.

Meteor Crater. After the Grand Canyon and the Petrified Forest, Meteor Crater ranks highest on the list of natural wonders along Route 66 in Arizona. For many years explorers and residents knew of the place but did not know what it was, theories about its origin ranging from volcanic crater to giant steamhole. Whatever its origin, those in the area were delighted to find so many chunks of meteoritic-iron lying around the area that a local industry started and fifteen tons of iron were shipped to market on the railroad. In 1903 Daniel Barringer, a Philadelphia lawyer and mining engineer, appeared. Barringer explored the crater and determined that it was created by a meteorite hit. He thought that the main mass of the meteorite would be buried in the bottom of the crater and that it could be mined. He formed a mining company and set to work, getting a patent to the land in the process, so that he became the owner of the crater. For years he drilled, spending a fortune. Finding nothing, he changed his theory, believing that the meteorite came in at an angle and would be buried in a sidewall rather than the center. The results of his efforts can be seen today, and are one of the interesting sights. Barringer continued almost obsessively until the stock market crash of 1929 stopped him. Since that time the crater has been developed as a tourist attraction. Still privately owned, the place is very well managed and maintained, with paved entrance road, parking lots and all the amenities.

The Tom Reed Mill in Oatman, about 1920—OP

Oatman. Mining towns are beloved in folklore and all too often writers have exaggerated their history. While Oatman's legendary image is that of a rip-roaring boom town and mock gunfights are staged on its streets today as a way of celebrating its past, it was actually a quiet and well-ordered place. The Black Mountains in which Oatman is located are rich in minerals and for years prospectors roamed their craggy peaks and desolate valleys looking for paydirt. In 1902 Ben Taddock made a big find, but lacked the funds to develop his strike so he sold out. His property changed hands several times before the Vivian Mining Company set up actual operations. Another group of claims was organized into the Tom Reed Gold Mine which went into sustained production in 1909 and was the town's most reliable long-term operation. There were geological quirks in the district which baffled miners until 1913 when engineers figured out the oddities and opened the United Eastern Mine, which produced almost $15 million from 1917 to 1924, the richest gold mine in Arizona's history. The boom in Oatman was just launching into the stratosphere when the National Old Trails Highway was created. Money talks and Oatman had lots of it, enough to steer the highway over the mountains and through its main street. When Route 66 replaced the Old Trails, the Oatman alignment was followed until late 1952. The name Oatman was adopted on June 24, 1909. Legend says this was in honor of Olive Oatman, a girl captured by Indians in 1851 and released five years later to tell her highly sensationalized story to the press. Figures concerning the population of Oatman and the value of the gold produced there vary. The height of its boomtown glory was 1915 when the number of residents was 3,500 or 15,000 or something in between. Estimates of the amount of gold produced range from $18 million to $36 million. The glory days lasted about a decade, and many substantial buildings were constructed. What one sees today are the meager remnants that survived three major downtown fires. By the 1930s Oatman was in decline, supported as much by Route 66 as by the dwindling resources of its mines. The mines were dealt a crippling blow in 1942 when the federal government declared that gold mining was not essential to the war effort and ordered closure of the gold mines so that the miners could work in copper mines instead. After that Route 66 was Oatman's livelihood and that was taken away in 1952 when the Yucca bypass, rerouting 66, was opened. Rittenhouse found a population of 737 in 1946. In 1960 another writer pegged the number of residents as 60, showing the impact of losing Route 66. Today Oatman survives on tourism from Historic Route 66 and is a colorful and interesting place to visit.

Parks. This was known as Maine until the late 1920s. It has been said that the later name came from a man named Parks who built a store there, though we have not found any confirmation of this. For many years it advertised itself as Parks in the Pines, a tradition carried on by the present store. It has been a favorite camping ground for years, and was the junction for an auto road to the Grand Canyon used from 1921 to about 1931.

Peach Springs. Flowing springs were found in this area centuries ago by Indians. Beale gratefully used the spring waters in 1858. When the railroad came through in 1882 it staked claims to the water and set up facilities there. Peach trees are not native to the area and there is speculation that Mormon pioneers planted them. For a time Peach Springs enjoyed a railroad boom, but it was short-lived, and the community settled down to a quiet life as headquarters for the Hualapai Nation. The Old Trails Highway and Route 66 came through the sleepy town, giving it a new life. In 1926 it had a hotel, Indian trading post, garage, service station, and general store. Later a cafe was added as well as motels, but it was always a small place. When I-40 was built, the bypass devastated the tourist business in Peach Springs, as it has no access to I-40. The present revival of interest in Route 66 has given it a boost, but it is staking its future on tourism, developing roads to the Colorado River, in an area owned by the tribe and referred to as the Western Grand Canyon. A paved road, modern motel and restaurant and other facilities are just starting to kick tourism into high gear.

Petrified Forest-Painted Desert. In order to protect this special place, President Teddy Roosevelt created the Petrified Forest National Monument in December 1906, an area of 90 square miles, all of it lying south of the railroad. In 1911 the size was reduced to 40 square miles. In 1930 President Hoover expanded the monument to include the Blue Forest and Newspaper Rock. In September 1932 Hoover added 2,500 acres to the north, incorporating the Painted Desert and Black Forest. In that same year a bridge was built across the Puerco River, allowing easy passage through the monument. The Painted Desert Rim Drive was opened in 1937, a scenic northern loop that connected with Route 66 on both ends, making an easy detour available to Mother Road travelers. In 1962 National Park status was granted, and in 1970 a 50,000-acre wilderness area was added.

Sanders. Now a school center for the Navajo Nation, Sanders got its start as a trading post due to springs nearby. A railroad section house was established there. In the days when Route 66 came through it, there were a few roadside businesses.

Seligman. Miles of broad flat grasslands attracted ranchers into this area in the early 1880s, but there was no community until 1886 when Thomas Bullock built the Prescott & Arizona Central, a railroad line that branched from the Santa Fe and ran south to Prescott, the territorial capital. He named the settlement that grew up around the terminus Prescott Junction. The Prescott & Arizona Central railroad was so poorly managed that a competing line, the Santa Fe, Prescott & Phoenix, was built in 1893, originating from Ash Fork. It put the P&AC out of business, after which the line going south from Seligman was torn up. Since the town was no longer the junction for Prescott, the name was changed to Seligman, after a family of New York financiers who had invested in northern Arizona. The Santa Fe moved its western terminus and roundhouse from Williams to Seligman in 1897, giving new life to the town. The Santa Fe constructed a nice Harvey House, El Havasu, in 1905. Route 66 brought the tourist industry to Seligman. As auto travel grew, train travel shrank, causing the railroad to close El Havasu in 1954. The building still stands and is used for railroad offices but is closed to the public. In February 1985 the Santa Fe ended Seligman's status as a division point, eliminating dozens of jobs. In 1978 I-40 bypassed Seligman, dealing the little town a terrific blow. Seligman has rallied behind the efforts of two of its native sons, Angel and Juan Delgadillo, who have been leading lights in the Route 66 revival. It was in Seligman in 1985 that Angel called the first meeting of the group that became the Historic Route 66 Association of Arizona. His efforts in publicizing the glories of the Mother Road and in getting it re-signed as Historic U. S. 66 sparked the 66 revival. Today Seligman shows the damage inflicted by the I-40 bypass but it retains an interesting downtown. Note: some early publications state that the line for the Mountain Time Zone ends at Seligman and that westbound travelers must set their watches back one hour there. This has not been true since 1950. Don't reset your watch until you reach the Colorado River at Topock.

Topock. The reason that anything exists here is that the railroad chose this narrow point as the place to string a bridge across the Colorado River. As a bridge port, a little settlement took shape in 1883. When the residents applied for a post office in 1915, they took the name Topock, which the railroad was using for the place. Its origin is unknown. Today you see the Topock post office as you drive through Golden Shores, but when you get to the river there is no town or community, only a marina known as Topock on a bay formed by the river—66 did not run through it. At the river itself there is an industrial installation run by Pacific Gas & Electric, but it is in no sense a town.

Truxton. The name Truxton came from Lt. Edward Beale of Beale Road fame in 1858 when he named a spring for his wife, whose maiden name was Truxton. The community of Truxton was founded in 1951 by D. J. Dilts, who built a cafe and gas station there. Truxton is a community that made its living entirely from Route 66, with motels, cafes and service stations being its only industry.

Twin Arrows. This trading post is famous and has become a Route 66 icon because its owners picked an advertising gimmick that worked, two telephone poles stuck in the ground, given plywood "feathers" and arrowheads and gaudy paint. Its stock in trade was much like that of any other post along the road. For many years it was operated by the Troxells, who advertised their Jean & Trox photo business almost as heavily—and effectively—as Troutner's Store For Men. After the bypass, several people tried to keep it going but failed. It is closed.

Two Guns. This has one of the most colorful histories of any 66 trading post. Canyon Diablo was bridged in 1915, making the site of this trading post a strategic point. One can see the old business buildings while driving by, but the recent owners have barred it to the public.

Whiskey Row in Williams 1880s—OP

Valentine. Valentine is not so much a town as a school site for Hualapai Indian children. Six hundred and sixty acres were set aside here for this purpose in 1900, and several school buildings were constructed as well as living quarters and a post office. The post office was first known as Truxton but in 1910 was moved onto private land about a mile away and changed to Valentine in honor of Robert Valentine, Commissioner of Indian Affairs. There was never a roadside business on the school tract, but at the later post office site there was one. From about 1950-1960 there was a fad for sending valentines to the Valentine Post Office to be remailed using the heart-shaped Valentine cancellation stamp on Valentine's Day. The most recent postmistress was murdered on the site in 1990, after which her husband razed the buildings, so that only empty land remains today.

Walnut Canyon. This ancient cliff-dwelling site is one of our favorite places. It was made a National Monument in 1915 in order to protect it from looting and vandalism. At the Visitor Center is a good museum. There are excellent hiking trails at Walnut Canyon. We think it is well worth a visit.

Williams (2,842). The area around the town of Williams was first explored by Mountain Man William S. Williams, Old Bill. The first settlers were ranchers, who came into the area in 1876 and the town site was created by cowboy C. T. Rogers in 1879. Railroad workers put Williams on the map in 1880 when they set up a construction camp at the foot of Bill Williams Mountain. By 1881 the camp had enough inhabitants to qualify for a post office and they picked Williams as the name, in honor of Old Bill. The railroad reached Williams in 1882, opening it to the world. It had few laws and plenty of single young men, who thought that a little gunplay was helpful every now and then to liven things up. A newspaper in 1885 called Williams the most lawless town in Arizona Territory. The town's second industry, lumbering, was added in 1893 when the Saginaw Lumber Company (later the Saginaw and Manistee) moved to town. Tourism became the third industry when the Santa Fe began running a train from Williams to the Grand Canyon in 1901 making it The Gateway to the Grand Canyon. This made Williams a major draw for Route 66 travelers who wanted to visit the Canyon and by the 1940s Route 66 was the town's lifeblood. Williams watched anxiously as town after town was bypassed by I-40 and resisted its own bypass so ferociously that it became the last remaining town on Route 66. It was in Williams, on October 13, 1984, that Route 66 made its last stand as an official US highway when the Williams bypass was opened and traffic was diverted to the north of town. The town observed the occasion with a sad ceremony. Bobby Troup appeared and sang his immortal *Get Your Kicks on Route 66*, a ribbon was cut and Route 66 ceased to exist. Williams, the last town on Route 66, has become a Mecca for Route 66 enthusiasts.

Winona. Winona began as a railroad section house. When the National Old Trails Highway came through and made a railroad crossing at Winona, Billy Adams, a local rancher, who owned the adjacent land, set up a tourist operation. Eventually it developed into a two-story hotel with cabins, a service station, curio store—the works. After World War 2, Adams sold the place to the Pill family, which owned and operated it until 2000. The business is still active.

First St. in Winslow about 1908—OP

Winslow (9,520). Winslow was *the* railroad town in northern Arizona. When engineers from the Atlantic & Pacific laid out their line from Albuquerque to California, they knew that they would need a place midway along the track in Arizona for a division point. They chose Winslow because of its location and the abundant water in Clear Creek. The town was named after a railroader, Edward Winslow. A roundhouse and other major facilities were built and Winslow became a company town. The arrival of Route 66 diversified the economy. In 1929 Winslow opened a major airport, by far the best in northern Arizona, and became an air hub, with TWA regularly landing flights there. In 1930 the Santa Fe Railroad built a major Harvey House, La Posada, in Winslow, designed by Mary Colter. In the 1950s the major railroad facilities were moved to Barstow. Then the airlines quit using the airport because modern planes did not need to refuel there. Finally Route 66 was bypassed by I-40 on October 9, 1979 at 4:00 PM. The town has struggled to recover ever since.

USEFUL WEBSITES

Flagstaff
http://www.flagstaff-arizona.com/
http://www.museumclub.com/
Grand Canyon
http://www.thetrain.com/
Historic Route 66 Association of Arizona
http://www.azrt66.com
Holbrook
http://www.ci.holbrook.az.us/
Kingman
http://www.kingmanchamber.org/
National Route 66 Association
http://www.national66.com/
Oatman
http://www.roadsidepeek.com/rte66/westariz/oatman/index.htm
Route 66 Magazine
http://www.route66magazine.com/
Seligman
http://www.angelsbarbershop.com/
Williams
http://www.williamschamber.com
http://www.route66place.com/
Winslow
http://www.winslowarizona.org/main.htm
http://www.wmonline.com/cities/winslow.htm

INDEX

Mileage Chart

Total distance across Arizona is **382** miles *611 km*	Ash Fork	Flagstaff	Holbrook	Kingman	Lupton	Oatman	Pet. Forst.	Seligman	Topock	Williams	Winslow
Ash Fork		53	144	111	217	139	169	23	164	19	110
Flagstaff	53		91	164	164	192	116	76	217	34	58
Holbrook	144	91		254	74	283	25	167	307	125	33
Kingman	111	164	254		328	28	279	88	53	130	221
Lupton	217	164	74	328		356	49	240	381	198	107
Oatman	139	192	283	28	356		308	116	25	158	250
Pet. Forst.	169	116	25	279	49	308		192	332	150	58
Seligman	23	76	167	88	240	116	192		141	42	134
Topock	164	217	307	53	381	25	332	141		183	274
Williams	19	34	125	130	198	158	150	42	183		92
Winslow	110	58	33	221	107	250	58	134	274	92	

The Fun Run

The highlight of Route 66 activities in Arizona each year is the **Fun Run**, usually held early in May. Check on the Route 66 website at http://www.azrt66.com for information.

The run starts in Seligman and goes to Topock, with stops and activities along the way. You can enter any vehicle: it does not have to be a classic or anything fancy. The idea is to allow everybody who wants to participate a chance to join in the fun. Give it a try! We think you'll like it!